Tinnitus

Treatment and Relief

Jack A. Vernon
Oregon Health Sciences University

Allyn and Bacon
Boston • London • Toronto • Sydney • Tokyo • Singapore

Executive Editor: Stephen D. Dragin
Editorial Assistant: Elizabeth McGuire
Editorial-Production Administrator: Joe Sweeney
Editorial-Production Service: Walsh & Associates, Inc.
Compositor Buyer: Linda Cox
Manufacturing Buyer: Suzanne Lareau
Cover Designer: Suzanne Harbison

Internet: www.abacon.com
America Online: keyword: College Online

Library of Congress Cataloging-in-Publication Data

Vernon, Jack A.
    Tinnitus : treatment and relief / Jack A. Vernon.
        p.   cm.
    Includes index.
    ISBN 0-205-18269-0
    1. Tinnitus—Popular works.   2. Tinnitus—Miscellanea.   3. Patient
education.   I. Title.
    RF293.8.V47   1997
    617.8—dc21   97-19661
                                                                                CIP

Printed in the United States of America

10   9   8   7   6   5   4   3   00   99   98

Dedication

With all due respect, this book is posthumously dedicated to Dr. Charles Unice. I have often said that most, by far, of what we know about tinnitus has been taught to us by the patient. Never has that statement been more true than in the case of Charles Unice. It all came about in the following manner:

In the early spring of 1973, I received a phone call from Dr. Charles Unice in Downey, California. He said he wanted to come to see us. I replied that we were honored by his attention but confused as to why he wanted to visit with us. He answered that the National Institutes of Health had informed him that we were the only group in the United States, at that time, that was trying to study tinnitus, and therefore he wanted to be seen and treated by us. I hastily explained that we were working on tinnitus but that our efforts were an attempt to establish an animal model of tinnitus; that we did not see tinnitus patients and we most certainly did not as yet have any treatment to offer tinnitus patients. It took some effort, but, finally, I thought I had convinced Dr. Unice that he would be wasting his time to come to Portland to see us.

Three days later he showed up on our doorstep. I didn't know what to do with him but suggested that he might help us if we could identify the qualities of his tinnitus sound or sounds, and therefore we spent the entire morning trying to produce sounds that were similar to his tinnitus. We found that his tinnitus was a tone and not a noise, and I think we found that it had a pitch that corresponded to a frequency of about 10,000 Hz. When lunchtime came, a group of us at the lab took Charles Unice to a local sandwich shop that bordered on one of the many pocket parks that flourish in Portland. Our plan was to eat lunch out of doors and enjoy one of the Northwest's rare spring days. This particular park contained an elaborate water fountain. It was designed to represent flowing water cascading over various rock layers like streams coming out of the mountains with a set of waterfall locks on one side. Dr. Unice walked over to and stood by the cascading water coming down the waterfall locks for such a long time that one of our group turned to me and said, "Do you think he is all right?" I said I would check, so I walked up behind Dr. Unice and said, "Chuck, are you O.K?" "Sh, sh," he said, holding out his arms as though to prevent my invading his newfound sanctuary. "Standing right here I cannot hear my tinnitus! It's the first time I have been unable to hear that unconscionably wretched sound since it began over two years ago. This is wonderful!"

At that moment the idea for using masking as a relief procedure for tinnitus fell in place for me. It was obvious that we could not park Dr. Unice by that water fountain for the rest of his life, but we could most assuredly arrange to place a similar sound in his ears. We spent the rest of the lunch period discussing the possibility of, and implications for, masking as a relief procedure for tinnitus and how best to do it. Dr. Unice convinced us that he would gladly and willingly wear almost any device that produced as much relief as did the sound of that water fountain.

That luncheon period with Charles Unice was a benchmark episode, a milestone, a ninth-inning, game-winning home run for our studies of tinnitus. As a result of our discussions, we started a tinnitus clinic with the active participation of Dr. Alexander Schleuning (now Chairman of OHSU's ENT department) and were soon seeing tinnitus patients. That tinnitus clinic is in operation to this day and by now has seen over 6,000 patients with severe tinnitus.

Dr. Unice made another and very significant contribution to the area of tinnitus. He founded the American Tinnitus Association. In his initial efforts to establish such a foundation he quickly discovered that technically and legally it was much more difficult to establish such an organization in the state of California than anywhere else in the Unites States. Therefore, he asked if it might be possible to establish the American Tinnitus Association under the aegis of the Oregon Medical School. It was through that mechanism that ATA came to life. Since those early days, ATA has become independent of our school and is a standalone organization daily serving many thousands of tinnitus patients under the very able direction of Dr. Gloria Reich.

It is impossible to overestimate the importance of the contribution that Charles Unice has made to the study of tinnitus. I am sure he would not agree. However, for the thousands who suffer with tinnitus it is a fortunate thing that Charles Unice acquired tinnitus, leading him to do all he did. It is with a profound sense of humility and gratitude that I dedicate this book to him.

Respectfully,
Jack Vernon, Ph.D.

Contents

Preface

Almost every tinnitus patient has encountered the statement "you will have to learn to live with it." For most patients this is not only very discouraging but a depressing state of affairs as well. In some cases, the induced depression becomes a reality that when treated by certain medications can lead to increased tinnitus.

It has been said before but needs repeating here, "It is immoral to give desperate patients false hope but it is worse to give them no hope."

The purpose for this book is to demonstrate to tinnitus patients that there is hope and that relief procedures have been developed. Moreover, it is highly likely, almost a certainty, that new and better treatments for tinnitus will be developed in the future. The future for the tinnitus patient does not have the gloomy approach of past years. The future looks bright.

Each contributor to this book was asked to present his or her approach in the simplest fashion possible. It is not that the contributors are talking down to you, but rather that so little is known about tinnitus that a highly technical language about it has not developed. At the end of each chapter is a list of questions that the tinnitus patient might logically ask of each author and the author's answers to those questions. Each of you will undoubtedly think of unasked questions; and, to that end, we encourage you to write your special questions to Jack Vernon, Ph.D., Oregon Hearing Research Center, NRC04, 3181 Sam Jackson Park Road, Portland, Oregon 97201-3998.

In this book you will find a discussion of the most frequently used relief procedures for the treatment of tinnitus. That there are many different treatments is due, in part, to the fact that there is no one treatment that works for everyone. This is partially because there are so many different possible causes for tinnitus. Since it is not possible to select the treatment best suited to a given individual, it becomes the task of the patient working with his or her primary health care individual to try the different approaches offered here. It can be helpful for you to pass along information about your experiences with treatments to other tinnitus patients but remember—that which works for you may not necessarily work best for others.

Mention has been made of the future for the tinnitus patient; and, in that regard, it is our hope that this book will be out of date and obsolete in very short order, having been replaced by new and better treatments.

In closing, I would like to take this opportunity to express unending appreciation to Ms. Barbara Lighthizer, without whom this book would not exist.

Introduction

JACK VERNON, Ph.D.
Professor of Otolaryngology
Director, Oregon Hearing Research Center
Oregon Health Sciences University
Portland, Oregon

When something goes wrong in most parts of the human body, the signal that something is amiss is usually pain. Once that signal is given, it then usually goes away shortly thereafter, or at least it does not become a permanent condition with which to reckon. To be sure there are cases of intractable and continuing pain, but usually the purpose of pain is to give the indication or signal that something is wrong and then go away. The ear, however, appears to have two signals to indicate malfunction: pain in cases of infection and the like, and tinnitus, which serves as an indicator for almost all auditory problems.

The incidence of severe tinnitus in the United States is extremely high, having been estimated at 7.2 million by one census and 12 million by an American Tinnitus Association estimate. These estimates are restricted to the number of patients with severe tinnitus, that is, the patients who hear tinnitus all the time, the patients who are "climbing-the-walls" with this problem, the patients whose quality of life has been seriously compromised. It is further estimated that 36 million Americans have some form of tinnitus. Many of those with mild tinnitus may be the younger generation given to listening to loud music and for whom continued exposure to such loud sounds will ultimately produce permanent severe tinnitus. Thus, the number of patients with severe tinnitus is very likely to increase over the coming years.

The considerations at issue in this book are for those patients with severe tinnitus. The treatments that are available today are probably most appropriate for those with tinnitus in a severe form and not those who have only a mild or temporary form of tinnitus. For those more fortunate with mild or occasional tinnitus, it is probably sufficient to admonish them to protect their ears against loud sounds, otherwise they can convert their mild and acceptable tinnitus into a severe and most undesirable condition.

In the practice of medicine it is often stated, almost as an inviolate doctrine, that one should not attempt to treat a symptom. Presumably efforts should be expended only to treat the cause of the symptom and not the symptom itself. Sound as that admonition may be, it is not possible in the case of tinnitus. For tinnitus one must, in almost all cases, treat the symptom since that is all that is known. From the Tinnitus Data Registry of the Oregon Hearing Research Center, 47 percent of patients with severe tinnitus have no idea as to what started their tinnitus or even what was associated with its start-up. Noise exposure accounted for 25 percent, ear pathology accounted for 7 percent, head injury for 6 percent and the remaining 15 percent are distributed over a wide variety of possible causes including 2 percent due to whiplash. That tinnitus can result from a whiplash does not mean that there is necessarily a connection between the ears and the neck. Tinnitus produced by whiplash is, most likely, brain trauma resulting from the brain being violently moved about within the cranium.

Even in cases where the cause of tinnitus is known, it is often not possible to treat that cause. For example, tinnitus known to be produced by exposure to excessively loud sounds does not represent a treatable condition. In addition, the fact that the underlying mechanism of tinnitus is unknown means that the direction of potential treatments is undetermined. It is likely that many health care professionals have failed to attempt to treat tinnitus for the reason that they object to treating a symptom. Moreover, as we will see in what follows, the treatments that are presently practiced seriously lack any consensus as to the cause of tinnitus or the mechanisms that underlie its occurrence.

In reading this book one will most likely be impressed not only by the number of different treatments that have been practiced in recent times but also by the number of patients listed as having benefited by each of these treatments. Not infrequently it is difficult to determine what is meant by "benefited." Thus, one must be careful in evaluating patient reaction to treatments. For one thing the tinnitus patient is grateful to any health care professional who will simply pay attention to his or her problem because this patient has been shunned and ignored in so many of his or her attempts to seek help. Or the patient has been victimized by unscrupulous professionals who have conducted an inordinate number of useless tests. For example, we know of one tinnitus patient who repeatedly underwent blood sampling every hour for entire days at a time to the tune of $1800 each day when in fact no attempt was made to relieve the tinnitus (the symptom).

All too often tinnitus patients have been turned away by the health care professional with the statement, "nothing can be done for tinnitus; you will have to learn to live with it." Thus, to these patients statements such as "I think we may be able to help you" or "there are several relief approaches we can try" are eagerly sought-for words of encouragement. And all too often patients who are grateful for positive attention are apt to overestimate the amount of tinnitus reduction actually produced. On the other side of this issue is the fact that studies involving a placebo trial seldom obtain more than 5 percent positive response for the placebo condition.

The contents of this book will reveal that there are many therapies that have been attempted for the relief of tinnitus. Some are more effective than others, and, as should be expected, there is no single treatment that appears to work for all or even for the majority of tinnitus patients. Because tinnitus can be due to so many different causes, it is understandable that many different kinds of treatment ultimately will be required in order to take care of the majority of the tinnitus population.

The fact that a variety of therapies have evolved in recent times is encouraging. As these efforts continue, it is undoubtedly the case that more and more effective treatments will become available.

Note that the word "cure" has not been used. There are no cures for tinnitus and sometimes it is this about which the patient can become confused. When the patient is told there are no cures, it does not mean that there are no relief treatments. Take the simple example of headache. We may not know what has caused the headache, but aspirin is nevertheless prescribed, which you will note is a treatment of the symptom. The aspirin relieves the headache and fortunately in the meantime, nature corrects the causal problem. As investigative efforts continue, as well as attempts to identify the underlying mechanisms of tinnitus, it is undoubtedly the case that cures for tinnitus will be developed. I think it is undoubtedly wrong to give false hope, but I think it is far worse to give no hope.

The following are some bits of information about severe tinnitus that may help the reader to understand what follows. These data are taken from the Tinnitus Data Registry collected at the Oregon Hearing Research Center.

THE QUALITY OF TINNITUS

In a sample of 1544 patients 79 percent described their tinnitus as a relatively pure tone as opposed to 6 percent who described their tinnitus as a noise, and the remaining 15 percent described it as a mixture of both a tone and a noise. The most frequently occurring pitch was a tone of 8000 Hz. To orient you, remember that the highest note on the grand piano is slightly above 4000 Hz.

THE LOUDNESS OF TINNITUS

In a sample of 1503 patients 88 percent had a loudness of 11 dB sensation level (SL) or less. The overall average loudness was 5.7 dB SL. Unfortunately, some health care professionals consider the low level of tinnitus loudness as evidence that those who complain about their tinnitus must have a psychological problem of some sort. On a Visual Analog Scale (0 to 10) for loudness given to 1544, patients the average rating was 7.5 for those with tonal tinnitus and 5.5 for those with noise type tinnitus.

THE MINIMUM MASKING LEVEL

In a sample of 818 patients with severe but maskable tinnitus 40 percent could be masked with a band of noise (2000–12000 Hz) at 8 dB SL or less, 68 percent could be masked with 14 dB SL or less. Recall that normal speech reaches the ears at about 60 to 65 dB.

RESIDUAL INHIBITION

Residual inhibition is defined as a temporary period of suppressed tinnitus immediately following a period of masking. The routine clinical test for residual inhibition is to apply the minimum masking level of noise (2000–12000 Hz) plus 10 dB for 60 seconds. In a sample of 1445 tinnitus patients tested for residual inhibition 91 percent displayed some form of residual inhibition. For some, the residual inhibition was complete disappearance of the tinnitus, while for others it was a partial reduction of tinnitus. On average the residual inhibition lasted 102 seconds.

WEARABLE TINNITUS MASKERS

There are three general forms of wearable tinnitus maskers that can be fitted as either in-the-ear or behind-the-ear units. In a study of 913 patients who could be successfully masked, hearing aids achieved this effect in 16 percent of the cases, tinnitus maskers were successful in 20 percent, and the combination unit (both a hearing aid and a tinnitus masker) was successful in 64 percent of the cases.

PERCEIVED LOCATION OF THE TINNITUS

In a sample of 1932 tinnitus patients the tinnitus was perceived as being located in both ears in 55 percent of the cases, for 20 percent it was located in one ear only (11 percent in the left ear and 9 percent in the right ear), for 24 percent it was located in the head. For 1 percent the location varied. Very rarely is the tinnitus perceived as being located outside the head. Occasionally during partial residual inhibition, a patient will perceive the tinnitus to have moved outside the head as a very faint signal, and, then, as the tinnitus returns to its normal loudness, it appears to move closer and closer until finally it is back inside the ear or head in its usual position and loudness.

NUMBER OF TINNITUS SOUNDS

In a sample of 1664 patients the tinnitus was composed of only one sound in 54 percent of the cases. It was composed of two sounds for 26 percent, three sounds for 9 percent and for 6 percent it was four or more sounds and 5 percent were unsure how many different sounds they heard.

TINNITUS AND HEARING LOSS

Almost 90 percent of the patients seen in the Oregon Tinnitus Clinic have a hearing loss, but only 15 percent of those patients present to the clinic wearing hearing aids although 80 percent confess they have difficulty understanding speech, especially in the presence of background noise. As will be seen in the chapter entitled "The Masking of Tinnitus" by Robert Johnson, the hearing aid can provide relief of tinnitus for a certain number of patients who in most cases have low frequency hearing losses and low pitched tinnitus.

DOES TINNITUS INTERFERE WITH SLEEP?

Of 1113 patients asked this question 78 percent replied in the positive. From these data we conclude that sleep interference can be one of the tinnitus effects contributing to the severity of the condition.

In the chapters that follow there is no prioritizing order beyond the first chapter. The first chapter, by Dr. Alf Axelson, instructs us how to evaluate treatments that are offered to relieve tinnitus. So, naturally, it should be read prior to all else.

We have listed the address of each author in the event that you the reader/patient wish additional information. There are more people today working on tinnitus than ever before so that what is written today will be out of date in short order only to be replaced by better and more effective treatments. Indeed, it seems highly reasonable to me to begin to dream of the day when a cure will be available for tinnitus.

Finally, we need to say that although there are many different therapies considered in this book, nevertheless we have not covered all the various procedures that some patients have found effective. As a general rule we have eliminated those anecdotal reports and claims that have not been subject to serious scrutiny and proper testing test. We have not made it a practice to ignore anecdotal reports. Indeed, we frequently use anecdotal reports to select some procedure or some therapy to test in a more rigorous manner. Anecdotal reports were the beginning of the test of the drug Xanax about which more will be offered later.

Many patients ask how they can keep informed about new advances in the treatment of tinnitus. The answer is simple. Become a member of the American Tinnitus Association, P.O. Box 5, Portland, Oregon 97207.

▶ 1

How to Evaluate Treatments for Tinnitus

ALF AXELSSON, M.D., Ph.D.
Department of Audiology
Sahlgrenska University Hospital
Göteborg, Sweden

INTRODUCTION

Some years ago a device called Audimax was introduced by Doctors Shulman and Tonndorf for treatment of tinnitus. The device was applied on a headband and an emitter with swept ultrasound was placed behind the tinnitus ear. Encouraging results made the device popular for some time. In 1986 there was a report published by Bob Dobie and his group in Seattle. They had performed a controlled study. This meant that they tested the patients with the device on and off without the patient knowing if the device was active or inactive. The patients had to indicate if their tinnitus loudness decreased or not. The study showed that there was no statistically significant effect of Audimax. However, interestingly enough, there was one patient who always noted that his tinnitus decreased when the device was switched on (without the patient knowing this). At the same time (1986) another study from Sweden by Leif Lyttkens' research group reported the same results in a control study of Audimax, that is, with no statistically significant effect. Again, there was one patient who could always tell whether the device was on or off because his tinnitus decreased when it was on. These two studies focus on a number of interesting points concerning the evaluation of treatment for tinnitus:

1. A skeptical attitude to open studies is motivated.
2. Controlled studies are more reliable.
3. From the statistical point of view, Audimax had no effect on tinnitus.
4. In reality, there were at least two patients who benefitted from the treatment.

THE CURE OF TINNITUS

At present, we can state that few patients with tinnitus can be completely cured. These are mainly patients in which the tinnitus comes from vascular disorders or middle ear disorders that can be treated surgically. Similarly, some diseases of the cochlear nerve, such as acoustic neuromas or blood vessels compressing the nerve, may be cured by surgery but definitely not consistently. Other curable causes of tinnitus are those associated with spontaneous otoacoustic emissions, myoclonus, Eustachian tube patency, anaemia, drug-taking effects (e.g., quinine, aspirin), too-rapid drug withdrawal (e.g. from benzodiazepines). It is probably true that in a random sample of patients with tinnitus only a few percent can be completely cured. However, patients with tinnitus from many causes can definitely be improved by different measures even if they are not completely cured.

LITERATURE SURVEY

In the medical literature there are a significant number of articles showing quite surprisingly good results from very different treatments. If one believes these articles, tinnitus treatment would certainly not be a clinical problem. It is not uncommon that many studies report an improvement in as high as 2 out of 3 of the patients treated and sometimes as many as 50 percent completely cured by the treatment. For anyone who works with major patient material such reports are in dramatic contrast to the humble results from clinical experience, and they leave a skeptical attitude towards these studies.

OPEN STUDIES

In an open study a particular treatment is offered to the patient, for instance, some kind of medicine. The patient is asked to perform the treatment in a prescribed manner, for example, one tablet three times a day for two weeks, and then come back to report on how the medication influenced his tinnitus. Many studies performed in this way are those that report very good results of tinnitus treatment with many different remedies. An open study can be somewhat refined by making a severity grading of the tinnitus symptoms before and after treatment with the patient not necessarily "remembering" how he graded his tinnitus before, during, and after treatment.

A definite problem of the open studies of tinnitus is the lack of an objective measure since the tinnitus symptom is completely subjective. The advantage with an open study using the patient's subjective response to the treatment is that this method is rapid and gives an indication whether the treatment can be considered worthwhile to be tried in a more scientifically reliable manner, that is, in a controlled study. They also give the clinician some experience with the treatment and its side-effects, which can be helpful later in design and handling of the controlled study.

What are, then, the explanations for the unrealistically positive treatment results? A common reason is probably that the patient wants to show his appreciation for the care, which may not have been his previous experience. The physician performing the open study may also show particular interest in the patient's statements concerning the tinnitus symptom, which makes the patient respond to the treatment attempt in a positive way. Also, in many tinnitus patients there is probably a basic attitude, a sincere wish, for improvement; and this positive attitude may influence the treatment attempt. Another reason may be that the physician performing the study influences the patient consciously or unconsciously to be more positive to the treatment than what is true. The physician may also have an authoritative attitude giving the nonstated but clear message, "You can rely on me—this treatment will help you." Some patients may fear that the physician would respond in a negative way if they report a negative outcome of the treatment attempt. Cultural attitudes affecting the doctor/patient relationship may also be important. The physician may also have an attitude of being "convinced" that the treatment is good for tinnitus, conveying this positive feeling to the patient unknowingly.

In many of the open studies a particular technical, electrical, magnetic, or other device has been tried or even more common, a recognized pharmacological agent or some kind of alternative medicine. There is no doubt that in many of these investigations the responsible physician has received payment from the manufacturer of the device or medicine for the examination of the report. I think it is only fair to state that such economic transactions may also influence the reported results. But, apart from that, there is a natural wish by the clinician for this trial to be successful and this can lead to observer bias in interpreting the patients' reports.

CONTROLLED STUDIES

In a controlled study the treatment is compared with so-called placebo treatment, that is, one trial period consists of active treatment, for instance, one tablet three times a day for two weeks; and during a second trial period, the patient gets inactive placebo tablets of the same configuration, taste, and dosage as the other tablets but without the active substance. An initial treatment of placebo or active treatment is randomly distributed among the patients. At the end of the study the patient can make a preference for one of the treatments or consider them equal. Again, the results can be somewhat refined by using different scales of severity grading. In cases for which the control study shows positive results there is an obvious need for further detailed studies. Since tinnitus has many different causes, there might also be different mechanisms involved in the origin of tinnitus. Consequently, it would be important to study those cases with a positive result in more detail to see what they have in common—gender, age, diagnosis, hearing, tinnitus characteristics, and so on. The result of such detailed studies could be that a certain treatment is recommended for certain cases of tinnitus. From the scientific point of view this type of study is much more reliable than the open study. However, there is another problem with the controlled study and that is from the statistical point of view.

STATISTICS

In statistics one often uses the term "significance level." It is common to use figures like 90, 95, or 99 percent significance level. If we look at adult males, we can state that it is probably true that adult males are between 5 and 7 feet tall (150-210 cm). This is probably statistically true at a 99 percent level, that is, the heights of 99 out of 100 adult males are within this range. However, as we all know there are extremely short as well as tall males outside of the given figures. In order to cover all adult males in the world we would probably have to give figures in the range of 3 to 9 feet. Since there are extremely few adult males who are between 3 and 5 feet or 7 and 9 feet, it is practical to use a statistical significance level covering 90 or 99 percent of a population. So, returning to the above Audimax example, this treatment had no "statistically significant" effect on tinnitus, which was the truth for most tinnitus patients but not for the two positive responders. It is very important to find scientific methods to identify even those few responders to any tinnitus treatment.

As is well-known, there are symptoms and diseases that can be cured in 100 percent of the cases, and at the other extreme, there are diseases that are completely incurable. There is no doubt that the symptom of tinnitus is very difficult to cure. Suppose that we had 1000 tinnitus patients who tried 1000 different suggested treatments. Suppose also that each one of these 1000 patients found one treatment that was effective for them only and not for any of the 999 other patients. Obviously, from the statistical point of view such a treatment would not give significant benefit. So, on the one hand, we can state that open studies have a tendency to give results that are too positive, and, on the other hand, controlled studies tend to give results that are too negative (from a statistical point of view).

In conclusion, there is a surprisingly large number of uncontrolled open studies showing good results with treatment for tinnitus by very varying measures. On the other hand, there is a substantial lack of controlled studies. These may show a too negative result because of the resistant nature of tinnitus to treatment. There is no doubt that if there was a good cure for tinnitus available this would be known world-wide today considering the rapid spread of information.

At present, we would like to recommend the following approach: In tinnitus clinics with a substantial number of patients, obviously many different treatment attempts are made. The patient should report the outcome of the individual treatment attempts and these should be collected and reviewed in order to investigate what type of treatment would be appropriate for a subsequent controlled study. If, for instance, 50 patients have tried preparation X and only one patient has benefitted from this, it would probably not be appropriate to perform a controlled study. However, if 10 patients reported subjective benefit from the treatment, this could indicate that the treatment would be worthwhile for a controlled trial. A useful approach is that of a preliminary open study and a subsequent controlled study for those who reported positively to the preliminary open study. This is called an "enrichment study" and is probably one of the best ways of applying a scientific approach to a condition with a fairly low response rate.

ETHICS

It is natural that in a disease that is basically incurable "everything" has been tried. This is also the case with tinnitus treatment. All kinds of different medications have been tried including various surgical procedures and different forms of so-called "alternative" medicine. It is also probably true that some unethical persons try to introduce treatments that often are fairly expensive in order to make money. It is not uncommon that the remedy is advertised accompanied by one patient's photograph and this particular patient states that he has benefitted or was cured by that remedy. It is also natural that people with an incurable disease are willing to try "everything" with the hope of getting rid of their troublesome symptom. The experienced tinnitus reader has certainly seen this type of advertisement over the years and there is no need here to specifically review such treatments. I suggest that it is important for the patients to have a skeptical attitude. It is important to find out where the reported study was made, in a well-recognized hospital or university clinic, or by an unknown private practitioner. It is also good if the patient questions the method of investigation.

ADVICE FOR THE INDIVIDUAL TINNITUS PATIENT

It is natural that tinnitus patients who meet each other also share their experiences of tinnitus as well as of its treatments. It is also very natural that someone who had a positive experience from some kind of treatment tries to convey this positive experience to other tinnitus patients. Since they often consider themselves lucky in finding some kind of beneficial treatment, they would also unconsciously try to convince others to try the same treatment. However, as we know, a particular treatment may help one patient but very few others. The attitude should rather be, "It worked for me, but of course I cannot guarantee that it will work for you," rather than "It worked for me; I think it will work for you, too."

Since there are mostly negative experiences of different treatments and very few positive, from the psychological point of view, it is easy to understand that most patients would rather accept the positive report from other tinnitus patients than negative reports from clinical trials. Obviously, from the scientific point of view, these kinds of statements are not very valuable; and from the patient's point of view, usually lead to recurrent disappointments and an attitude towards tinnitus that tends to slow down the normal process of learning (to some extent) to live with it.

If you as a tinnitus patient have found some kind of treatment that seems to decrease your tinnitus, you probably would not continue this treatment for the rest of your life. It is very important that you consult your physician about the side-effects, about the effect of long-term use of the treatment, and so on. I think it is also wise, once in a while, to force an intermission in the treatment to see how the tinnitus "behaves." Maybe you will have a remaining positive effect for some time such that you can then try an intermittent treatment. Also, if the tinnitus deteriorates and you try your treatment again, and it works again, this tells you that it is even more true that this particular type of treatment works for you. Again, since in many cases we are talking about treatment attempts that will last for years, it is very important that you try to "force" your physician to give you answers to your questions. It is a fairly common experience that patients are too shy to press their doctors on such specific points that they subsequently have to turn to Readers' Queries in medical magazines to get a satisfactory answer.

FUTURE ASPECTS

Today there is no particularly successful remedy for tinnitus. The best treatment available is probably a combination of counselling and psychological cognitive measures combined with relaxation. The aim of the treatment today has to be to change the psychological attitude of the patients, trying to make them accept the tinnitus. However, it is also obvious from the psychological point of view that people want to try new suggested measures. They want to take chances rather than accept the sad fact that they will have to live with the tinnitus symptoms for the rest of their lives. This, of course, must not result in a nihilistic attitude from researchers in trying to find a remedy that cures tinnitus.

PATIENT'S QUESTIONS AND ANSWERS

1. *Question:*   Since tinnitus is a sound we hear in the head or ears, how can you test it?

Answer: Testing is primarily done by introducing comparison sounds, such as tones, until the patient finds one that is similar to their tinnitus. Once the sound similar to tinnitus is determined, it is then used to determine the loudness of the tinnitus.

2. *Question:*   You used the term "placebo." What is a placebo?

   Answer: Placebo means a fake, useless treatment; it is like a sugar pill. The purpose of the placebo is to determine whether or not the treatment effect is real or imagined. In conventional drug tests that include a placebo trial, it is customary for a substantial number of the placebo trials to obtain positive responses.

3. *Question:*   The controlled studies of the Audimax always found one person who got relief of tinnitus by its use. Is it worthwhile for each of us to be tested with this equipment?

   Answer: The outside chance that you might be that one person who gets relief with the Audimax might be worthwhile if there were no other treatments available. As it is, however, your time would be more profitably spent exploring current and effective treatments of tinnitus.

▶ 2

Therapeutic Blind Alleys

ROSS COLES, M.D.
Institute of Hearing Research
University Park, Nottingham
United Kingdom, England

As a medical student in London in the late forties and early fifties, I well remember the wisdom of one of the clinical teachers who told the students that "You can always tell how little we know about any condition by the number of treatments listed in the textbooks: the more numerous the treatments, the less is known." If I recall correctly, he was referring to dermatology, disorders of the skin. But the same truism could be applied to many other conditions. Certainly tinnitus would be one of them and, up to a point, it still is.

In fact, we do know quite a lot about tinnitus these days and how to help people with it, and in a few cases cure it. But the fact is that there is as yet no quick, easy, and highly effective treatment for the majority of people with tinnitus. And this often leads them to endless searches for cures.

In a sense, looking for a cure is not always a good thing for the person with tinnitus, because in the end the majority of them do indeed have to learn to live with their noise. They get annoyed when doctors tell them that; it is so easy to say, so difficult to do. In fact, what the doctor says is quite right; but of course there are different ways of saying it. The emphasis we have been teaching in our annual (since 1981) British, and now European, instructional courses on tinnitus has been to add "but we are going to help you to do so."

The trouble with looking for a cure is that it concentrates the mind on the tinnitus and leads to ever increasing frustration and anxiety when each attempted treatment fails. All this tends to wind up the tinnitus and delay the time when the person starts wholeheartedly to look for ways of living with tinnitus and adjusting to it, which the vast majority do, sooner or later. That is not to say, of course, that most of them would still not like to be without their tinnitus; but at least in most cases they reach a state in which it is no longer something that discolors their whole life. Perhaps the ideal target is that expressed to me by a worker in heavy industry with noise-induced tinnitus. At one time he was quite desperate with his tinnitus; but now he says that although it is just as loud as originally, it no longer troubles him. He added, "Indeed I would only notice it if it went."

Nevertheless, many people want to look for devices, drugs, dietary managements, and so on to help them with their tinnitus. And while the story of research on cures is a somewhat dismal one, as might be predicted on scientific grounds, there are a few people who appear to benefit from almost every treatment recommended (see Chapter 1 by Alf Axelsson). The important thing, I think, is that when you read about someone else's successful management of tinnitus you do not automatically accept it as gospel truth. By all means give it a try if it is safe and is not too harmful to your pocket, but do not expect a lot and be philosophical about the high probability of being disappointed.

There is another aspect to all this too. Although medical science has in fact many limitations, some people seem to misinterpret TV programs and newspaper articles about the marvels of modern medicine as meaning that the cause of everything is now understood and that any failure to diagnose or cure is the fault of the doctor. From the professional point of view, too, we have to be careful not to become arrogant and think we know it all. There is still plenty of room for the unexpected and the unexplained. So each report of benefits from some particular latest therapy needs to be given serious consideration. For the last decade and a half I have been doing that, somewhat unofficially, on behalf of the British Tinnitus Association. The problem is, though, that if a proper clinical trial were given to every new treatment and every *cure* reported by individuals, a very large proportion of the nation's available research staff, funds, and time would be used up in largely fruitless trials.

My own policy therefore has been to look critically at what has been claimed to be helpful, to ascertain how much evidence there is of its benefit according to the people who have tried it: but in that I need also to bear in mind that people who have not benefitted from it seldom report the fact. I look at its possible scientific explanation and then, if it still looks sufficiently promising, I give it an open trial.

The purist scientist holds up his hands in horror at open trials. This is where a number of patients are simply given the treatment, to see how they get on with it. Of course if we get a positive result, then that cannot be interpreted as a success. But the result may be regarded as an indication for going on to a proper controlled trial. On the other hand, a negative result can be interpreted firmly as indicating that the treatment is giving little, if any, benefit.

A weakly positive trial has to be viewed with great suspicion as there is always the risk of wishful thinking by the person with tinnitus that it has helped, or perhaps even a desire to please the doctor (see, again, Chapter 1). To get over this tendency, I always give my patients very strong negative counselling about these trial treatments. This involves saying that I do not really expect the treatment to work, but that I think there is just enough chance that it might do so that I think it worthwhile for me to spend a bit of time in giving it a trial. I also ask them to be very careful in their reports on the treatment to be critical as to whether their tinnitus has really improved, and they must certainly not try to please me with their reports.

On the whole, I have been satisfied with this approach to trying various remedies, although I often feel two slight anxieties. The first is that by keeping a list of patients who would like to try any new remedy, their search for a *cure* may serve to delay their coming to terms with their tinnitus. On the whole, though, they tend to be patients who have tried all or most of the more conventional treatments and have not obtained sufficient benefit such that they would like to try something new if it came along. My other anxiety is that such a body of people may be a self-selected group of non-responders to any treatment (if such people exist). When working with some drug companies, they have not been too happy with my body of subjects for trials; but my response is that nobody wants to take drugs if they can avoid doing so, and therefore any tinnitus treatment involving drugs must be reserved for those whom it has been impossible to help sufficiently by more conventional and non-drug means. Thus, I think I have in fact had the right target population for drug trials.

Over the years I have investigated a considerable number of claimed remedies, and they all proved negative. These included oxygen inhalations, and then carbogen (a mixture of oxygen and carbon dioxide) inhalations, in 16 patients without benefit; multiple vitamin B preparations in 50 patients, with possible benefit in 6 patients; carbonium suphuratum salts used in 11, without success; likewise with ERA-Q salts; TENS, transcutaneous electrical nerve stimulation, as used in treatment of pain, without success in 13 tinnitus patients; and sodium fluoride, which did not seem to have any effect on the tinnitus itself in 17 patients with otosclerosis, but probably has a place in preventing the advance of deafness in that condition.

During the last few months before my retirement, in 1992, acupuncture became available locally within the National Health Service (NHS). In discussion with the acupuncturist, in fact she was a specially trained physiotherapist working in the Pain Clinic, we thought that patients having both tinnitus and neck or jaw disorders might be most appropriate for this. Indeed, all three patients that I referred did quite well. I am not sure if the tinnitus was actually reduced, but the neck and jaw discomfort did and therefore their overall ability to cope with the tinnitus improved. But three cases does not prove anything, it is just encouraging.

I also referred a few cases to a local hypnotist, as fee paying patients, but that did not seem to help them much. On the other hand, more recent experience with the use of hypnosis in the hands of Dr. Arleta Starza, an NHS clinical psychologist, was much more positive; and she found it to be very helpful in many cases as an adjunct to relaxation training. A word is needed here to say that this use of hypnosis, and self-hypnosis, is poles apart from what might be called *stage hypnosis*. In that, you can imagine someone being rather theatrically hypnotised and then told that when the hypnotist wakes them up they will no longer hear their tinnitus. That simply does not work, just as it does not work for chronic pain.

DRINKS, FOOD, ALCOHOL, TOBACCO, AND MEDICATIONS

Before going on to the particular trials about which I have been asked to write, I would like to take this opportunity to say a few words on the theme of the effects on tinnitus of certain drinks, foods, and medications, and of alcohol and tobacco. Tinnitus people are sometimes advised not to drink tea and coffee because of their high content of caffeine and to avoid red wines, ports and such like, and to avoid certain foods. But to tell tinnitus people generally to avoid a list of drinks and foods usually has no effect on their tinnitus and merely detracts further from their quality of life. The same goes also for smoking and alcohol, there being no evidence that these are harmful to hearing or cause tinnitus, except possibly from severe chronic alcoholism: indeed there is weak scientific evidence that smokers and moderate drinkers actually hear better and have less tinnitus. There are of course other reasons for advice against smoking, but tinnitus is not one of them.

What people need to do if they wish to try and search out whether some particular food or drink, or tobacco or alcohol, is temporarily aggravating their tinnitus is to go on a system of *withdrawal and rechallenge.* You withdraw from the suspected aggravators for a matter of one or two weeks: if the tinnitus then seems to be rather better, then deliberately go back onto them, what we call rechallenging the system, and see if the tinnitus gets worse again. But tinnitus can fluctuate so much at times, and particularly with perhaps some hopeful expectation of benefit, that you need to do this withdrawal and rechallenge at least three times before you can be sure that they are really upsetting your tinnitus. You can then consider the degree of relief given by avoidance of these things and decide on whether the advantage outweighs the loss of enjoyment in doing without them. If you experience improvement, and you cut out all these suspected aggravators, you can then go further to find out if it is really necessary to go without all of them, by deliberately relaxing (rechallenging) one of these items at a time.

With respect to medications one has to be a bit more careful. The drugs are presumably being taken for some good reason and to stop them could be hazardous to health. So any trial withdrawal and rechallenge from a particular drug suspected of causing (temporarily) or aggravating tinnitus has to be done in consultation with your doctor. The principle is the same though. In fact, there are not many drugs that cause permanent harm to your hearing and tinnitus, the ones that do being quite rarely used drugs. These are mainly certain lifesaving antibiotics that are given in very serious infections and some of the anticancer drugs. Quinine and similar drugs in very high doses may cause permanent harm in a few people, but the evidence for this is thin. It is even thinner for aspirin and other pain relieving drugs and for the loop-diuretics, drugs that act on the kidney to increase the excretion of urine, for instance, in treatment of high blood pressure, heart failure, or fluid retention. Such drugs usually do not damage the hearing but, coupled with some of the other drugs or high noise levels, may very occasionally do so. The other drugs that are said to cause tinnitus do so infrequently and only temporarily, just while on the drug, and it is often possible to switch to another drug of the same general type.

You may wonder why so many drugs have tinnitus listed as a side effect. This is simply because tinnitus can arise as a temporary symptom of distress from the body against something that is upsetting it. The drugs that are most commonly blamed for doing this are the nonsteroidal anti-inflammatory drugs, the kind of drugs you take for chronic arthritis; also the beta-blockers, most commonly taken to control the heart beat and blood pressure; and also some of the antidepressants. You will note that these drugs are used in treating conditions that are common in the middle aged and elderly. Tinnitus is also more common in the middle aged and the elderly, and purely coincidental associations between onset or increase in tinnitus and the taking of such a drug must be common. It seems probable that these coincidences largely account for why so many of these and some other drugs are reputed to cause or aggravate tinnitus. In most cases they have not in fact had any such effect, but occasionally they really are (temporarily) to blame. If that is suspected, then it becomes a matter of withdrawal and rechallenge, or switching to another drug to check the cause.

MAGNETS IN THE EAR CANAL

The story of my involvement in this starts with the arrival through the post of a small airmail parcel with a Japanese stamp on it. It was from a doctor whom I had met some years previously and who had been involved in trying some powerful rare earth magnets, placed deep in the ear canal as a treatment for tinnitus. This had been written up in one of the lesser known Japanese journals devoted to ear, nose, and throat work. In 56 patients Dr. Takeda reported tinnitus reduction in 37, no change in 18 and an increase in one. The benefit was said to take several days to develop but would last for at least three weeks and sometimes even longer. I discussed the matter with physicists and physiologists at the Institute of Hearing Research, but this did not reveal any reasonable explanation of how the magnets might affect the ear. But there I was, with a number of tinnitus patients looking for help and what appeared to be quite a simple remedy on my desk, so I conducted one of my open trials. The magnets themselves were very small, little disks about 2 mm in diameter and 1 mm deep. An assistant mounted these in cotton wool and placed one close to the ear drum of each tinnitus ear, with the north pole of the magnet facing inward as recommended by Dr. Takeda. In 42 patients who tried them, 14 reported some improvement.

We felt that the open trial gave sufficient grounds for optimism for us to set up a proper trial. This was conducted in my own clinic in Nottingham jointly with colleagues in a tinnitus clinic in Birmingham. We used placebo magnets, which were made of identical material and size, but not magnetized, as controls. The trial was double-blind—the patients did not know whether they were having the active treatment or the placebo, and neither did the clinical observer. Another member of staff at each of the two sites did, of course, know because they had to choose and insert the correct magnets. Only after the trial was over was the double-blind code broken to reveal what kind of treatment, active or placebo, each patient had had. This procedure ensured that there was no bias in either the patients' reports or the observing doctors' interpretation of them.

In all, we treated 51 patients. One had to be excluded at an early stage because he discovered that he was on the active treatment. He decided to scratch his ear with a metal paper clip and suddenly the magnet flew out of his ear and attached itself to the clip, much to his embarrassment and to our amusement. Another patient had quite a major change in her hearing state that in itself would have affected her tinnitus, and so she was not a fair subject to include in the analysis. In the end 26 patients had active magnets: in 7 their tinnitus improved, and in 7 it got worse. Twenty-three patients had the placebo magnet: 4 improved and 3 got worse. You do not have to be a mathematician to see that these results indicate no significant benefit from this treatment; at any rate, in the way we applied it, which followed closely the methods described by Dr. Takeda. It also illustrates the potentially misleading results that can arise from open, uncontrolled trials.

We went on to try pulsed electromagnetic stimulation, which is sometimes used in medicine and in veterinary work for treatment of disorders of the muscles, ligaments, and joints. There had been a report that a patient had also noticed a reduction in his tinnitus. But in an open trial in about 12 patients, we got no satisfactory results using an electromagnetic stimulator of the kind used for the other treatments.

I thought the story on magnetic treatment was going to stop there, but more recently the subject has been reopened. With a different kind of electromagnetic stimulator, another patient had tried it on his head and it seemed to reduce his tinnitus. A formal trial was set up in Liverpool by an ear, nose, and throat surgeon, Nick Roland, together with some of his otological and audiological colleagues. The results were published in the journal Clinical Otolaryngology in 1993. From their double-blind placebo-controlled trial involving 58 patients, there were slight but statistically significant more frequent benefits in those on the active treatment. The authors concluded their paper by saying, "However, we feel these initial positive results have shown sufficient promise to embark on a major study involving a larger number of patients with tinnitus."

Their second study has now been completed. It also has been rather inconclusive; it seems that electromagnetic stimulation with that particular form of stimulator is not markedly beneficial for tinnitus. Whether or not further research will be carried out is uncertain. The treatment remains a possibility, though, but not a very promising one. The fact remains that the instrument (Therapak) is in use in the United Kingdom, with regular advertisements of it in *Quiet,* the journal of the British Tinnitus Association (BTA), and occasionally, patients are reporting benefit from it. The BTA has no objection to such advertisements since the treatment is unlikely to do any harm whatsoever, occasionally seems to benefit some patients, and the firm refunds all but £5 of the cost of the equipment (£55) if the treatment is not found to be successful and the instrument is returned within six weeks. Not a bad deal really, but whether this line of treatment will ever prove to be something more useful seems rather unlikely. I am sure any good news of it would soon spread to the professional journals and the newsletters of the national tinnitus associations, and I can simply invite readers to "Keep your eyes on this space."

LIDOCAINE (LIGNOCAINE, XYLOCAINE)

Lidocaine, lignocaine, and xylocaine are names given in different countries to the same substance, the local anaesthetic that the dentist frequently uses. But when it is injected into a vein of a tinnitus patient, it will abolish the tinnitus in about half of the cases and much reduce it in many of the others. The duration of the relief is only a matter of minutes up to perhaps a couple of hours, occasionally longer. But intravenous injections having such a short duration of effect are not really a practicable treatment. They also have to be done under careful safety control in a hospital environment, and repeated injections maybe somewhat toxic to the liver.

On the other hand, tinnitus sufferers can take enormous encouragement from this finding, which has been repeated in quite a number of countries, notably New Zealand, the United States, and the United Kingdom. It proves that tinnitus can be abolished by a drug. That is, it is not something that is totally untouchable by medical means. But we already knew that tinnitus was not necessarily permanent, since in some patients it is intermittent and its fluctuations are not associated with any change in hearing or anything else that we can measure, apart from the tinnitus.

What we need now is to find an oral analogue, a drug that can be taken by mouth that has the same effect and is fairly free of side-effects. Lidocaine is thought to work by what can be called a "membrane stabilizing" action. Therefore, there have been numerous trials of other membrane stabilizing drugs that can be taken by mouth to see whether they have any effect on tinnitus. The two main groups of such drugs are those that act on the central nervous system and are or can be used in the treatment of epilepsy; and those that are used in the treatment of overactivity of the heart muscle, causing irregularities of the heart beat. Of the first group, the tranquilizers seem to help. Of these I personally favor clonazapam since it is less addictive and seems to work in a very low dosage (0.5 to 2mg a day). But I suspect it works by calming the person and reducing tension rather than by any direct effect on the tinnitus. Xanax has been used for this purpose in the United States but is banned for use in the United Kingdom because of its highly addictive properties. Probably the best of the anti-epilepsy drugs is carbamazepine (Tegretol). Occasionally this seems to reduce tinnitus, and in the same way it can also help with chronic pain, but it is quite an unpleasant drug for many people and also has some effects on the blood quality that need careful monitoring. I regard it as a last resort drug. Recent evidence from Birmingham in the United Kingdom suggests that the cardiac anti-dysrhythmic drug nimodipine may be useful, but we must really await the results of further research on that and other new drugs.

So at present we have not found any drug that can be taken by mouth that will have the same effects as lidocaine given into a vein. As a result two other approaches have been made with lidocaine to try to get it into the internal ear, where it has been thought by some to have its effect in reducing tinnitus. In Germany they studied the use of iontophoresis for this. This is a technique previously developed in the United States, for anaesthetizing the ear drum prior to minor surgery on it. A solution of lidocaine is put into the external ear and a weak DC electric current is passed through the solution to cause the lidocaine to pass through the ear drum. First reports from Germany for its use in treating tinnitus were very promising, although they did not do a properly controlled study. The result was that at the Third International Tinnitus Seminar, held in Münster in 1987, the conference registration documents included an advertisement for an instrument called the Tinnicur. In fact it was just an iontophoresis instrument, presented as a tinnitus treatment. But subsequent studies from elsewhere in Germany, in the Netherlands, the United Kingdom, and probably elsewhere have all failed to repeat the original results from Germany, and I do not think this treatment has any merit. I myself tried it in 15 patients, without any useful benefit resulting.

The next method of trying to get lidocaine into the internal ear was even more dramatic. That was to actually inject the lidocaine solution through the ear drum and then position the head so that the fluid pooled over the round window membrane, the membrane separating the middle ear from the internal ear. First reports from Japan, where this has been tried out extensively, recorded reduction in tinnitus severity in 42 out of 58 ears treated. Work from Israel also reported some good results. The Japanese went on to give injections into the middle ear of a steroid, dexamethasone. Our attention was drawn to this work by a member of the British Tinnitus Association who keeps a watch on research papers and has been very helpful to us at times, although he must be disappointed with the outcomes of his work. So we tried this treatment in Nottingham, starting with the dexamethasone and then, if that did not work, going on to the lidocaine.

We ended up by using it on only seven patients, for reasons that will become apparent. The dexamethasone seemed to do nothing, but the lidocaine produced extremely unpleasant side-effects. The trouble is that the internal ear contains not just the hearing organ but also the balance (vestibular) organ, which the lidocaine temporarily paralyzes. The action of this can be compared with the engines of a twin engine aircraft. The aircraft flies along a straight course provided both engines are going at the same speed. But if one engine suddenly slows down or stops, the aircraft immediately goes off course, as do we, in a violently giddy way, if one of our balance organs suddenly fails. The aircraft pilot would then correct his rudder to put the plane back on the right course. Likewise, our brain can compensate for a vestibular imbalance, but it takes a period of several weeks for the brain to do that. In the meantime, if the imbalance between the left and right ears continues, there is severe vertigo often with nausea and vomiting.

Every one of our seven tinnitus patients thus treated suffered such severe vertigo that they had to be admitted to the hospital until the effects of the lidocaine wore off. This is hardly a treatment that recommends itself for management of tinnitus, especially as it did not seem to help the tinnitus either. And at about the same time, a similar open trial of this treatment had been carried out by my friend and colleague Alf Axelsson in Göteborg, Sweden. He tried it in only six of his tinnitus clinic patients. In none of his cases was there any longstanding relief, and in most cases there was such violent vertigo, nausea, and vomiting for several hours that he also discontinued this as a possible line of treatment for tinnitus.

GINKGO BILOBA

Extract of Ginkgo biloba (EGB) is probably the most popular of herbal treatments that have frequently been thought to be helpful for tinnitus, and some years ago there was a lot of correspondence in the then *Newsletter of the British Tinnitus Association* about it. It largely arose from a report from Germany by Sprenger in 1986. In 62 patients with hearing impairment Sprenger reported improvements in hearing for 22 patients, and in the 33 having tinnitus, it was abolished in 12 and reduced in 5. Such a report, reinforced by several others, could not be ignored.

Consequently, we undertook an open, uncontrolled trial along the lines I have already described, using our usual procedures to discourage, as far as we could, unrealistic expectations of benefit from the treatment. Twenty-three tinnitus clinic patients took part, each taking one 14 mg tablet of EGB three times a day for twelve weeks. Twenty-one patients completed the trial. Eleven reported no change in their tinnitus, two said it was slightly less, and two very slightly less. But two reported that their tinnitus had become very slightly worse, two slightly worse, and one markedly worse. There were some side-effects, too, but in only two of these did they necessitate interruption of treatment, one due to indigestion and one due to depression.

Evidently from this study, even though it was an open uncontrolled one, EGB given in this way was not beneficial overall. Several other more recent studies have given similar results with no statistical advantage over a placebo drug. One or two patients who had apparent benefit wanted to stay on it, and I certainly had no objection to them doing so. The results illustrate something commonly experienced in tinnitus—that for many people it is far from a static condition, tending to wax and wane. This makes studies of treatment very difficult. Ginkgo then is almost a perfect example of how one must not get too excited about a few people reporting benefits from some treatment. You have to look at the whole picture, and then you often find that there are many other patients who seem worse *on* the treatment. But they only rarely volunteer that information. The result is that anecdotal reports on supposed remedies for tinnitus tend to be one-sided.

Nowadays I certainly do not stop patients from trying EGB, although in the United Kingdom it is only available in homeopathic strengths. I do not think it can do any harm, perhaps some people may get some benefit, and it is not expensive. My attitude is rather the same toward other herbal remedies and homeopathic preparations. The latter defy the ordinary concepts of medicine but nevertheless have many followers, and I would not be so arrogant to declare categorically that they are wrong. But I do not positively encourage patients to try these treatments; and I do warn them that repeated searches for a cure tends to be counterproductive to development of adaptation to their tinnitus.

FALSE RESULTS AND FALSE HOPES

I think the false hope given by individual people in reporting how a particular therapy has worked for them is probably explained by the sort of results reported in the trials of ginkgo and the magnets. Tinnitus often fluctuates in intensity; and if by chance someone is trying some remedy and this happens to coincide with a spontaneously better period of tinnitus, this then appears to be a successful treatment. The same fluctuation, of course, explains why so many drugs are blamed for making tinnitus worse when in fact the worsening tinnitus and the taking of the drug is in most cases nothing more than coincidental.

Why some medical and scientific reports claim such marvelous results is more difficult to explain. It is sufficient to say that among those working on tinnitus we have come well used to these claims and we take them all with a large pinch of salt. We say, "Well let us see if that stands up to further trial in another center." Indeed, there are so many allegedly successful treatments for tinnitus that if they were all true, or indeed any of them were true, there would be no need for any further research. Quite plainly there is such need. So what has gone wrong in these research studies that claim such good results?

One hates to say it, but there is always the risk of frank dishonesty. I think the vast majority of medical research scientists and doctors are honest, however, they can delude themselves. Also, in the Japanese studies I have mentioned, I wonder whether they have been influenced by an Oriental dislike of losing face or causing their doctor to do so. And in some countries the doctors are held in great awe and they speak to their patients in a very authoritarian way, almost ordering the patient to take the treatment and get better. Perhaps some patients are then afraid to say that the treatment has not worked. I am sure that some patients respond well to this approach and feel less anxiety about their condition, which in turn allows the tinnitus to wind down a bit and there is a real improvement. I have often wondered if my own approach to patients is too gentle, and whether it might have been better for my patients if I had been less truthful and more forceful.

So while we can take hopeful encouragement from research reports of success with some new treatment, we must not allow ourselves to get too excited about them until they have been studied further. And we must be prepared to be disappointed by their results. In the meantime, research continues on many fronts, and I am sure that sooner or later we will get a drug or some other treatment that will bring speedy relief for the most commons forms of tinnitus.

PATIENT'S QUESTIONS AND ANSWERS

1. *Question:*   I see that you make reference to a British Tinnitus Association. Is there an American Tinnitus Association?
   Answer: Yes, indeed. The American Tinnitus Association was the first of its kind. Its address is ATA, P.O. Box 5, Portland, Oregon 97207. ATA publishes a quarterly journal that provides general and up-dating information about tinnitus.

2. *Question:*   You report that 12 percent of those using a multiple vitamin B preparation got relief of their tinnitus. Did these patients display a vitamin B deficiency?
   Answer: No, not clinically. We did not test their blood specifically for that. Vitamin deficiency in the general population of developed countries is very rare.

   On the other hand, the possibility of vitamin B_{12} deficiency is covered in detail in Chapter 10. This reports a study of military personnel in Israel, which revealed that those with measured B_{12} deficiency were more susceptible to noise-induced hearing loss and noise-induced tinnitus. The data are not totally clear cut. For example, in the group with noise-induced hearing loss and noise-induced tinnitus, 47 percent also had a vitamin B_{12} deficiency, as compared with 27 percent in those with noise-induced hearing loss but no tinnitus, and 19 percent in those with normal audiograms and no tinnitus. In Nottingham, UK, in reaction to this work, we checked blood B_{12} and folate levels in about 50 of our Tinnitus Clinic patients but found no significant difference between them and the general population. A few cases with abnormally low levels were treated appropriately but without any effect on their hearing or tinnitus. Perhaps there is some racial, geographical, or occupational factor accounting for the much higher rates of B_{12} deficiency in Israeli military personnel.

3. *Question:*   I have heard of at least one patient who found that red wine relieved his tinnitus. Does that make any sense?
   Answer: That which might be effective for one patient is not necessarily effective for other patients. Indeed, the result of some procedure for one patient is very different from a full blown study of that procedure. I will bet that if we question a group of tinnitus patients about the effect of red wine, we will find many for whom red wine makes tinnitus worse. I would guess that the relaxation produced by the red wine is more likely what that one patient actually experienced.

4. *Question:* The results with injected lidocaine are impressive. Is there an oral form of that drug?

Answer: That is partly covered in this chapter. More tales are that a drug called tocainide is a close oral form of lidocaine; but when it was tested in three different centers in the USA and in our clinic here, the results were very disappointing. Roughly one person in 20 got tinnitus relief, while the rest experienced many side effects. Another such drug is flecainide, but trials of this in our clinic and in the USA have also been disappointing. Moreover, occasionally these drugs can produce life-threatening side effects, such that my own feeling is that use of these drugs for treatment of tinnitus is not justified.

5. *Question:* I understand your reluctance to accept anecdotal reports from patients but to wait for properly controlled study seems to take a long time.

Answer: That is true, and, for the most part, it is probably permissible for you to try treatments about which you have heard positive things. Just keep in mind that many of these so-called positive cases are unlikely to be effective treatments in general and be prepared to be disappointed.

3

Medical Aspects of Tinnitus

ALEXANDER SCHLEUNING, M.D.
Chairman, Department of Otolaryngology,
Head and Neck Surgery
Oregon Health Sciences University
Portland, Oregon

Medical diseases and emotional factors not only may cause, but may greatly affect, the severity of tinnitus. Since tinnitus is a symptom, it is often regarded as a non-medical entity. However, our own experience and medical literature reveals that there are a number of clinical conditions in which tinnitus is the major symptom. There are two types of tinnitus that the physician and the patient are apt to experience: (1) *objective* and (2) *subjective.*

OBJECTIVE TINNITUS

When the patient's tinnitus can be heard by the physician, certain conditions are suspected. This is called audible or objective tinnitus and should be considered when the sound is blowing in character, corresponds to respiration, when it is pulsating, or rough in character, or when there is a rapid succession of clicking or popping sounds. The physician may be able to hear this tinnitus by placing his or her ear (or stethoscope) against the patient's external canal or mastoid bone. A tube from the external ear of the patient to the physician can also be used to transmit sound from the patient to the observer.

Tinnitus that corresponds with breathing, usually indicates an abnormally patent (open) eustachian tube. This tinnitus is extremely distressing and may frequently occur after weight loss or in debilitated individuals who have experienced a long term illness. It may also occur without apparent cause. Fortunately, most patients who have this symptom only experience it for a short time (days or months). Symptoms can be relieved by lying down or by putting the head in a lowered position. Individuals with this complaint should generally see their physician because there are a variety of both medical and surgical methods to relieve the symptoms if they are persistent.

Occasionally, a patient will have tinnitus that is characterized by sharp or irregular clicks heard for several seconds to minutes at a time. This type of tinnitus is generally intermittent, although it may occur repeatedly during the day. The cause is not well understood, but the mechanism is. The sound is produced by contractions of the muscles of the soft palate or, in some instances, muscles of the middle ear. The fluttering that occurs is very much like the fluttering of an eye that individuals may experience with fatigue or stress.

Tinnitus that is synchronous with the heartbeat and pulsating in nature may indicate a variety of cardiac or vascular abnormalities. This may be due to abnormal vascular flow from arteries to veins somewhere in the head and neck (A—V abnormalities) or secondary to turbulence in major vessels from arteriosclerosis or narrowing of a vessel by kinking or bending. The most common site of irregular shunting of blood from artery to vein tends to be intracranial (within the brain) or in vessels about the ear. Occasionally, this alteration of blood flow can be controlled by occlusion of the vessel.

A soft rushing or flowing type of tinnitus may also be heard in vascular tumors in the middle ear, which, although uncommon, may give very pronounced symptoms. These are usually diagnosed by external examination and by CAT scans.

Causes of objective tinnitus are generally quite rare when one considers the number of patients seen with this complaint.

SUBJECTIVE TINNITUS

Subjective tinnitus is the more frequent problem encountered. The incidence of this complaint has been variably estimated to affect 30 to 40 million Americans. Almost everyone experiences this complaint at one time or another. One must keep in mind the ear itself makes noise, and when one is subjected to a totally quiet circumstance, it is not uncommon to perceive a noise or sound in one ear which is internally generated and is not notable on occasions other than complete quiet.

It is important to keep in mind that there are a variety of medical conditions that either cause or affect the presentation of subjective tinnitus. These include (1) otologic disease, (2) cardiovascular abnormalities, (3) metabolic illnesses, (4) neurologic disorders, (5) pharmacologic or drug induced symptoms, (6) dental factors, and (7) psychologic or emotional factors.

Otologic Causes for Tinnitus

Otologic (ear) disease is the most common cause of tinnitus in any age group. Over 90 percent of people who complain of tinnitus have some form of ear disease. Neurosensory (nerve type hearing loss) is the most frequent finding. Of the patients seen in our Tinnitus Clinic, over three–fourths had a 30–dB–or–greater hearing loss in the higher frequencies (from 3KHz to 8KHz). Thus, high frequency hearing loss represents the most common measurable feature in any group of patients complaining of tinnitus. As a result, it is necessary for all patients who have tinnitus to have a thorough hearing test.

This high frequency hearing loss is most often a result of aging or prolonged noise exposure. Improvement of the tinnitus can often be achieved with the use of hearing aids or masking devices that relieve a portion of their loss. A large proportion of mild, high pitched tinnitus is related to this high frequency hearing loss.

There are many other specific ear disorders, however, that can cause tinnitus and that may or may not result in high frequency hearing loss. Meniere's disease, chronic suppurative otitis media (chronic draining ear), recurrent viral infections of the ear, otosclerosis, and sudden hearing loss are all factors in causing moderate to severe tinnitus. In addition, the first symptom in many patients with acoustic neuroma (a benign tumor of the VIII nerve) may be tinnitus. This is a special consideration when the tinnitus and hearing loss is unilateral. Tinnitus from a tumor is a quite uncommon occurrence (1:100,000 people). Although the majority of patients with tinnitus may have hearing loss or some other form of ear disease, surprisingly few consider it the major causal factor, generally relating their tinnitus to some activity or other occurrence. As a rule, however, hearing loss is considered the most common cause of tinnitus.

A surprisingly large number of patients complain of associated dizziness. At least a third of the patients have dizziness sometime during the course of their tinnitus. This percentage is higher than found in the nonaffected population. These symptoms of dizziness, unsteadiness, or true vertigo (sensation of motion) all merit medical evaluation.

Cardiovascular Disorders

Not surprisingly, cardiovascular problems are frequently associated with tinnitus. Because tinnitus is more common in the older population group, cardiovascular complaints are relatively common. We have noted that 37 percent of patients who have tinnitus have one or more cardiovascular complaints. Although not common, it has remained our persistent opinion that high blood pressure can be a factor in the onset or severity of some patients' complaints. One percent of individuals relate some specific cardiovascular incident to the onset of their complaint. Other vascular problems that must be excluded in a medical evaluation include anemia (in which tinnitus is secondary to the increased heart rate and cardiovascular output) and extensive arteriosclerosis in which calcific plaques frequently cause vascular turbulence. Both of these disorders cause a low pitched pulsating sound. More rarely alteration in venous blood flow in the head will result in a low frequency soft hum. The fact that many venous causes can be altered or stopped by compressing the jugular vein in the neck is helpful in diagnosis if not treatment. Again this type of problem should be evaluated by a physician.

Metabolic Disease

Metabolic abnormalities are common in patients who complain of tinnitus. However, the number may not be more than a matched similar age population. Diabetes and thyroid disease may be factors resulting in tinnitus, but only rarely will the patient or individual identify these disorders as instigating their ear noise. In those without diabetes the development of arteriosclerotic plaques and the development of neurosensory hearing loss is more common than in nonafflicted individuals. Also, with hyperthyroidism, the cardiac output is increased causing a tinnitus that tends to be rushing or pulsatile in nature. Recent literature has implicated high cholesterol levels and general hyperlipidemia as a factor causing tinnitus, particularly when associated with acute hearing loss or dizziness; therefore, a low fat diet is useful in those people with abnormal cholesterol levels. Vitamin deficiencies are extremely uncommon and despite play in the general press have not been identified as a major factor.

Neurologic Disease

Head trauma can cause tinnitus. In referral centers treating patients with severe tinnitus, 10 percent of patients have had some associated head trauma, either skull fracture or severe closed head injury. Though there are no reliable figures that define the percentage of patients who have had skull fracture and develop tinnitus, the percentage is probably quite high. This is the result of damage to the internal structure of the inner ear with nerve or hair cell damage creating a persistent and very troublesome tinnitus. Very often, the symptom is not noted immediately following the head injury because of other associated trauma, but the individual will experience this symptom appearing later. Generally tinnitus, as a result of trauma, will diminish over a period of time following the accident. It may take several years. Tinnitus also may be noted in patients who have had whiplash injury suggesting that nerve input from the neck and shoulders along with concussion damage to the inner ear may be involved. Only rarely, however, do individuals suffer any permanent disability because of this complaint. Other disorders of the central nervous system implicated in causing tinnitus include meningitis and multiple sclerosis, with or without hearing loss.

Pharmacological Factors

A relatively high percentage of patients will relate the onset of their tinnitus to a change or initiation of specific medications for other illnesses. All types of drugs can be considered as a possible cause for increased tinnitus. The most frequent medications causing this symptom are anti–inflammatory drugs, (2) antibiotics, (3) sedatives or antidepressants.

It is generally well known by most people, that aspirin or aspirin-containing compounds will cause tinnitus. But many patients are unaware that they are receiving aspirin-containing drugs. The dosage is not necessarily large and as few as two to three aspirin a day can create symptoms. Aspirin–containing medications, such as Percodan, Darvon compound, Bufferin, or Ecotrin are often not considered by the patient as a cause of the tinnitus. Nonsteroidal anti–inflammatory drugs, (naprosin or ibuprophen) are also frequently implicated as causing tinnitus, although the symptoms are not generally as severe as those from aspirin. Certain antibiotics, particularly the aminoglycosides, for example, Streptomycin, Kanamycin, Gentamicin (all aminoglycosides), will cause tinnitus, although they are more apt to cause symptoms when given concurrently with diuretics. They may also be associated with vestibular abnormalities and hearing loss.

Quinine–containing compounds given for muscle cramps or arrhythmia may cause ringing. Heavy metals, such as mercury, arsenic, and lead in high doses, can cause symptoms but are very rare. Individuals or family members who drink from well water that has not been tested for heavy metals would be wise to have the water tested to exclude that possibility if they experience symptoms.

Any discussion regarding medications that might cause tinnitus must include tobacco and caffeine, which have long been known to increase ear noise. Both the nicotine and caffeine are stimulants and in some cases may actually constrict blood vessels so that the association of increased tinnitus with smokers or caffeine addicted individuals is not surprising. Many physicians feel that at least 50 percent of the patients who complain of tinnitus can be markedly improved by stopping smoking and significantly reducing their caffeine intake. All patients are advised that these drugs may accentuate the symptoms. The medical explanation is that stimulants may make the cells of the inner ear (cochlear) more irritable and therefore more likely to randomly discharge.

Dental Factors

Patients with tinnitus may describe active temporomandibular–joint (TMJ) problems. Temporomandibular–joint problems are quite common in the general population. However, it is felt by most physicians testing patients with tinnitus that temporomandibular–joint disease can often be associated with increased symptoms. Tinnitus, which is secondary to TMJ problems, is usually of lower pitch, often related to jaw activity, or jaw trauma. Grinding of teeth, misalignment, and painful teeth are frequent complaints. Ear pain is not uncommon.

Psychological Factors

Most sufferers of tinnitus realize fatigue and stress play a major role in the severity of their complaint. It is likely that stress increases the perception of the problem rather than causes it. There have been some studies that suggest a majority of patients with *severe* intractable tinnitus has many features of depression. It is hard, however, to state whether the depression is a result of the tinnitus or the tinnitus is a result of the psychiatric disorder. In a large referral tinnitus clinic, such as ours, 15 to 20 percent of the patients have had depression during the course of their illness. There may be many more unwilling to admit this complaint. There undoubtedly is a significant population in which depression plays a major role, and in patients who are depressed, treatment must be directed at managing the depression as well. Fatigue and stress make symptoms worse. This may be related to the individuals inability to suppress or tolerate the complaint.

Tinnitus is a *symptom* and not a specific disease problem. As such, many medical disorders are associated. Many patients can be relieved of their symptoms by medication or other forms of medical treatment. A thorough medical evaluation and physical examination are imperative in understanding and developing a therapeutic plan with thought and reason.

PATIENT'S QUESTIONS AND ANSWERS

1. *Question:* Does tinnitus occur in children?

   Answer: Though rare, this does occur. It is usually related to middle ear infections or their residua—chronic serous otitis. Ear infections almost always cause pain and a hearing loss, but occasionally children will complain of tinnitus early in an infection. The usual questions to ask children with this complaint concern whether their hearing appears dull, whether they've had a cold, and whether they have ear pain, and so on. However, tinnitus does not relate to the severity of the infection. Tinnitus also can occur in children with profound neurosensory hearing loss, although they rarely complain about it. When asked, they often describe a variety of sounds, including popping, hissing, and roaring.

2. *Question:* What is the relationship of tinnitus to otosclerosis?

   Answer: Otosclerosis is a disorder of the middle ear in which one bone [the stapes (stirrup)] becomes fixed by new bone. As a result, there is a slow progressive hearing loss over years. The hearing loss usually becomes noticeable in the patients' late 20s or early 30s. Fortunately, this loss does not equally affect the eighth nerve or cochlea. Therefore, the hearing loss is conductive in nature (meaning sound is prevented or blocked from entering the inner ear). Patients with otosclerosis frequently complain of tinnitus with their hearing loss. This tinnitus tends to get more severe as the hearing loss becomes more profound. The tinnitus is more commonly low–pitched than that which is noted with noise trauma or aging. Surgery for this hearing loss (stapedectomy) diminishes or relieves the tinnitus in approximately 75 percent of individuals. The decrease in symptoms is felt secondary to the masking effect of improved hearing. In other words, the patient is able to hear better; therefore, the normal sounds about him tend to mask the tinnitus.

3. *Question:* Can wax or debris in the ear cause or affect the tinnitus?
   Answer: Occlusive wax filling the ear canal can decrease hearing and, therefore, increase the tinnitus. Often, in older individuals, hair in the canal can rest against the tympanic membrane and cause a rough, low–pitched rumbling tinnitus as well. This is relieved by removing the wax and hair from the ear.

4. *Question:* What is the significance of unilateral tinnitus?
   Answer: Unilateral tinnitus is much less common than bilateral and is an important sign if there is associated hearing loss. A concern of physicians about this combination is that there might be an acoustic neuroma causing the complaint. It must be remembered, however, that the occurrence of an acoustic tumor is quite rare—1:100,000 population—and that the frequency of unilateral hearing loss is much more prevalent. Thus, one must exclude other causes of unilateral tinnitus, which include explosions or loud noise close to the affected ear, or head trauma involving the ear. In almost every instance, unilateral tinnitus merits medical evaluation.

5. *Question:* How often is tinnitus secondary to trauma?
   Answer: Tinnitus frequently occurs after head injury, and almost every patient who has been knocked unconscious will have this complaint. It may not be very noticeable initially. It is not uncommon to have dizziness or unsteadiness as well. What is significant about tinnitus secondary to trauma is that it is difficult to manage with masking or by medical means. Fortunately, it tends to resolve very slowly over a period of time.

6. *Question:* What is the significance of tinnitus secondary to temporomandibular joint problems?
   Answer: The exact cause of tinnitus associated with temporomandibular joint problems (or even dental problems) is not clearly known. Usually the tinnitus tends to have a low–pitched quality, and, as such, may be related to muscle spasm. It is frequently seen in association with occipital headaches and shoulder and neck spasm. This particular complaint can be managed by dental or temporomandibular joint physical therapy, muscle relaxants, heat, and avoidance of excessive chewing of hard foods.

7. *Question:* What is the significance of tinnitus in a totally deaf ear?
   Answer: Tinnitus can occur in a patient who has no hearing. It is suspected that tinnitus can be generated from any point along the course of the auditory nerve or higher neural pathways. It, therefore, can occur in patients without usable hearing. Treatment in these cases, of course, is difficult and frequently may require medication since physical therapy, masking, and other techniques are not often successful. One might read about the possibility of cutting the eighth nerve but this surgical procedure has associated risks and is only successful in approx-

imately 50 percent of cases. Because one also affects the balance mechanism in cutting the nerve, it is rarely advised.

8. *Question:* What makes tinnitus worse?
   Answer: Noise, noise, noise! In addition, stress, fatigue, and lack of sleep all accentuate the patient's complaints. The use of stimulants, coffee, tobacco, any caffeinated beverage, and chocolate all can accentuate the patient's problems. These factors account for many cases of troublesome tinnitus.

9. *Question:* Does tinnitus occur secondary to surgery?
   Answer: Tinnitus can occur secondary to surgery and, as one would expect, most commonly after ear surgery. The noise of the drill used for surgical dissection and associated trauma to the inner ear can substantially increase tinnitus. This complaint, however, is relatively infrequent. Tinnitus has also been reported following other surgical procedures, including open heart surgery. It is felt that this may represent changes in blood flow during the course of the operation, which may affect or damage certain nerve fibers in the high–frequency range.

10. *Question:* What is significant about tinnitus in patients with normal hearing?
    Answer: After evaluating a patient for any medical factors that might accentuate or cause tinnitus, there are still those with increased sensitivity to noise, heightened hearing acuity, and loud—almost painful—tinnitus. These patients are exceedingly difficult to manage and through the course of the years have been the most complex problems faced by the physician. Generally, devices to decrease the amount of sound reaching the ear are only partially successful and, in some instances, may even increase the tinnitus. The nature of the tinnitus in these patients is no different than in those with hearing loss, basically being high–frequency with a rather wide range of sound. Patients with this complaint, because of the sensitivity, are extremely anxious, and the most successful treatment has been directed toward the patient's developing anxiety. This treatment frequently includes psychotherapy and medication.

4

Pulsatile Tinnitus

ARISTIDES SISMANIS, M.D., F.A.C.S.
Medical College of Virginia Hospitals
Department of Otolaryngology
Richmond, Virginia

Pulsatile tinnitus is the type of ear noise perceived by the sufferer as a "whising" or "thumping" sound that oftentimes is synchronous with the arterial pulse. Pulsatile tinnitus is a symptom and not a disease and should always be thoroughly investigated because, in some cases, it can be caused by a serious underlying condition. In contrast to the continuous type of tinnitus, which is more common, pulsatile tinnitus is treatable in the majority of patients. Pulsatile tinnitus usually originates within vascular structures (blood vessels) inside the head or neck regions when turbulent blood flow occurs. This results from either increased blood flow volume or narrowing of the lumen of the vascular structure. According to the vessel of origin, vascular pulsatile tinnitus can be classified as either arterial or venous. Pulsatile tinnitus originating from other structures is classified as non-vascular. Pulsatile tinnitus is called "objective" when it is audible to both patient and physician and "subjective" when audible by the patient only.

All patients with pulsatile tinnitus deserve evaluation by an otolaryngologist-head and neck surgeon (ear, nose, and throat physician) who is familiar with the work-up and management of this problem. Examination of the ears and head and neck region is of utmost importance. Following examination, a hearing test, performed by an audiologist, should be obtained, since in some cases there is an associated hearing loss. Appropriate radiologic testing, which depends upon the clinical findings (history, examination), should be next in order. Head magnetic resonance imaging (MRI) coupled with magnetic resonance angiography (MRA) and/or computer tomography (CT) are usually requested on pulsatile tinnitus patients. Carotid artery angiography (a radiologic test that involves the injection of a radiopaque fluid into the arteries of the neck that outlines them) is indicated for very selected patients only. In cases of suspected neurologic head conditions, such as benign intracranial hypertension, a consultation with a neurologist is necessary. Finally, in the work-up of patients with pulsatile tinnitus, carotid artery ultrasonography, a noninvasive way of determining the blood flow of the carotid arteries in the neck, and lumbar puncture, for determination of the cerebrospinal fluid pressure, may be needed.

Explanation to the patient of the exact cause of their pulsatile tinnitus and reassurance is very important. The majority of these patients feel greatly relieved when they know the exact nature of their problem and especially when this can be corrected. The following sections describe the most common conditions that can produce pulsatile tinnitus.

BENIGN INTRACRANIAL HYPERTENSION (BIH) SYNDROME

BIH syndrome (also called pseudotumor cerebri or idiopathic intracranial hypertension) is a condition characterized by increased pressure of the fluid that bathes the brain (cerebrospinal fluid or CSF) of obscure origin. It is strongly suspected, however, that patients with this syndrome have decreased absorption of the CSF resulting in brain edema (swelling). The majority of these patients are young females and are usually overweight. In my experience, this has been the most common cause of pulsatile tinnitus in female patients. Other symptoms of this syndrome include hearing loss, ear fullness, dizziness, headaches, and visual disturbances (blurred vision and visual loss). Table 4–1 summarizes the etiologic factors and related disorders causing BIH syndrome. Management of this condition should include weight loss, administration of a diuretic (water pill), and, rarely, cortisone by mouth. Most of the patients with this disorder will improve dramatically with weight reduction alone. Surgery is indicated very seldom and only when conservative treatment fails.

TABLE 4–1   **Etiologic Factors and Related Disorders of BIH Syndrome**

1. Obesity	9. Lupus erythematosus
2. Menstrual irregularities	10. Oral contraceptives (without sinus thrombosis)
3. Pregnancy and postpartum (without sinus thrombosis)	11. Nitrofurantoin
4. Hypothyroidism	12. Indomethacin
5. Hyperthyroidism	13. Tetracycline
6. Cushing's syndrome and disease	14. Nalidixic acid
7. Vitamin A (excessive intake, deficiency)	15. Iron deficiency anemia
8. Vitamin D deficiency	16. Idiopathic (primary)

GLOMUS TUMOR

Glomus tumors are benign vascular tumors located usually in the ear or in the area just below the ear corresponding to the skull base. One of the initial manifestations of glomus tumor is pulsatile tinnitus. Hearing loss is also a common symptom. Upon examination of the ear, a red mass behind an intact tympanic membrane is found. Treatment depends upon the age and general condition of the patient, location and extension of the tumor. Young individuals are usually treated with surgery, and older individuals may need no treatment at all since these are very slowly growing tumors.

ATHEROSCLEROTIC CAROTID ARTERY DISEASE

Atherosclerosis (collection of cholesterol in the wall of a blood vessel) involving the carotid arteries (neck arteries) reduces the lumen of these vessels resulting in turbulent blood flow that produces pulsatile tinnitus. This condition usually occurs in older individuals with a history of hypertension, elevated blood cholesterol, diabetes mellitus, angina, and smoking. The management of these patients is conservative and surgery is reserved for individuals with neurologic symptoms and findings (loss of consciousness, neurologic deficits).

HYPERTENSION

I have seen several patients with high blood pressure and pulsatile tinnitus that started soon after they went on medications to control their elevated blood pressure. Tinnitus subsided in most of these patients four to six weeks after initiation of treatment. If tinnitus continues, the patient may have to be switched to another medication for their elevated blood pressure.

TORTUOUS (TWISTED) ARTERIES

Pulsatile tinnitus can result from a tortuous (twisted) artery of the head and neck and usually does not need any treatment. The majority of these patients will do well with reassurance alone.

FIBROMUSCULAR DYSPLASIA

Fibromuscular dysplasia is a condition that narrows the lumen of the carotid arteries of usually young female patients and can manifest itself with pulsatile tinnitus. Other associated symptoms include headaches, dizzy spells, and loss of consciousness. Management is usually conservative with surgery reserved for very selected cases.

INTRACRANIAL VASCULAR LESIONS

Intracranial vascular lesions include aneurysms (dilatation of the vessel wall) and arteriovenous malformations (abnormal communication between arteries and veins). These lesions are very uncommon but when they do occur they may present the symptom of pulsatile tinnitus. Evaluation by a neurologist or neurosurgeon is imperative. Many of these lesions can be treated by a neuroradiologist with embolization (occlusion of the lumen of the particular vessel with appropriate material). In some patients, a neurosurgical procedure may be necessary.

NONVASCULAR ETIOLOGIES

Nonvascular causes of pulsatile tinnitus are uncommon. Palatal myoclonus, one cause of this type of tinnitus, consists of rhythmic involuntary contractions of the soft palate and can result in pulsatile tinnitus. Table 4–2 summarizes the various causes of pulsatile tinnitus.

TABLE 4–2 **Etiologies of Pulsatile Tinnitus**

Arterial	**Venous**	**Nonvascular**
Intra and extracranial arterio-venous malformations	Benign intracranial hypertension	Vascular neoplasms of the skull base and temporal bone
Intracranial arterio-venous fistulae and aneurysms	Jugular bulb abnormalities	Palatal, tensor tympani, and stapedial muscle myoclonus
Atherosclerotic carotid artery disease and subclavian artery disease	Abnormal condylar and mastoid emissary veins	Patulous eustachian tube
Atherosclerotic occlusion of the contralateral common carotid artery		Cholesterol granuloma of the middle ear
Fibromuscular dysplasia of the carotid artery		
Extracranial carotid artery dissection		
Intrapetrous internal carotid artery dissection		
Brachiocephalic artery stenosis		
External carotid artery stenosis		
Ectopic intratympanic carotid artery		
Persistent stapedial artery		
Aberrant artery in the stria vascularis		
Vascular compression of the eighth cranial nerve		
Increased cardiac output (anemia, thyrotoxicosis, pregnancy)		
Aortic murmurs		
Paget's disease		

It is obvious from the aforementioned that all patients with pulsatile tinnitus deserve a thorough evaluation by a team of professionals consisting of an otolaryngologist-head and neck surgeon, audiologist, neurologist, and neuroradiologist in order to determine its exact cause. In the majority of patients, a benign underlying process is found; however, in some patients, a serious problem can be present that, if neglected, can result in a catastrophic event such as a stroke. Finally, most patients with pulsatile tinnitus can be helped by medical and/or surgical treatment.

PATIENT'S QUESTIONS AND ANSWERS

1. *Question:* You indicate that one possible test for patients with pulsatile tinnitus involves MRI of the head region. I have been told that MRI is excessively loud, and I do not want to do anything that will increase my tinnitus.
   Answer: You are quite correct. MRI is loud and we always have the patient wear ear plugs during the test. One test of MRI found the sound level within the chamber to be in excess of 93 dB. Ear plugs should reduce that sound level to about 73 dB, which should be safe even for tinnitus patients.

2. *Question:* My tinnitus is exactly in phase with my heart beat and appears to be in the left ear only. Does that indicate anything about its possible cause?
   Answer: Most likely your kind of tinnitus is due to some arterial abnormality in the left side of your upper neck. Of course we can be sure only by examination. However, pressure applied to the left upper neck that alters the perceived tinnitus would lend support to the possibility of some kind of arterial abnormality.

3. *Question:* If I had an arterial abnormality, should it have been present from birth?
   Answer: That could be the case or it is also something that can develop at any time. Plaque can build up and produce blockage. Arteries can become twisted and blocked. Injury can produce local edema. Many things can cause your kind of pulsatile tinnitus, and I do not think I have seen a case of pulsatile tinnitus that was present from birth.

4. *Question:* I have heard that masking can be used to relieve tinnitus. Would it work for pulsatile tinnitus?
   Answer: I am told by the Oregon Hearing Research Center that masking, in its usual form, does not work for pulsatile tinnitus. However, they go on to explain that typical tinnitus maskers are relatively high pitched and, therefore, above the pitch usually associated with pulsatile tinnitus. The final answer on masking is always that produced by an actual test. You might want to try low frequency sound to see if your pulsatile tinnitus can be relieved in that manner. But allow me to warn you, even if masking does work for you, be sure you have a thorough examination by a physician to determine the cause of your tinnitus. You do not want to hide something that might later lead to some catastrophic event.

5. *Question:* Can pulsatile tinnitus come and go, being present sometimes and not others?
   Answer: Yes, pulsatile tinnitus can fluctuate but usually it is constant. If your pulsatile tinnitus fluctuates, it will be necessary for you and your physician to make arrangements to test you when it is present.

6. *Question:* Does the fact that I can hear my heart beat mean that I'll likely have a heart attack?
   Answer: No, not at all. However, the examination given you by your physician will allow him to determine whether you should see a cardiologist.

7. *Question:* Does the fact that I can hear my tinnitus in phase with my heart beat mean that I have high blood pressure?
   Answer: That is a possibility but not a very high one. Blood pressure does not seem to be related to tinnitus in any direct way. For people who have fluctuating tinnitus and fluctuating blood pressure, there does not appear to be any correlation between the two fluctuations.

8. *Question:* It appears that I have two different forms of tinnitus. One is pulsatile and one is a continuous high pitched tone. Of the two, the pulsatile tinnitus bothers me the most. Will treatment of the pulsatile tinnitus also provide relief for the continuous tinnitus?
   Answer: Since the pulsatile tinnitus is the most bothersome to you, we should treat it first, but I doubt that such treatment will have any effect upon the continuous tinnitus. If after treating the pulsatile tinnitus the continuous tinnitus remains, we will then see about relief for it. It is entirely possible that the continuous tinnitus may not bother you once the pulsatile tinnitus is relieved. It can easily be the case that one can have two very different things malfunctioning at the same time. We consistently see patients with hearing loss due to one cause and tinnitus due to some other cause. Usually we treat the tinnitus in one manner and then treat the hearing loss with hearing aids or with whatever is required.

9. *Question:* I have pulsatile tinnitus. If it turns out to be caused by intracranial hypertension, will reducing the hypertension remove the tinnitus, and, if so, will the hypertension build up again to reintroduce the tinnitus?
   Answer: Most likely the answer to all your questions is, yes. However, notice that reoccurrence of the hypertension may require a long time, and even if it does happen, we now know what to do to relieve it.

5

Are There Any Safe and Effective Drugs Available to Treat My Tinnitus?

ROBERT E. BRUMMETT, Ph.D.
Department of Otolaryngology, Oregon Hearing Research Center
Oregon Health Sciences University
Portland, Oregon

Most people that I have met, regardless of which country they come from, have some unexplained mystical feelings about drugs. People seem to think that every disease has some drug that will cure it. If their original physician fails to prescribe the miracle cure, patients will seek out other physicians who, they hope, will prescribe the desired remedy. Tinnitus is no exception. Most everyone, physicians and patients alike, seems to think there is a magic bullet that will cure tinnitus. The only problem today is that this bullet has not yet been identified.

There are many reasons why we do not yet have a drug cure for tinnitus. We do not know the mechanism by which the many different agents, such as drugs, trauma, noise, and even different diseases, can cause tinnitus. Because we do not know how or even where, with any specificity, tinnitus is generated, it is very difficult to rationally design a drug that would be expected to remedy the malady.

The good news is, that some drugs have been demonstrated to control the symptom of tinnitus. The first drug to be tested in carefully controlled clinical trials and shown to be efficacious was lidocaine. Lidocaine is a local anesthetic that is used extensively in both dental and medical practice. Many people still think of the local anesthetic that they receive from their dentist as being novocaine. In fact novocaine is rarely used today, and for the last fifteen to twenty years has been replaced with the much safer drug lidocaine or other even newer local anesthetics that are similar to lidocaine. Lidocaine, despite having been proven to relieve tinnitus, is not a useful drug for this purpose. It is a very dangerous drug because of serious toxicity, must be given intravenously, and the effect only lasts for about fifteen to thirty minutes. The excitement generated in the researchers for a drug for tinnitus relief by the observations that lidocaine could relieve tinnitus was not that a treatment had been found but that if one drug could work, it may be possible to find another drug that would work and still be useful.

To be proven effective, drugs must undergo very rigorous testing. The conventional terminology is that studies must be "double-blind, placebo controlled, randomly assigned, and prospective" in nature. This means that neither the patient nor the investigators can know which patients are receiving the actual drug and which patients are receiving the so-called sugar pills, the inactive placebo. Patients must be assigned treatment in a random manner. If they are not randomly assigned, then any systematic method of patient selection could result in some unknown selection of patients so that the results of the study would be biased either for or against the treatment under study. So that all of the criteria described thus far can be met, the study must be prospective in that all of the needed criteria must be met before the patient receives treatment.

The reason why studies of drug therapy need to be so carefully controlled is that many people who have almost any disease will get better whether they are treated or not. If that was not the case, the human race would not have survived until the advent of modern medicine. If everyone who got seriously ill died, there would not have been enough people around to be our great, great, great, great, great, great, great grandparents. It is obvious that we did survive, even without the best of medical care. Most people get well despite their treatment. If they are being treated when they get well, most people believe that it was the treatment that made them better. In reality, this may or may not be the case. Take, for example, the situation that everyone who ate dill pickles over 150 years ago is dead. We all know that the dill pickles had nothing to do with everyone dying despite the fact that everyone who ate dill pickles is dead. This is easy to see because it is such an absurd example, however it is still an example of someone taking something, having something happen, and then jumping to the conclusion that the first event was causal to the next. This is true for both drug treatment and drug adverse events or toxicity. Many people get better when they take drugs, and many people have adverse effects when they are taking drugs. In both instances the drug may or may not have had anything to do with making the patient better or causing the adverse reaction.

Claims for beneficial effects of drugs that are not based on carefully controlled studies are always suspect. This does not mean that the investigators or anyone involved with the drug are dishonest or cheats. They may have the best of intentions, but their data must be accepted with much skepticism. For someone who is desperately ill with any disease, the needed degree of skepticism is often very difficult to acquire. Consequently, when patients take any remedy and get better, it is not unnatural for them to assume that the treatment taken was responsible for the cure. In fact, many such individuals are willing to write letters, either solicited or unsolicited, to the manufacturer of the medication telling them of the miraculous effects of their drug. Such letters are called testimonials, and all you need to do is go to some health food store and read the literature attached to many of the products to find examples of what I mean. Just because a drug has not been subjected to a rigorous clinical trial does not mean that it is worthless. It only means that it has not been *proven* to be effective.

All drugs are poisons. The drugs found in health food stores, or so-called nature stores, are no exception. As a culture we seem to have developed the idea that just because something is "natural" it is good and safe. Despite the fact that this is not true, it is often extended to the belief that natural products are somehow not dangerous and drugs found in pharmacies are. The fact is that all products found in health food stores and pharmacies are poisons. Most people think that (1) prescription medication is potentially dangerous, otherwise its sale would not be restricted, and (2) the relatively uncontrolled products are not dangerous. Aspirin, a drug taken by millions of people worldwide that can be obtained almost everywhere, kills many people every year, especially children. A related natural product, methyl salicylate, otherwise known as oil of wintergreen, is very toxic as well, and a dose as small as one teaspoonful could be fatal. Products such as strychnine, cyanide, arsenic, lead, tobacco, cocaine, marijuana, morphine, methane, botulinus toxin—the list is very, very long—and all natural products are also very toxic substances.

When we take drugs for medical purposes, all of the considerations just discussed must be taken into account, that is, what benefit can you expect to receive from the drug and what are the adverse effects that can be expected. These considerations should be made by your physician with you participating in the decision. Your physician should be trained to make such evaluations.

When you take any form of medication, whether it is labeled as a "food supplement" by the health food industry to get around federal regulations or a prescription drug obtained from your pharmacist, you should expect the product to do what it is supposed to do. You should also have been made aware of possible adverse effects to determine if you are willing to take the risk for the potential benefit and so that you can watch for them as soon as you begin treatment. In other words, every drug has a risk benefit ratio and reliable information should be available to your physician and you so that a proper decision can be made. This decision will not necessarily be the same for everyone. Some people are willing to risk more for a potential benefit than others, and therefore, everyone must assume some of the responsibility for making the appropriate decision.

Our laboratory participated in the controlled studies demonstrating the efficacy of lidocaine to reduce tinnitus. Because of the initial success, we all believed that some other drug should be useful. The characteristic of lidocaine limiting its use for the treatment of tinnitus is that it is metabolized very rapidly by the liver when it is taken orally. When any drug is taken orally, it *passes through* the liver before it reaches the rest of the blood system so that it can be carried to where it will exert its effect. When a drug such as lidocaine is given intravenously, it is carried by the blood to where it can exert its effect *before* it gets to the liver where it is destroyed.

Lidocaine is not only a local anesthetic used by surgeons and dentists, it is capable of correcting abnormal heart beats known as ventricular fibrillation. Because ventricular fibrillation can be fatal, much effort was made by the pharmaceutical industry to develop a drug that had the beneficial effects of lidocaine on the heart but was not so rapidly metabolized by the liver that it was destroyed before it could be carried by the blood to the heart. Shortly after lidocaine had been shown to alter tinnitus, the structural analog of lidocaine called tocainide was developed. Tocainide could be taken orally and enough could be absorbed to help the heart. It was our belief that it might also benefit tinnitus patients in a similar fashion. We participated in a rather large study supported in part by the drug company that makes tocainide to determine if it was really beneficial. In the part of the study done at our institution we treated 20 patients with tocainide. Only one patient claimed any beneficial effect, and most of the 20 experienced many unpleasant side effects. The one patient who had a beneficial effect did not appear to have serious side effects, and he elected to continue taking the drug for several years after the study was over. We finally lost the patient to follow up so we do not know if his tinnitus returned after he stopped taking the drug. In fact we do not really know if the tocainide actually made the tinnitus go away. He only had a beneficial effect while he was receiving it and not when he received the placebo. Because of the fact that only one patient out of 20 seemed to benefit and that most of the patients experienced unpleasant side effects, we decided that tocainide was not an appropriate drug for the relief of tinnitus and began looking for other more promising drugs.

During 1991 we heard from a number of tinnitus suffers who reported that when they had been given the drug Xanax or alprazolam their tinnitus got much better. Based solely on these anecdotal reports we decided to perform an open study to determine if in fact alprazolam was able to decrease tinnitus in a small number of patients. For this study ten patients with tinnitus that had been present at a constant loudness for over two years were chosen. In an open study both the investigators and the patients know that everyone in the study will get the active drug. This is *not* a controlled study. Every patient had difficulty sleeping before drug therapy started, and after being on the drug, everyone had *no* difficulty sleeping. The initial dose was 0.5 mg given two times a day. At the end of the first week of treatment we intended to increase the dose to 0.5 mg three times a day if the patients did not report any change in their tinnitus. After completing the tinnitus measurements and finding no change, we decided not to increase the dose because all of the patients complained of excessive daytime sedation; and in two patients we decreased the dose to 0.25 mg two times a day for the same reason.

At the end of the second week of treatment five out of the ten had their tinnitus reduced to very low levels, and two of the others had some reduction in their tinnitus. By now, the daytime sedation had decreased for most of the patients. The dose of drug was then tapered down to zero over a period of six days. One of the patients who had reported no change in his tinnitus called to report that when he finally stopped all drug intake his tinnitus increased. He felt then that maybe his tinnitus had in fact been reduced, but the change was so slow that he had not been aware of it. We did not change this patient to the helped group, but we did feel that it was a very interesting observation. Based on the encouraging results from this open study we decided it was worth going to the expense and effort to conduct a full-blown controlled study. In open studies you maximize the chances of success. The patients are told that they are going to receive a drug that might make their tinnitus better, and they all know that they are getting the drug and not some placebo. Furthermore the investigators know that everyone is getting the active drug and in most likelihood, even unknowingly, encourage the patients in a way that they will get better.

It is generally accepted that about 30 percent of patients treated with a placebo will get better. We used to do an experiment with pharmacy and medical students years ago, when such activities were permitted, in which all students in their first pharmacology laboratory had their threshold to pain measured. They were then given a capsule that they were told contained aspirin. After one hour they had their pain threshold measured again. Virtually every student had their threshold increase about 30 percent even though half the students received lactose or milk sugar in their capsule instead of aspirin. In most years, however, the students getting the aspirin had their thresholds increase a little more than the students getting the milk sugar, but the difference was usually not significantly greater. Because of this suggestion or placebo effect, we had to do an experiment in which neither the investigators nor the patients knew who was getting the active drug and who was not.

For the controlled experiment we chose 40 patients who had tinnitus that had remained rather constant for at least two years and who lived within a reasonable distance from Portland, so that the required many visits to the laboratory would not be a burdensome problem. Because most tinnitus sufferers are so desperately seeking help, we do not have a difficult problem finding adequate volunteers. Most of the patients for our studies are selected from patients who have been to the tinnitus clinic at our laboratory and have been entered into the tinnitus data registry.

Before drug treatment was started all potential subjects were tested as follows:

1. Tinnitus loudness level (dB in sensation level). This is how loud the tinnitus appears to the individual in dB above the determination threshold of the patient to hear sound at the tinnitus frequency.
2. Tinnitus subjective evaluation. This is a 10 point visual scale on which the patient was instructed to rate their tinnitus from one to ten, one indicating the tinnitus is just noticeable and 10 indicating the worst sound they can imagine.
3. Minimum masking levels (dB in sensation level). This is the intensity of the sound at the tinnitus frequency that was needed to cover up or mask the patient's tinnitus.

4. Tinnitus frequency match, determined by asking the patient to choose sounds of different frequencies until the patient can repeatedly match one sound as their tinnitus frequency.
5. Hearing thresholds (this was the traditional audiogram to determine how well the patient can hear).
6. A medical examination to make sure there were no medical reasons that would preclude the patient taking part in the study.

As the patients were entered into the study, the treatment they received was determined by chance, that is, the drug treatment was randomly assigned. The treatment could have been the active drug (alprazolam) also known as Xanax or the placebo (lactose) also known as milk sugar. Both drugs looked alike in that the alprazolam tablet was placed in a blue capsule and the remainder of the space filled with lactose. The placebos were filled with lactose. Neither the patient nor the investigators evaluating the patients knew who was getting what, that is, the study was double-blind.

The starting dose was 0.5 milligrams (mg) given at bedtime. This is a very small dose, and one of the side effects of drugs like alprazolam is that they cause drowsiness and drowsiness at bedtime is not likely to cause a problem. In most cases this drowsiness decreases over a few days and becomes less bothersome for the patient. This dose was continued for seven days. At the beginning of treatment periods the patient was given sufficient medication to last three days past the next scheduled visit. This prevents medication lapses in case the patient is not able to make it to the laboratory on the day scheduled. It also allows us to check on the reliability of the patients taking the medication. By counting the remaining capsules we could determine if the proper number was missing. If too many remained, we must assume that the patient did not take the medication as prescribed.

At the end of the first seven days the patients returned for evaluation and the dosage was increased to 0.5 mg at bedtime and 0.25 mg two times during the day. This was continued for another twenty-one days, and the patients returned for evaluation and the dose was increased to 0.5 mg three times a day. The patients stayed on this dosage for another fifty-six days (8 weeks) at which time they came back for a final evaluation of their tinnitus and were questioned about any adverse reactions that they experienced while taking the medication. Finally, each patient was given sufficient medication to "taper" off the drug. This was done by reducing the daily dose by 0.5 mg every three days. Thus each patient took 0.5 mg two times a day for three days, then 0.5 mg once a day for three days, and then all medication stopped.

In the final evaluation, only 19 of the 20 patients receiving the placebo and 17 of the 20 patients receiving the active drug (alprazolam) completed the study. The one patient in the placebo treated group who did not complete the study failed to return for the final dose increment. Two of the alprazolam treated group dropped the treatment because of excessive drowsiness during the daytime, and one failed to comply with the dosage regimen in that he only took the medication occasionally as "he felt like it."

As expected there were no changes in hearing thresholds of any of the patients. There was also no significant change in the minimum masking level in the patients in the study. There were significant reductions in both the tinnitus loudness level and subjective tinnitus loudness (10 point scale) measures in the patients receiving the alprazolam, and no significant changes in the patients receiving the placebo. It was the conclusion of the authors that alprazolam did in fact reduce the sensation of tinnitus in some patients with tinnitus.

There were also some adverse effects noted in the patients taking alprazolam. Two patients dropped from the study because of excessive daytime drowsiness. One patient reported having what was considered to be mild withdrawal symptoms when the drug therapy was terminated after the taper off period. Five patients reported they had some difficulty "getting started in the morning." Four patients claimed that they had more dreams while on the medication.

It was concluded that alprazolam (Xanax) could be a drug to treat some tinnitus patients. It was also concluded that because of the similarity to the other benzodiazepine drugs that alprazolam could be addicting. For this reason it was recommended that patients not take the medication for longer than four months and, at that time, the drug dose should be slowly reduced by 0.25 mg every three days

TABLE 5–1   **Benzodiazepine Drugs**

Generic Name	Trade Names
Alprazolam	Xanax
Bromazepam	Lectopam
Chlordiazepoxide	Librium
Clonazepam	Klonopin
Clorazepate	Gen-XENE
Diazepam	Diazepam Intensol
Estazolam	ProSom
Flurazepam	Dalmane
Halazepam	Paxipam
Ketazolam	Loftran
Lorazepam	Ativan
Nitrazepam	Mogadon
Oxazepam	Serax
Prazepam	Centrax
Quazepam	Doral
Temazepam	Restoril
Triazolam	Nu-Triazo

until the patient is off medication for at least one month. At this time therapy could be restarted if so desired. Alprazolam is an effective and relatively safe drug for tinnitus relief. It does not cure tinnitus. However, like all drugs including aspirin it does have some adverse side effects.

It is possible that other benzodiazepine drugs would provide relief of tinnitus in a manner similar to that provided by alprazolam. However, all of these drugs, while similar, have some differences in effect. I would not be at all surprised if most of these drugs would provide relief similar to that provided by alprazolam, however, there are no scientific data to support this belief. There are some anecdotal reports that I have had from some patients that they have received benefit from other benzodiazepine drugs such as Klonopin, Ativan, as well as valium.

PATIENT'S QUESTIONS AND ANSWERS

1. *Question:*   I have not tried any relief procedure for tinnitus. I was told by my doctor to go home and learn to live with it. Should I try Xanax to see if it works for me?
   Answer: I would recommend that after a good medical examination by an otolaryngologist you try the noninvasive procedures first and, if they do not work, then try Xanax. In our Tinnitus Clinic at the Oregon Hearing Research Center they first try masking, and, if that does not work, the patient is sent to their primary physician to discuss the possibility of a trial period with Xanax.

2. *Question:*   I have now been on Xanax for six weeks and my tinnitus is all but gone. What do I do now?
   Answer: I would recommend that you continue with your present dose schedule for an additional ten weeks. At the end of that time gradually taper off the drug paying careful attention to the effect upon your tinnitus of the tapered dose. Stay off the drug for one month, and then, if necessary, go back on the drug at the same dose level you are currently using. If it turns out that your tinnitus has not returned at the end of the one month break or is so low that it does not bother you, wait until the tinnitus has returned to a bothersome level before reinitiating the Xanax.

3. *Question:*   If the Xanax completely removes my tinnitus, will it remain removed after I stop taking Xanax?
   Answer: We do not know the answer to that question, but we think it is most likely that the tinnitus will return, at least at some level, after you stop taking Xanax. Xanax is not a *cure* for tinnitus.

4. *Question:*   My tinnitus fluctuates, so can I take Xanax just when I need it?
   Answer: Probably not. In our investigations we have found little or no effect of the drug on tinnitus until between the first and second week of treatment.

5. *Question:*   I have heard that one cannot drink alcohol with Xanax, but I find that a glass of wine helps my tinnitus. Are alcoholic drinks harmful while taking Xanax?

    Answer: Xanax enhances the effects of alcohol so that one drink is more like several. We generally recommend that one not drink at all when taking Xanax.

6. *Question:*   Is it possible that Xanax and masking might interact to give more tinnitus suppression than afforded by either one alone?

    Answer: We have not studied such a possible interaction, but it is something you could attempt on your own. If Xanax reduces your tinnitus, you might determine if FM radio static will reduce it more. As a general statement, the lower the level of tinnitus the easier it is to be masked. Thus, if Xanax has lowered the tinnitus, it may be possible to effect an interaction with masking for additional suppression.

▶ 6

Antidepressant Drugs and Tinnitus

ROBERT A. DOBIE, M.D.
Department of Otolaryngology
The University of Texas

MARK D. SULLIVAN, M.D., Ph.D.
Health Science Center at San Antonio
San Antonio, Texas

INTRODUCTION

Readers of this book already know that tinnitus is a common problem that affects different people in different ways. Most people who have tinnitus manage somehow to live with it fairly comfortably. They may only notice it in very quiet places, and even then, can read or sleep or do whatever they wish to do without much bother. *How* they do this is a bit mysterious; there should really be more research on the ways people cope successfully with problems like tinnitus, so that those who have greater difficulty coping can learn from those who seem to do so easily.

Most people assume that loud tinnitus would be more distressing than soft tinnitus, but that doesn't seem to be true. While we can't measure tinnitus directly, we can estimate its loudness by asking a person with tinnitus to compare his or her own tinnitus to external tones generated by an audiometer or similar instrument. These "matching" studies have shown that very soft tinnitus can be just as distressing as loud tinnitus; it seems to depend not so much on the tinnitus sound as on the person who owns the sound.

Some people with tinnitus become depressed. Since simply getting rid of the tinnitus is usually not possible, it's important for patients and doctors alike to know about depression and its treatment.

DEPRESSION

In casual conversation, *depression* means something like sadness. When doctors refer to *major depression* (MD), they mean something more severe, more prolonged, and out of proportion to external causes (this distinguishes MD from normal grieving, for example). MD is more than just a persistent sad mood; it also includes interference with several aspects of daily life. People with MD usually lose interest in things that they used to enjoy. They have difficulty concentrating and feel more tired than usual. They often feel guilty and worthless. While many people with MD lose their appetites and lose weight, others eat more and gain weight. The same is true of sleep; depressed people may sleep more or less than is typical for them. Frequent nighttime and early morning awakenings are particularly common in MD. People with MD may have suicidal thoughts, and some attempt suicide.

Criteria for diagnosis of MD have been published by the American Psychiatric Association. However, it must be stressed that people—including doctors—should not diagnose themselves. A useful guide to self-referral is the modified Beck Depression inventory reproduced as Table 6–1. A score of 8 or greater indicates that a visit to a physician (ideally, a psychiatrist) or psychologist is in order, to determine whether MD is present.

MD is quite a common disorder; some have called it the "common cold of psychiatry." On any given day, about 5 percent of the adult population has MD, but the percentage in doctors' waiting rooms is much higher—about 10 percent. MD is more prevalent in medical offices for two reasons: first, medical illness of any type can trigger depression; and second, depressed people often see the doctor about symptoms they would otherwise ignore or perhaps not even notice. Many people are uncomfortable discussing problems with moods and feelings and assume that if they don't feel well, it must be due to a medical problem.

About 15 percent of people have one or more bouts of MD during their lifetimes; this includes 10 percent of men and 20 percent of women. Most of these are "depression-prone" individuals who have multiple bouts of MD over the years. In other words, some of us are prone to MD and others are not, for reasons that are still unclear. Studies of identical twins raised apart suggest that vulnerability to depression is, in part, genetic. Negative life events, particularly those involving losses, also play an important role. There is no biological test to determine definitively whether someone has a major depression, though often there are major changes in the levels of stress hormones (like cortisol) and neurotransmitters (like serotonin). At this point, major depression remains a clinical diagnosis, made by your doctor, based upon the symptoms you have.

Without treatment, MD usually runs its course over a period of six to eighteen months, although about 15 percent of depressed people get worse and eventually commit suicide. Even for those who recover, the costs can be great in terms of personal suffering, lost income, medical costs, and effects on family and friends.

Treatment of MD usually involves either psychotherapy, or drugs, or both. Studies have shown that depression of mild to moderate severity responds equally well to antidepressant medication or to specific psychotherapy (cognitive-behavioral or interpersonal). Severe depression responds better to medication than to therapy alone. Many psychiatrists consider combined treatment the best way to obtain rapid symptom relief and avoid relapse. The traditional antidepressants were called tricyclics due to their chemical structure. There are newer medications called heterocyclics, and the newest medications are called the selective serotonin reuptake inhibitors (SSRIs). The most famous of the SSRIs is Prozac. One month the popular press portrays Prozac as all good and the next month as all bad. The truth is somewhere in between. It is significantly easier to take than the tricyclics, but it has risks and needs to be monitored carefully by the prescribing physician.

Drug treatment must of course be prescribed by a physician. While psychiatrists have years of special training in the use of antidepressant drugs, many internists and family practitioners are also quite experienced with these drugs. Your own doctor can advise you whether referral to a psychiatrist for diagnosis and/or treatment is necessary.

Psychotherapy occurs in many different settings. Some primary care physicians offer counseling in their offices, but most individual psychotherapy involves psychiatrists and psychologists. Specially trained psychiatric social workers and nurses also conduct psychotherapy, usually in group sessions.

TINNITUS AND DEPRESSION

Before discussing the association between tinnitus and depression in detail, it's important to emphasize that most people with tinnitus do not visit otolaryngologists (ear, nose, and throat specialists), and most of those who do are satisfied by the treatment and counseling they receive. Several years ago, we ran a tinnitus research clinic at the University of Washington Medical Center, seeing *only* patients who had been to another otolaryngologist but were still unsatisfied. These patients did not represent a cross-section of the 40 million or so Americans who have frequent or constant tinnitus; instead, they were some of the worst cases.

About 60 percent of our patients at the Tinnitus Research Clinic had MD as well; this was six times higher than we would have expected for an average outpatient clinic. What was more remarkable was the strong correlation between MD and the degree of tinnitus-related disability in these patients' lives. Patients with minor problems, for example, difficulty concentrating because of tinnitus once in a while, were much less likely to have MD than patients who reported severe problems, in areas as diverse as sleep, thinking, social activities, and sexual relationships. The point was *not* that depression is especially common in people with tinnitus (that may or may not be true), but that people who are *severely* bothered by tinnitus are quite likely to be depressed as well.

At this point in the story, people always ask the chicken-and-egg question: which came first, the tinnitus or the depression? We don't have any solid evidence one way or the other, except that about half of our depressed tinnitus patients had had at least one previous bout with MD, prior to ever having tinnitus. We believe that some people are more predisposed to depression than others and that tinnitus is one of many internal and external triggers that precipitates MD in susceptible individuals. While it is possible that depression could cause tinnitus directly (both disorders involve brain chemicals called neurotransmitters), it's at least equally likely that depression could cause people to notice, and complain about, sensations like tinnitus that had been ignored before. Obviously, we have here the makings of a classic "vicious circle," with tinnitus and depression each making the other worse. In the final analysis, it doesn't really matter which came first; we need to do something about it. While psychotherapy and other treatments discussed elsewhere in this book may effectively break the tinnitus-depression cycle, we decided to investigate the use of antidepressant drugs.

ANTIDEPRESSANT THERAPY

Our studies used nortriptyline (NT), a frequently-prescribed "tricyclic" drug (brand names include Pamelor and Aventyl); other tricyclics include amitriptyline (Elavil), and desipramine (Norpramin). Newer agents in the SSRI category include fluoxetine (Prozac), sertraline (Zoloft), and paroxetine (Paxil). We chose NT because it can be measured directly in blood samples, making it easier for us to determine proper doses. It is generally well-tolerated and tends to produce some sedation when taken near bedtime, a desirable side effect in most instances. However, there is no evidence that NT works better than other antidepressants for people with tinnitus.

When we began to treat patients with NT, we noticed several favorable results. Patients were sleeping better, functioning better, and feeling better in general. Many even reported that their tinnitus was less loud, and most commented that it was less bothersome. As encouraging as these early results were, they didn't really prove that NT was working—patients might have gotten better without any treatment, or the improvement could have been due to any number of factors other than the drug, the sympathy and support of the doctor, for example.

The acid test for any drug treatment is a clinical trial comparing the drug to a placebo, a pill or capsule containing only inactive ingredients such as milk sugar, but indistinguishable from the active drug. Our placebo study was randomized (patients were assigned to receive either placebo or NT on a random basis—like the toss of a coin). It was also double-blind; neither the doctor nor the patient knew which capsule, NT or placebo, the patient was receiving. Thus, we could be pretty sure that any *differences* in results between the NT and placebo groups would be due to the drug itself.

Most of the genuine drug effects were predictable. Depressed patients improved, but those taking NT showed more improvement in their depression scores than those taking the placebo. Patients with severe insomnia were particularly likely to be helped by NT. Many patients in both groups reported less tinnitus, and the patients who took NT experienced greater reductions in tinnitus than those who took the placebo. However, the differences between the groups in this area were small and could have been due to chance.

There were three take-home messages from our placebo study:

1. NT effectively reduces depressive symptoms in patients with tinnitus and depression.
2. NT has, at best, a questionable effect on tinnitus *sensation* (the sound itself).
3. Placebo effects can be very strong in depressed tinnitus patients.

The third message is important. It confirms what many doctors suspected; time, support, and sympathy can do a lot of good. We also need to be cautious about accepting the validity of any therapy that has not been subjected to a similar placebo study.

SHOULD YOU TAKE AN ANTIDEPRESSANT?

Only your doctor can help you answer that question. The screening criteria in Table 6–1 may help you decide whether to discuss the possibility of MD with your doctor. Should the decision be to try an antidepressant drug, it may be worth knowing a bit more about them.

TABLE 6–1   **Beck Inventory**

Instructions

In each group of statements below, pick out the one statement which best describes the way you feel today, that is RIGHT NOW!! Circle the number next to the statement you have chosen. If several statements in the group seem to apply equally well, circle each one.

BE SURE TO READ ALL THE STATEMENTS IN EACH GROUP BEFORE MAKING YOUR CHOICE.

1. 0 – I do not feel sad.
   1 – I feel sad or blue.
   2 – I am blue or sad all the time and I can't snap out of it.
   3 – I am so sad or unhappy that I can't stand it.

(Continued)

TABLE 6–1 *Continued*

2. 0 – I am not particularly pessimistic or discouraged about the future.
   1 – I feel discouraged about the future.
   2 – I feel I have nothing to look forward to.
   3 – I feel that the future is hopeless and that things cannot improve.
3. 0 – I do not feel like a failure.
   1 – I feel I have failed more than the average person.
   2 – As I look back on my life, all I can see is a lot of failures.
   3 – I feel I am a complete failure as a person (parent, husband, wife).
4. 0 – I am not particularly dissatisfied.
   1 – I don't enjoy things the way I used to.
   2 – I don't get satisfaction out of anything anymore.
   3 – I am dissatisfied with everything.
5. 0 – I don't feel particularly guilty.
   1 – I feel bad or unworthy a good part of the time.
   2 – I feel quite guilty.
   3 – I feel as though I am very bad or worthless.
6. 0 – I don't feel disappointed in myself.
   1 – I am disappointed in myself.
   2 – I am disgusted with myself.
   3 – I hate myself.
7. 0 – I don't have any thoughts of harming myself.
   1 – I feel I would be better off dead.
   2 – I have definite plans about committing suicide.
   3 – I would kill myself if I had the chance.
8. 0 – I have not lost interest in other people.
   1 – I am less interested in other people than I used to be.
   2 – I have lost most of my interest in other people and have little feelings for them.
   3 – I have lost all of my interest in other people and don't care about them at all.
9. 0 – I make decisions about as well as ever.
   1 – I try to put off making decisions.
   2 – I have great difficulty in making decisions.
   3 – I can't make any decisions at all any more.
10. 0 – I don't feel I look any worse than I used to.
    1 – I am worried that I am looking old or unattractive.
    2 – I feel that there are permanent changes in my appearance and they make me look unattractive.
    3 – I feel that I am ugly or repulsive looking.
11. 0 – I can work about as well as before.
    1 – It takes extra effort to get started at doing something.
    2 – I have to push myself very hard to do anything.
    3 – I can't do any work at all.
12. 0 – I don't get any more tired than usual.
    1 – I get tired more easily than I used to.
    2 – I get tired from doing anything.
    3 – I get too tired from doing anything.
13. 0 – My appetite is no worse than usual.
    1 – My appetite is not as good as it used to be.
    2 – My appetite is much worse now.
    3 – I have no appetite at all any more.

TABLE 6–2 **Common Side Effects of Tricyclic Antidepressants**

All more common in elderly	May be present in any age group
Drowsiness	Increased appetite
Dizziness	Headache
Confusion	Fatigue
Blurred vision	
Dry mouth	
Constipation	
Difficulty in urination	

Source: Advice for the Patient: Drug Information in Lay Language, United States Pharmacopeaial Convention, Inc., Rockville, MD, 1993.

Tricyclic drugs are generally quite safe but may induce side effects; some of the more common are listed in Table 6–2. Special precautions are listed in Tables 6–3 and 6–4. Some people are more likely to have side effects, and some shouldn't take these drugs at all, but this can best be determined by discussion between patient and physician. As mentioned earlier, the SSRI drugs tend to have fewer side effects, interactions, and precautions than the tricyclic drugs.

The proper dose for a tricyclic antidepressant varies from one person to the next. Many doctors prescribe NT at bedtime, beginning at the 25 mg dose level, then gradually increasing the dose until an adequate blood level is reached. In our studies, we used blood tests to determine dose; most of our patients required 75 to 100 mg at bedtime. In clinical practice, changes in the patient's symptoms and side effects usually determine the dose. It is important to take enough medicine for a long enough time, usually measured in weeks, if NT or any other antidepressant is to be effective. Patients are often undertreated.

TABLE 6–3 **Medical Problems Affecting the Use of Tricyclics**

Alcohol abuse	Heart disease
Asthma	High blood pressure
Blood disorders	Kidney disease
Convulsions (seizures)	Liver disease
Diabetes	Mental illness
Difficult urination	Overactive thyroid
Enlarged prostate	Stomach problems
Glaucoma (increased eye pressure)	

Source: Advice for the Patient: Drug Information in Lay Language, United States Pharmacopeaial Convention, Inc., Rockville, MD, 1993.

TABLE 6–4   **Drugs That May Interact with Tricyclics**

Medicine for mental illness, including
    Pimozide (e.g., Orap)
    MAO inhibitors (e.g., Nardil)
Medicine for high blood pressure, including
    Clonidine (e.g., Catapres)
    Guanadrel (e.g., Hylorel)
    Guanethidine (e.g., Ismelin)
    Methyldopa (e.g., Aldomet)
    Metyrosine (e.g., Demser)
    Rauwolfia alkaloids (e.g., Serpasil)
Medicine for overactive thyroid
Gastrointestinal medicines, including
    Cimetidine (e.g., Tagamet)
    Metoclopramide (e.g., Reglan)
Appetite Suppressants (diet pills), including
    Amphetamine (e.g., Obetrol)
Medicine for asthma or breathing problems, including
    Isoproterenol (e.g., Isuprel)
    Epinephrine (e.g., EpiPen)
    Ephedrine (e.g., Quadrinal)
Medicine for colds, sinus problems, hay fever, or allergy, including
    Phenylephrine (e.g., Neo-Synephrine)
Medicine for itching, including
    Trimeprazine (e.g., Temaril)
Medicine for nausea, including
    Promethazine (e.g., Phenergan)
Medicine for hyperactivity, including
    Pemoline (e.g., Cylert)
X-ray contrast agents, including
    Metrizamide
Sedatives, tranquilizers, and sleeping pills
Narcotics (including prescription pain medicines)
Medicine for seizures

Source: Advice for the Patient: Drug Information in Lay Language, United States Pharmacopeaial Convention, Inc., Rockville, MD, 1993.

Some patience may be required in dealing with side effects. Often, these will go away in time, without requiring any reduction in dosage. Once a stable dose is found, most patients should stay on the antidepressant drug for at least six months, after which a gradual withdrawal is appropriate.

Antidepressant drugs probably don't relieve tinnitus directly in most cases, but they can certainly help many tinnitus patients. When using these drugs, our goal is to convert a patient whose daily life is being disrupted by tinnitus into one who can cope and function, who can say, "I have tinnitus, but it doesn't bother me."

PATIENT'S QUESTIONS AND ANSWERS

1. *Question:*   I have read that nortriptyline can exacerbate tinnitus. In your experience, did that ever happen? If it did happen as a side effect, did the exacerbation gradually habituate?
Answer: Tinnitus is an uncommon side effect of nortriptyline. In other words, occasional patients treated for depression with this drug complain of tinnitus when they did not have it before treatment. However, the situation is different for people with *pre-existing* tinnitus. We have reanalyzed our randomized trial data, defining "worse tinnitus" as a 5 dB or greater increase in tinnitus match level (1 kHz, worse ear) after therapy. Seven out of 47 nortriptyline subjects (15%) had worse tinnitus at the end of the trial compared to 12 of 42 placebo subjects (29%). In other words, tinnitus was *less* likely to increase in subjects taking nortriptyline.

2. *Question:*   I find it difficult to get a good night's sleep. Will the sleep enhancing effect of nortriptyline wear off?
Answer: One of the real advantages of antidepressants is that sleep improvement usually will not "wear off." If this does happen, we would suspect a worsening depression and consider more aggressive treatment.

3. *Question:*   Since newer antidepressants are now available, do you plan to study them?
Answer: One of us (M.S.) has had good clinical success with tinnitus patients using newer drugs such as Prozac, Paxil, and Zoloft. However, we are not presently planning a study using these drugs.

4. *Question:*   If a patient gave a positive response to the placebo, how did you proceed to treat them? Leave them on the placebo?
Answer: No, all patients were told at the end of the study which type of pill (nortriptyline or placebo) they had been taking. They were then offered a choice of nortriptyline versus reconsidering other treatment options such as masking.

5. *Question:*   If I stay on the drug, will I become dependent or addicted?
Answer: Fortunately, this does not happen with drugs like nortriptyline, in sharp contrast with the benzodiazepines, (e.g., Valium, Xanax) that frequently are associated with drug abuse and dependence when used for prolonged periods.

6. *Question:*   When should I consider stopping the drug?
Answer: We recommend at least six months therapy with antidepressant drugs if the initial adjustment trial period has shown successful improvement of symptoms.

7

Drug Treatments for Tinnitus at Tulane University School of Medicine

P.S. GUTH, Ph.D.*; J. RISEY**; R. AMEDEE, M.D.**
Department of Pharmacology (*) and Otolaryngology (**)
Tulane University School of Medicine
New Orleans, Louisiana

There are many causes of tinnitus ranging from exposure to loud noises, trauma to the head, allergic reactions to medicines or permanent damage to the inner ear caused by drugs. All of these agents cause damage to the inner ear, and this may result in tinnitus. Even though most tinnitus is thought to originate in the inner ear, the actual steps that lead to tinnitus are unknown. Also, it is likely that the steps that lead to tinnitus may not be the same for all causes of tinnitus.

The actual process that produces tinnitus is incompletely understood. Being uncertain about the process of tinnitus generation makes the development of effective treatments very difficult. Since our knowledge about how tinnitus is produced is limited, treatments are directed at relieving the symptom rather than curing the underlying problem. Just as we take an aspirin for a headache knowing that the aspirin will not remove the cause of the headache but only dull the pain, certain treatments for tinnitus will only reduce the awareness of its presence without getting at the cause.

In some instances there may be medical problems that can be treated successfully with either surgery or medicines. Problems with blood vessels or evidence of previously undiagnosed medical problems such as diabetes are examples of problems that can cause tinnitus. These conditions can usually be treated directly and successfully. Treating these types of conditions will eliminate or dramatically reduce the patient's tinnitus complaint because the medications administered are aimed directly at the problem itself. In many cases, though, the actual cause for the tinnitus cannot be determined, and medicines are prescribed to suppress the patient's tinnitus rather than to cure the underlying problem.

Having said that, the reader should not jump to the conclusion that progress in the treatment of tinnitus has not been made. In fact, progress has been and is being made in that many treatments currently in use are chosen because of their selectivity and for more logical, knowledge-based reasons than in previous years. For instance, one treatment that was in vogue some years ago was the drug lidocaine. You may know lidocaine as the drug your dentist uses to deaden your nerves before working on your teeth. It works and all nerves can be deadened by lidocaine. In fact, all the cells in your brain can be deadened by lidocaine, if you use high doses. When lidocaine was used to treat tinnitus, it was able to suppress tinnitus, but it also affected nerves all over the brain. The unwanted side effects resulted in numbing of the lips, slurring of speech, and in one instance a loss of memory for a short period of time. These are called side effects and were predictable from what we knew about lidocaine. Using lidocaine was like using a shotgun to kill an insect! If there were a drug that acted only on the inner ear, there would be no side effects elsewhere in the body.

FUROSEMIDE

Our own experience is primarily with a drug called furosemide (trade-name, Lasix) that acts primarily on two organs, the kidney and the inner ear. It is therefore a drug that should have only a few effects. Furosemide is used primarily as a diuretic (it increases urine flow), but it is also used to treat some cases of high blood pressure and to reduce fluid in the lungs from congestive heart failure. Its action in the inner ear is shared by only a few other diuretics (ethacrynic acid and bumetanide) or, said in another way, not all diuretics affect the inner ear as furosemide does.

HOW THE IDEA FIRST CAME TO US

In the hearing part of the inner ear (called the cochlea) there is a chemical process by which a small electrical voltage is created between two fluid compartments. This voltage is called the endolymphatic or endocochlear potential. The voltage is about 1/100 that of the commonly used 9-volt battery but is absolutely essential for normal hearing function. As such, this electrical potential can be thought of as the *inner ear's battery!* This *battery* has properties that make it unique to the inner ear.

Furosemide and certain other drugs (ethacrynic acid, bumetanide, and aminooxyacetic acid, AOAA) are known to reduce the endocochlear potential. This reduction in the inner ear's electrical potential caught our attention when a former student, William Sewell, demonstrated that this reduction went hand-in-hand with a lessening of activity of the hearing nerve. Now, it is not exactly known whether tinnitus in humans is accompanied by an increase (or a decrease) in activity of the hearing nerve. But when drugs known to cause tinnitus such as aspirin are given to animals, activity of the hearing nerve and the hearing part of the brain are increased. If—and it is a big *if*—tinnitus in humans is characterized by a similar increase in nerve activity, then a drug might suppress tinnitus by reducing the endocochlear potential.

In fact, the first test of this idea that a reduction in the endocochlear potential would suppress tinnitus was carried out with the drug AOAA. In a well-controlled study AOAA did prove to suppress tinnitus in about 20 percent of our 60 patients. Unfortunately, it also had severe drawbacks in that it caused nausea and dysequilibrium.

When Sewell demonstrated that the endocochlear potential and the hearing nerve activity were reduced by furosemide, we decided to try furosemide for tinnitus sufferers. A decided advantage of this drug over AOAA was the fact that it had been in use for about 15 years at the time, and physicians were well acquainted with its use. Our first test of furosemide was by intravenous injection (80 mg) in a population of 40 patients with tinnitus. These patients were injected with either furosemide or another diuretic, one without effects in the inner ear. We used two diuretics, rather than a placebo, so that both would create the urge to urinate. This way the patients were not able to distinguish furosemide from the other drug. Since the patients were not informed as to which drug they had been given and since both produced an urge to urinate, the effectiveness of furosemide could be assessed without bias. We measured the changes in the severity or loudness of the patient's tinnitus after the administration of the diuretics using two different methods: (1) by a self-rating or subjective scale, and (2) by audiometric loudness matching procedures. Of the 40 patients in this trial, 20 reported a suppression (lessening of the severity or loudness) of their tinnitus with furosemide.

The next step was to determine whether furosemide would work when given by mouth and what the effective dose would be. To do this, 12 of the twenty patients whose tinnitus was suppressed by furosemide (i.e., they were furosemide-positive) were given various doses of oral furosemide. It is important to emphasize that these patients were already positive to the furosemide injection. (To this day, before oral furosemide is prescribed for a tinnitus patient in our clinic, an intravenous injection called the furosemide challenge is given to determine whether their tinnitus is furosemide-sensitive.) If the response to the furosemide challenge is negative, no oral furosemide is given. All 12 patients were started at 80 mg per day (2—40 mg tablets per day). Three of the 12 patients responded at this dose level. For the remaining patients, the dose was increased to 120 mg (3—40 mg tablets per day) for five days. An additional three patients responded at this dose. The remaining 6 patients were given 160 mg (four 40 mg tablets per day) for five days, and 4 of these 6 patients responded at this level.

In summary, a total of 10 of the 12 original patients were positive for oral furosemide. In fact, one of the patients dropped out of the trial so it could be said that 10 of 11 patients enjoyed suppression of their tinnitus by furosemide. Remember that these patients were already positive to intravenous furosemide. This initial positive, suppressive effect of the drug exerts a psychological effect that is difficult to factor into the therapeutic process but may be very important. That is, having realized a suppressive effect from the intravenous drug, these patients approached the oral medication with hope and perhaps a more positive attitude. This positive attitude or belief that the drug was going to have a beneficial effect on their complaint may have biased some reports on the effectiveness of the medication. On the other hand, using the injection to preselect patients for trial with furosemide insures that only those patients who are actually sensitive to this medication will be given oral furosemide. Dr. Robert Dobie of San Antonio, a highly respected otolaryngologist, performed an open trial with furosemide in his patients but without a prior furosemide intravenous challenge. His results were less encouraging than ours. One obvious reason is that Dr. Dobie's patients were not preselected for sensitivity to furosemide.

CLINICAL EXPERIENCE WITH FUROSEMIDE

Since our early trials in 1986, 800 patients have come to the Tinnitus Clinic at Tulane University. Of these, 180 have received the furosemide challenge, and 85 of these reacted positively to it and were given prescriptions for oral furosemide. You can see from these numbers that our original response rate of about 50 percent has held up over the years. Not all patients are given furosemide. First, patients are screened by a physician to rule out medical problems that may make it unwise to give furosemide, such as known heart disease, hypersensitivity to the drug, patients unable to make urine, patients with liver cirrhosis, hypokalemia, and patients already taking ototoxic drugs. During the oral trial with furosemide, a close watch was kept on the patient's plasma potassium levels as furosemide can cause a reduction in it. To date, none of our patients has experienced either decreased potassium levels or side effects other than the expected increase in urine production. Some of our patients have been on the drug for over four years. It may be interesting to note that some patients report that when taking furosemide they are able to operate in a noisy environment without any worsening of their tinnitus. Worsening of tinnitus after exposure to loud noises is frequently observed.

TINNITUS OF CENTRAL (BRAIN) VERSUS PERIPHERAL (INNER EAR) ORIGIN

It struck us as peculiar but interesting that only about 50 percent of our tinnitus patients responded positively to furosemide. Why was that? Furosemide, it turns out, has essentially no effects in the brain. Remember that it acts primarily in the kidney and inner ear. Therefore, it probably has effects only on tinnitus that comes from the inner ear and not the brain. Is it possible that 50 percent of tinnitus sufferers have tinnitus that comes from the brain? The conventional wisdom is that most tinnitus comes from the inner ear. We considered this information as something that might help shed some light on the differences between inner ear tinnitus versus brain tinnitus.

For instance, some tinnitus sufferers reach the limit of their endurance with their problem and turn to their ear surgeon for relief. They discuss cutting the hearing nerve in the hopes of eliminating the ringing that is presumed to be coming from the inner ear. Even once they are told that this will result in complete hearing loss in that ear, many patients are still willing to take that chance in order to stop the tinnitus. In a significant proportion of patients who chose to have this surgery performed the tinnitus remains *unchanged*. This experience is generally interpreted to mean that although the tinnitus may have originally come from the inner ear, by the time the surgery was done, the origin of the tinnitus must have moved to the brain. Therefore, destroying the inner ear or cutting the hearing nerve would not affect the tinnitus that is now coming from a more central source, the brain.

We recognize that patients who have tinnitus that appears to be coming from an ear without hearing represents a special kind of tinnitus sufferer. If our idea that furosemide only works on inner ear types of tinnitus is correct, then furosemide should have no effect if given to patients who have tinnitus coming from a completely deaf ear. We located 14 patients with tinnitus coming from a nonhearing ear as a result of a destructive surgery. These fourteen patients were given an injection of furosemide, as described above, and 12 of 14 patients reported no change in their tinnitus, as predicted. Two patients, however, reported that their tinnitus was improved after the injection. We have placed both of these patients, who reported that their tinnitus was better after the injection, on oral furosemide and intend to follow their progress. If they continue to receive positive benefits from furosemide orally, we may need to change our thoughts about how furosemide affects tinnitus. Additionally, though, we intend to consider alternate explanations as to why these patients may have responded positively to furosemide. We included patients who had destructive procedures of their inner ears (called labyrinthectomies) as well as patients who had tumors removed from their hearing nerves. In patients who had tumors removed it is most often the case that the hearing nerve is not actually cut but that the tumor is merely removed from the surface of the nerve. It may be that the tumor patients and the labyrinthectomy patients are not exactly the same with regard to the origin of their tinnitus. For labyrinthectomy patients the inner ear has literally been surgically destroyed, whereas in acoustic tumor patients, the inner ear is often unaffected and the hearing nerve may be left intact. In fact, the two patients whose tinnitus was suppressed by furosemide had had surgery for acoustic neuroma, and all the others had undergone a labyrinthectomy.

TINNITUS SUPPRESSION USING ANTIHISTAMINES

Terfenadine (trade name Seldane) is a nonsedating drug used in the treatment of nasal allergies. Many patients have reported that while on this medication their tinnitus appeared to be somewhat reduced. At the request of the manufacturer we conducted a controlled study of this medicine in patients complaining of tinnitus. Twenty-four subjects with tinnitus were enrolled in the study and each subject participated for ninety days. Each subject was given terfenadine for two of the three months they participated in the study. For the third month, the subject was given a placebo, which was supplied by the drug manufacturer. Neither the subjects nor the clinic personnel knew when each subject was on the real medication. The effectiveness of the medication was judged by use of both subjective rating scales and audiometric loudness measurements. Forty-seven percent of the subjects responded positively while on terfenadine, indicating a lessening of the severity of their tinnitus complaint. The average effect was a "slight" to "mild" suppression. The subjects who reported the greatest degree of improvement in their complaint were those who admitted to having had allergy problems in the past. The results of this study indicated that terfenadine is most effective in patients with tinnitus when they have some prior history of allergy problems but that the drug may also be useful in some nonallergic cases.

CONCLUSION

Given our experience with drugs in the treatment of tinnitus, it is our opinion that no single drug is the panacea. An entire armory of treatments including drugs must be at the disposal of the specialist who treats tinnitus patients. After establishing that a patient's tinnitus is not treatable by other means (such as surgery), the specialist should then consider drug therapy. The drug armory would include antianxiolytics, diuretics, antihistamines, calcium channel blockers, antidepressants, and even in some rare instances, aspirin. Until the exact causative mechanism is known, we must rely on these symptomatic treatments.

PATIENT'S QUESTIONS AND ANSWERS

1. *Question:* I have heard that diuretics can produce hearing loss, and hearing loss can make tinnitus appear to be worse. How safe are diuretics in treating tinnitus?
Answer: Certain diuretics have been linked with hearing loss (ototoxicity), but these effects were primarily seen in debilitated patients usually in an intensive care setting who were receiving antibiotics (aminoglycosides) for life-threaten-

ing infections that were also potentially ototoxic. Our own experience with furosemide (both I.V. and oral dosing) in nearly 200 patients has failed to produce any adverse changes in hearing, and no patient has noted a worsening of their tinnitus while receiving this treatment. As noted, thorough pretreatment screening in an effort to reduce possible side effects is essential.

2. *Question:*   Allergies are seasonal, so if my tinnitus is constant regardless of the season, does that mean that it is not due to allergies and that antihistamines will not work for me?

   Answer: Allergies may be seasonal (spring or fall months) or perennial (occurring year round). Tinnitus may also be episodic or constant, and when constant, it is often prone to periods of worsening and lessening. Allergic patients with constant tinnitus have been observed by us as experiencing a worsening in their tinnitus seasonally (usually the spring and/or fall pollen seasons). This is the group of patients in which antihistamines appear most useful. These drugs may not entirely suppress their tinnitus, but they have been shown to prevent (or lessen) the episodic periods of worsening during pollen seasons. Patients may also experience food allergies, and in this group antihistamines will not prove effective. For example, if every time a tinnitus sufferer eats whole wheat bread, their tinnitus worsens, then simply avoid eating the whole wheat bread. The best treatment for food allergies (and also seasonal allergies) is *avoidance.*

3. *Question:*   What are the rare cases when aspirin reduces tinnitus?

   Answer: This group of patients are thought to have measurable spontaneous otoacoustic emissions. Measurement of otoacoustic emissions represents a new technology that allows for the earliest detection of hearing loss and consists of spontaneous and evoked emissions. Fewer patients have measurable spontaneous emissions, but in those tinnitus sufferers with these emissions, aspirin has been postulated as a possible treatment for their tinnitus. No objective scientific data exist primarily because the number of patients with spontaneous emissions and tinnitus are *extremely* small.

   An aspirin a day (particularly a baby aspirin) in an attempt to reduce coronary artery disease will probably not promote the development or worsen the severity of tinnitus. But each patient with tinnitus using aspirin for this purpose needs to realize that they may now become more sensitive to the effects of one cup of caffeinated coffee or one chocolate bar consumed per day. When in doubt, consult with your primary care provider or your otolaryngologist.

4. *Question:*   If my tinnitus was created by two causes (loud noise exposure and later head trauma that added a second tinnitus), does that mean that my tinnitus cannot be treated?

   Answer: Neither form of tinnitus may benefit from treatment, both forms may benefit from treatment; or only one form of tinnitus may improve with treatment. Any combination is possible. This group of patients generally are the most difficult to treat, but even if only minimal improvement in one form of tinnitus is effected, these patients are usually extremely appreciative. Head trauma may be unavoidable, but generally loud noise exposure is preventable. These patients must be willing to conserve what hearing they have or certainly their tinnitus (and hearing) will worsen.

5. *Question:*   I was treated with lidocaine on one occasion and my tinnitus went away for the first time in 15 years. Unfortunately, it only lasted for about an hour. Why can't this effect be prolonged?

   Answer: No doubt the lidocaine was given I.V. and this form of therapy provided similar relief in many patients. Unfortunately, just as it "deadened" your tinnitus, it can do the same to your entire system, including the brain. Many patients treated with lidocaine experienced side effects and several had potentially serious problems. An oral form of this drug is not metabolized (or circulated throughout the body) in the same manner as the I.V. form. As mentioned, what we really are looking for is a narrowly aimed drug that acts on the tinnitus foci but has few effects (side effects) elsewhere in the body. This is one reason why research funds are so essential to the eventual "cure" of tinnitus.

8

Tinnitus Treatment with Transmitter Antagonists

DORIS-MARIA DENK, M.D.*; D. FELIX, M.D.**;
R. BRIX, M.D.*; K. EHRENBERGER, M.D.*
*ENT Department, University of Vienna, Austria
**Division of Neurobiology, University of Berne, Switzerland

INTRODUCTION

The symptom tinnitus may be due to a number of causes. Various diseases of the ear and nonotologic diseases can give rise to tinnitus. This complex pathogenesis brings about problems in the treatment procedure. Most frequently, the tinnitus originates in the inner ear. In about 60 percent of inner ear diseases, tinnitus occurs. We have developed a new therapy for a special form of inner-ear tinnitus, the so-called cochlear-synaptic tinnitus.

WHAT IS COCHLEAR-SYNAPTIC TINNITUS?

Cochlear-synaptic tinnitus, which is subjective and non-pulsatile, is caused by functional disturbances of the synapse (the place where nerve cells join) between inner hair cells and afferent dendrites of the auditory nerve (the nerve fibers leading from the inner ear to the brain). This synapse can be influenced by application of substances that are agonists or antagonists of the transmitter substance.

WHICH PATHOGENETIC FACTORS ARE RESPONSIBLE FOR COCHLEAR-SYNAPTIC TINNITUS?

In order to understand the pathophysiology of cochlear-synaptic tinnitus and the concept of our tinnitus therapy, we need to discuss the receptor-pharmacological working hypothesis about the functioning of the inner ear. It is based on the following aspects:

> *Glutamate, which is known to be one of the most important excitatory neurotransmitters of the central nervous system, works as transmitter substance in the afferent cochlear synapse (the synapse between inner hair cells and afferent dendrites of the auditory nerve). On the subsynaptic membrane of the afferent dendrites, two different types of receptors, which work as a dual receptor system, are excited by glutamate: (1) the NMDA (N-methy-D-aspartate)- receptor; and (2) the non-NMDA-receptors: quisqualate, kainate.*

When the synapse functions normally, this dual receptor system is responsible for a typical pattern of depolarization. Under pathological conditions the spontaneous depolarization patterns mimic sound-induced patterns, which may be perceived as tinnitus by the patient. This may, for example, happen under excessive stimulation of the receptors. Then glutamate induces neurotoxin activity. Calcium plays an important role in the resulting neurodegeneration.

In microiontophoretical animal experiments, which were performed by Ehrenberger and Felix, it was shown that in the afferent cochlear synapse subsynaptic spontaneous activity could be modulated by application of glutamate agonists or antagonists. During the application of glutamate, subsynaptic afferent activity increased. This effect could be antagonized in a reversible manner by application of glutamate antagonists. Based on these findings, we used transmitter antagonists in patients with cochlear-synaptic tinnitus. This therapy aims at influencing the afferent cochlear synapse and at reducing the tinnitus.

WHICH CLINICAL DIAGNOSES ARE COMPATIBLE WITH COCHLEAR-SYNAPTIC TINNITUS? WHICH IS THE INDICATION FOR TREATMENT WITH TRANSMITTER ANTAGONISTS?

Inner ear diseases, which are caused by functional disorders and not by mechanical damage, may lead to cochlear-synaptic tinnitus. Based on our working hypothesis, some clinical examples of cochlear-synaptic tinnitus can be given:

1. hearing loss in the elderly ("presbycusis")
2. sudden hearing loss- cochlear hearing loss
3. noise-induced hearing loss- normal hearing

Other forms of tinnitus are not of cochlear-synaptic origin, e.g., tinnitus caused by middle-ear diseases, cochlear-mechanic tinnitus, tinnitus caused by disorders of the auditory nerve (retrocochlear tinnitus). Why does tinnitus in Menière's disease or following blast injury not represent cochlear-synaptic, but cochlear mechanic tinnitus? These forms of tinnitus originate from a "decoupling" of the hair cells from the tectorial membrane, caused by an endolymphatic hydrops (as is the case in Menière's disease) or following mechanical trauma in the case of blast injury. This "decoupling" has been described by Tonndorf. In clinical practice, cochlear-synaptic tinnitus can be assumed after other tinnitus etiologies have been ruled out.

WHICH DIAGNOSTIC EXAMINATIONS SHOULD BE PERFORMED BEFORE THERAPY?

In patients who suffer from tinnitus, a thorough ENT and audiological examination is obligatory in order to rule out retrocochlear tinnitus causes (such as acoustic neuroma). The diagnostic procedure should also help to find out if a cochlear-synaptic tinnitus etiology can be taken into account. In such cases, a therapy with transmitter antagonists is indicated. In the following paragraphs, We would like to give a short survey of the diagnostic tests we perform in our department. The diagnostic battery consists of history, ENT examination, functional testing, tinnitus analysis, structural analysis, and, if necessary, other medical examinations (by an internal specialist, neurologist, ophthalmologist, orthopedist, orthodontist, psychiatrist).

History: The history gives us valuable hints regarding tinnitus etiology and helps us to determine which tests of the diagnostic test battery must be carried out. In addition to the general and ENT histories, a detailed tinnitus history is of great importance. The information we need is onset of tinnitus, tinnitus side (unilateral, bilateral, in the head), tinnitus character (especially differentiation between pulsatile/non-pulsatile tinnitus), interaction with everyday life. Also, a subjective scaling of the tinnitus helps to get an impression of the subjective impairment the patient has. The patients are asked whether they suffered from blast injury, ear surgery, trauma, and so on.

ENT Examination: The ENT examination comprises otomicroscopy and an orientating vestibular check-up with Frenzel's lens. If necessary, the functioning of the Eustachian tube is examined, and an endoscopy of the nose and epipharynx is performed. To decide upon the appropriate diagnostic procedure it is extremely important to differentiate between subjective (only the patient hears his tinnitus) and objective tinnitus (can be heard by the examiner).

Functional Testing: In each tinnitus patient a pure-tone audiogram is carried out. If required, stapedius reflex or tympanogram is recommended. Auditory evoked potentials (brainstem audiometry) are necessary for topodiagnosis of hearing loss and must be performed in any case of asymmetrical hearing loss. In some cases, a frequency discrimination test helps to exclude an endolymphatic hydrops. If the patient suffers from vertigo, electronystagmography must be performed.

Tinnitus Analysis: The evaluation of tinnitus is difficult. There are no general criteria for evaluation. Common tests for tinnitus analysis that we perform are tinnitus matching and masking. Tinnitus matching: This audiometric test determines character (noise or tone), pitch and loudness of tinnitus by stimulation of the contralateral ear. Most patients suffer from low-intensity tinnitus, but the loudness measured does not correlate with subjective impairment. Tinnitus masking: In this test the minimum masking level is determined by ipsilaterally presenting a narrowband noise under earphones.

Structural Analysis: It depends on the case as to which of the examinations available are chosen: high-resolution tomography of the temporal bone, magnetic resonance imaging of the head, sonography of the neck vessels, or angiography.

WHICH DRUGS ARE USED FOR THERAPY OF COCHLEAR-SYNAPTIC TINNITUS? HOW ARE THEY APPLIED? WHAT ABOUT THE DOSAGE?

The drugs we apply are antagonists of the transmitter substance glutamate. They protect the cells against calcium-induced neurotoxin activity. Therefore, they are neuroprotective substances. Therapy of cochlear-synaptic tinnitus with transmitter antagonists is not a symptomatic, but a causal, therapy. In the past, we used GDEE (glutamic acid diethyl ester), now we are using Caroverine. To guarantee an effective blood concentration of the drugs, they are given as slow intravenous infusion. In most cases, a single infusion is administered. The dosage depends on the tinnitus reduction achieved in the individual patient. If the tinnitus is fading, the infusion has to be stopped. No general recommendation regarding the dosage can be given. If in the individual case too much of the substance has been applied, the tinnitus that has been reduced can become louder again. Luckily, this effect is reversible and can be counterbalanced by application of glutamate. Therefore, the substances have to be applied carefully. The patients are asked to report any change of their tinnitus during therapy.

> *GDEE (GLUTAMIC ACID DIETHYL ESTER): GDEE is a Quisqualate antagonist (non-NMDA receptor blocker). This substance is not available as a registered drug, but it was possible to get it on special clinical request. At most, 20 mg GDEE are given in 100 ml physiologic saline solution.*

> *CAROVERINE: Caroverine is a glutamate antagonist at the non-NMDA and NMDA-receptor site in a dose-dependent manner. It is a registered spasmolytic drug commercially available in Austria and Switzerland. At most, 160 mg Caroverine is given in 100 ml physiologic saline solution.*

HOW CAN THE THERAPEUTIC EFFECT BE EVALUATED?

The evaluation can be done by subjective or objective methods. For subjective evaluation, we perform tinnitus rating and tinnitus matching immediately before and after the infusion with the neuroprotective substance. In clinical practice, tinnitus therapy is performed under subjective therapy control. For objective evaluation, the cochlear sum action potential can be measured in brainstem audiometry. Subjective tinnitus reduction correlates with a shortened latency period of Jewett I as a result of better cochlear synchronization. This proves the peripheral site of action of GDEE and Caroverine.

THE RESULTS OF GDEE/CAROVERINE THERAPY

GDEE: 130 patients with cochlear-synaptic tinnitus, from 22 to 78 years old, received a single infusion of GDEE. The diagnoses of the patients treated are shown in Table 8–1. One hundred patients (76.9%) noted a tinnitus reduction (Figure 8–1). In these patients, the improvement was observed in the subjective rating as well as in the tinnitus matching. The amount of tinnitus reduction after the infusion, as measured by tinnitus matching, was about 50 percent in absolute values. In 23.1 percent of the patients treated, no tinnitus reduction could be achieved.

CAROVERINE: In a pilot study, 72 patients, from 18 to 90 years old, with cochlear synaptic tinnitus were treated with a single infusion of Caroverine. The diagnoses are summarized in Table 8-2. Forty-eight patients (66.7%) had a significant tinnitus reduction according to the above-mentioned criteria. Twenty-four patients (33.3%) had no improvement of their tinnitus.

TABLE 8–1   **Diagnoses, Treatment with GDEE**

n = 130, 22 to 78 years old	
Diagnoses	**Number of patients**
normal hearing	22
presbycusis	45
symmetrical cochlear hearing loss	24
asymmetrical cochlear hearing loss	12
sudden hearing loss	17
asymmetrical combined hearing loss	10

TABLE 8–2   **Diagnoses, Treatment with Caroverine**

n = 72, 18 to 90 years old

Diagnoses	Number of patients
normal hearing	6
presbycusis	21
symmetrical cochlear hearing loss	17
asymmetrical cochlear hearing loss	17
sudden hearing loss	9
symmetrical combined hearing loss	1
asymmetrical combined hearing loss	1

How Would You Explain the Nonresponders?

The group of the nonresponders may be due to a multifactorial tinnitus etiology. In these cases, redundant pathophysiological mechanisms other than cochlear-synaptic pathology may be responsible for the development of tinnitus. Perhaps diagnosis was incorrect in some of these cases.

How Long Did the Tinnitus Reduction Last?

Interestingly, the duration of the therapeutic effect varied and could not be predicted. Tinnitus improved for periods lasting hours, days, or months. This may be explained by different tinnitus causes (noise, degeneration processes in the elderly, etc.) that led to the same pathophysiology of cochlear-synaptic tinnitus. This can be illustrated by the following example: a patient with noise-induced hearing loss is treated successfully. If he is exposed to noise again after therapy, the improvement of tinnitus will fade. The therapy with transmitter antagonists may be repeated. In some cases of successful therapy with Caroverine, the improvement could be stabilized by oral therapy with this substance

Did You Observe Any Side Effects?

In no case did we observe severe side effects. In the GDEE group, some patients reported a slight transient headache. In the Caroverine group, very few patients complained of a slight transient headache, dizziness, the feeling of a "hot head" or unusual taste in the mouth. These symptoms only lasted for a short time. In no case did therapy have to be stopped.

CAN DRUGS OTHER THAN TRANSMITTER ANTAGONISTS INFLUENCE COCHLEAR-SYNAPTIC TINNITUS?

Drugs, which are common in tinnitus treatment, can also be used symptomatically in cochlear-synaptic tinnitus, whereas transmitter antagonists may causally influence the mechanisms responsible for the origin of tinnitus. For practical reasons, the patients are given an oral medication with a serotonin antagonist (Sulpirid), the histamine agonist betahistine or the nor-adrenaline antagonist Tizanidine for one month before we start with the therapy with transmitter antagonists. If tinnitus does not improve, as is the case in most patients, Caroverine is applied.

CAN THERAPY WITH TRANSMITTER ANTAGONISTS DETERIORATE TINNITUS?

In all the patients treated we had no case with long-lasting tinnitus worsening. As mentioned earlier, if too much of the transmitter antagonists is applied, the effect of tinnitus improvement fades again, the tinnitus that has improved may become louder. This effect can be counterbalanced by application of the transmitter glutamate. In cases of tinnitus with "decoupling" of the inner hair cells from the tectorial membrane, infusion of large amounts of liquid may temporarily worsen tinnitus because of the "volume effect."

CONCLUSION

Scientific findings of inner ear research led to the therapeutic concept of cochlear-synaptic tinnitus with transmitter antagonists. The results of tinnitus therapy with GDEE or Caroverine confirm the working hypothesis about the functioning of the afferent cochlear synapse. The indication for therapy with transmitter antagonists is the cochlear-synaptic tinnitus. This is not a diagnosis in the conventional sense but describes a pathophysiological condition. Cochlear-synaptic tinnitus can be assumed after other possible tinnitus causes have been ruled out. For correct indication, thorough ENT and audiological examinations are therefore necessary. At the beginning, we used GDEE (Glutamic acid diethyl ester), now we are applying Caroverine. These transmitter antagonists prevent calcium-induced neurodegeneration. We treated 130 patients with GDEE and 72 patients with Caroverine. The results of therapy with these neuroprotective substances are very encouraging. In the GDEE group 76.9 percent of the patients treated and in the Caroverine group 66.7 percent of the patients treated had a significant tinnitus reduction. The dosage of the substances differs from patient to patient. If too much of the substances is applied, the tinnitus improvement may fade. Therefore, the application has to be done carefully to avoid overdosing. GDEE and Caroverine have proved to be effective substances in the therapy of cochlear-synaptic tinnitus.

PATIENT'S QUESTIONS AND ANSWERS

1. *Question:* You suggest it is important to rule out such things as acoustic neuroma. How is that accomplished?
   Answer: The aim of dignostics is to rule out other tinnitus causes than cochlear-synaptic ones. The brainstem evoked audiometry allows functional testing of the inner ear, the cochlear nerve, and the auditory pathway as far as brainstem level. If there is any suspicion of retrocochlear dysfunction in brainstem evoked audiometry, MRI is carried out. Testing for acoustic neuromas has become very precise by the use of MRI (Magnetic Resonance Imaging), which is a very refined way to visualize the various bodily regions. MRI is capable of displaying very small acoustic tumors. These tumors are very slow growing, and they are always benign. If an individual has tinnitus on one side only for which there is no known reason, the possibility of an VIII nerve tumor should be tested. MRI is a very loud machine and the patient undergoing MRI should always wear ear plugs.

2. *Question:* Does removal of an acoustic tumor also remove the tinnitus?
   Answer: In most cases, it does not. The VIII nerve tumor actually invades the acoustic nerve, and its removal may impart considerable damage to the remaining hearing with the consequence that, in some cases, the tinnitus is increased by the operation. It is for this reason that it is desirable to detect and remove acoustic tumors as early as possible.

3. *Question:* If an acoustic tumor is detected in an elderly patient, should it be removed?
   Answer: That is a very interesting question. Acoustic neuromas can be life threatening. On the other hand, they are very slow growing and in the very elderly patient, an initial acoustic neuroma may offer little threat to their well-being. It all depends upon the symptoms displayed by the elderly patient. One should also consider the therapeutic option of gamma knife.

4. *Question:* For tinnitus testing you indicate that the test tones are introduced to the contralateral ear. What do you do if the contralateral ear is a deaf ear?
   Answer: If the contralateral ear is truly deaf, it is then necessary to apply the test tones to the ipsilateral ear. Tests conducted in the U.S. suggest that tinnitus testing is equally accurate regardless of which ear is used as the test ear.

5. *Question:* Are there other tinnitus centers using GDEE or Caroverine?
   Answer: To our knowledge, there are no other centers using our treatment procedures and, yes, that may mean coming to Vienna to be treated by our method, although we expect other centers to adopt our techniques once they become more widely known.

9

Effectiveness of the Low Power Laser and Ginkgo Extract i.v. Therapy in Patients with Chronic Tinnitus

M. WALGER, Ph.D.; H. VON WEDEL, M.D.;
S. HOENEN; L. CALERO
*Klinik und Poliklinik für Hals-Nase
Ohrenheilkunde der Universit ät Ze Köln
Germany*

In a clinical prospective blind study on 155 patients suffering from chronic tinnitus, we tried to evaluate the effectiveness of a new therapy method: Low Power Laser in combination with Ginkgo extract, i.v. The patients were divided into four groups: (I) Laser/Ginkgo, (II) Ginkgo, (III) Laser, and (IV) Placebo. Each patient was treated in twelve successive sessions every 2 to 3 days with i.v. application of Ginkgo extract or NaCl solution. The laser was positioned at a distance of 2 cm above the tip of the mastoid and activated only in groups I and III. Before, during, and up to four months after the treatment, each patient underwent different audiological and psychometrical tests, such as pure-tone audiogram, estimation of tinnitus loudness and frequency, tinnitus-masking for pure-tones, narrow- and broadband noise, residual inhibition effects, psychometrical scaling of tinnitus loudness, intrusiveness and stress, and a special questionnaire for scaling the effectiveness of the treatment up to four months after the therapy.

No significant differences could be observed between the four groups in all of our investigated parameters, and there was no median change after the treatment. Individual improvements of tinnitus or hearing loss could be observed in patients within all groups. This has to be related to the psychological effect of an intensive therapeutical treatment (placebo effect). Besides the clinical study we evaluated the transmission energy of the low power laser to the human cochlea in 10 formalin fixed temporal bones with implanted photodiodes. These data clearly demonstrate the total absorption of the He/Ne-laser rays (wavelength: 632.8 nm). The pulsed infra-red rays (wavelength: 904 nm) were absorbed to an amount of about 0.01 percent of the primary power output. These results do not support theories of laser activated repair mechanisms within the inner ear of tinnitus patients.

INTRODUCTION

With the new therapy Low Power Laser in combination with Ginkgo extract i.v., Witt and Felix in 1989, tried to offer an alternative method for the treatment of hearing disorders including chronic tinnitus. After i.v. application of Ginkgo-extract, a combination-laser, consisting of a gas-laser (He/Ne, wavelength: 632.8 nm) and 5 pulsed, infra-red laserdiodes (Ga/As, wavelength: 904 nm), is positioned behind each ear of the patient and in twelve successive sessions the cochlea is stimulated every three to four days. The inventors of this treatment, in a report by Witt in 1989, postulate astonishing effects within the inner ear: activation of flavo-proteins, enhancement of ATP-synthesis, and the stimulation of repair mechanisms that finally result in a reduction or total relief of hearing disorders and tinnitus. But these effects have never been proven and sensational reports of 60 percent improvement or removal of chronic tinnitus were never confirmed in clinical studies!

To evaluate the effectiveness of the Laser/Ginkgo treatment, we performed a clinical prospective double-blind study in 155 patients suffering from chronic tinnitus lasting more than half a year. In all of these patients other treatments failed to reduce the complaints.

Additionally, we took an interest in determining the remaining laser energy that reached the cochlea. In this experimental study, we implanted photodiodes in 10 fixed human temporal bones at the level of the cochlea and measured the transmission of the two different laser rays at 632.8 nm and 904 nm.

PATIENTS AND METHODS

We were able to include 155 patients (99 male, 56 female) between 16 and 80 years of age who suffered from chronic and therapy-resistent tinnitus, lasting from six months to forty years (mean: 5.47 years; median: 2.25 years). Nineteen patients stopped the combination therapy, 6 of them because of tinnitus enhancement. These patients were excluded from the final evaluation of the results. Patients were randomized and distributed to the following four groups:

TABLE 9–1 **Four Groups in the Laser-Ginkgo Study**

Group LG n = 47	Group G n = 37	Group P n = 37	Group L n = 34
Laser— Ginkgo i.v.	Laser inactive— Ginkgo i.v.	Laser inactive— NaCl i.v.	Laser— NaCl i.v.
(laser active, 5–10 ml Ginkgo i.v.)	(laser inactive, 5–10 ml Ginkgo i.v.)	(laser inactive, 5–10 ml NaCl i.v.)	(laser active, 5–10 ml NaCl i.v.)

Each patient was treated in twelve successive sessions every two to three days with an i.v. application of Ginkgo extract (Syxyl, D3) in groups LG and G, or NaCl solution in groups L and P. Syxyl D3 (a homeopathic Ginkgo extract solution) was used in arrangement with the inventors of the therapy because of the superior effectiveness compared to other Ginkgo extracts like EGB 761 or Tebonin (Marchand, 1992). The low power laser was positioned at a distance of 2 cm above the tip of the mastoid and activated only in groups LG and G for 8 minutes in each session.

To evaluate the effectiveness of the therapy, different audiologic and psychometric methods were used in certain time intervals. For the audiologic measurements we performed a pure-tone audiogram, estimation of tinnitus loudness and frequency, tinnitus masking for pure-tones, narrow- and broadband noise according to Feldmann, and residual inhibition effects. The psychometric tests used were first of all a visual analog scale (VAS), which proved definite parameters of tinnitus such as loudness, intrusiveness, and stress. Furthermore, three to four months after finishing the study we surveyed the patients concerning the changes regarding the quality of tinnitus in a special questionnaire.

For the statistical elaboration we used the median-test, Kruskal-Wallis-1-way Anova-test, Mann-Whitney U-test, and the chi-square-test.

Results

First of all, we can mention that just in a few individual cases, but independent of the treatment we used, there was an improvement of tinnitus or hearing loss compared to the beginning of the treatment. In contrast to that, we also found patients with tinnitus-enhancement. The statistical evaluation showed, however, no significant differences among the groups.

Leading through the visual analog scale (VAS) after each single treatment, we could follow the development of the whole therapy. We combined the different parameters of tinnitus, loudness, intrusiveness, and stress, to one score. The next step

TABLE 9–2   **Final Results of Effectiveness**

n = 155 – 19	Tinnitus-Masking		Tinnitus, subjective		Audiogram	
	better	**worse**	**better**	**worse**	**better**	**worse**
Laser-G. (44)	11.4% (5)	9.1% (4)	6.8% (3)	6.8% (3)	4.5% (2)	0% (0)
Laser (31)	9.7% (3)	9.7% (3)	6.5% (2)	12.9% (4)	3.2% (1)	3.2% (1)
Gingko (31)	6.5% (2)	3.2% (1)	16.1% (5)	12.9% (4)	6.5% (2)	3.2% (1)
Placebo (30)	10% (3)	6.7% (2)	6.7% (2)	16.7% (5)	6.7% (2)	6.7% (2)

Three to four months after the treatment based on the evaluation of 136 patients

was to compare the beginning of the study with the end by the help of statistical methods, by using a graph. As mentioned before, there are no differences among the four investigated groups. Improvement as well as tinnitus enhancement were possible, but most of the patients left treatment without any change of tinnitus or hearing loss.

Table 9–2 summarizes the final results of the effectiveness of the combination therapy three to four months after the end of the treatment. As an "objective" parameter of tinnitus loudness, we determined changes of the masking threshold for pure tones, narrow- and broadband noise at the tinnitus frequency (see Table 9–2, Tinnitus-Masking). Improvement or tinnitus enhancement was defined as a change of 10 dB or more. We found no statistically significant differences between the four investigated groups, although there were some individual changes.

To have a view over the further development of the therapy, each patient was surveyed after three to four months concerning his subjective tinnitus assessment in a special questionnaire (Table 9–2, Tinnitus, subjective). We asked particularly for changes regarding the quality of tinnitus. At the end and even after three to four months, there was no difference among the groups.

The improvement of the hearing sensibility was determined by changes of at least 10 dB at two frequencies out of 1, 2, 3, or 4 kHz (see Table 9–2, Audiogram). It was shown in each group that some patients had improvement and others worsening with regard to their hearing ability. Again, there was no significant difference among the groups and therefore no significant difference among the therapies.

EXPERIMENTAL LASER STUDIES

Besides the clinical study we evaluated the transmission energy of the low-power-laser to the human cochlea in 10 formalin fixed temporal bones with implanted photodiodes (Hamamatsu, SI 1337-66BR). The measurement of the He-Ne-laser showed a complete absorption of the laser rays at a depth of 4 to 5 cm (level of the cochlea) in all investigated temporal bones. This result agrees with the well-known minimal transmission of this wavelength in biological tissues. In contrast to that we found a small transmission rate of the infra-red diodelaser at a wavelength of 904 nm. In this respect the pneumatization of the temporal bone was significant. The measured laser-power ranged from 0.3 μW (bad pneumatization) up to 3.77 μW (good pneumatization). The mean of the 10 evaluated temporal bones was 1.67 μW. This is in the range of 0.01 percent of the primary energy of the infra-red laser-diodes. Because of the missing skin and the loss of blood circulation in our experiments, we presume a much higher absorption in the native tissue.

Additionally we performed energy measurements with a special calorimeter (Scientech Laser-Power-Meter, Type 36-0001) using a comparable distance between the laserdiode and the inner ear (6 cm). We found only 1.1 mW per cm^2 for each laser-diode at a distance of 6 cm without temporal bone. In this respect a ray-treatment with a low power laser is comparable to an exposition in the sun (Schnizer, 1988).

CONCLUSION

Contrary to the reported success of up to 60 percent reduction of tinnitus described by the founder of the combination-therapy, the clinical studies proved contradictory results. Plath (1992) and Partheniadis-Stumpf (1993) reported upon prospective evaluations with a small number of patients less than forty. They had only a few improvements but considered their therapy as a successful one for individual therapy resistent cases.

In opposition to the postulated effectiveness of the combination therapy Low Power Laser and Ginkgo extract i.v., our study cannot confirm these results. No significant differences could be observed between the four groups in all of our investigated parameters. Therefore the individual improvements within all of the four investigated groups have to be related to the placebo effect by using modern techniques in the treatment of chronic tinnitus.

Besides the clinical evaluation on 155 patients we proved that a maximum of 0.01 percent from the laserdiode output at 904 nm could reach the cochlea and the He-Ne-laser rays are totally absorbed. So these and the clinical data do not support theories about the laser-activation of repair mechanisms within the human inner ear.

PATIENT'S QUESTIONS AND ANSWERS

1. *Question:*   Some doctors report about better hearing after this therapy. Can I possibly do without hearing aids after this treatment?

Answer: Reports about an improvement of hearing are very rare and in these cases, the improvement can definitely not be seen as an effect of the combination therapy. The grade of improvement of hearing determines whether the hearing aid can be removed after the treatment. This should be discussed with your doctor.

2. *Question:* Is it possible to use this therapy for the treatment of patients with acute onset of tinnitus?

   Answer: As the effectiveness of this therapy has not yet been proved, there is no reason for or against an application in acute tinnitus. But in any case, an acute tinnitus should be treated in the conventional way, for example, using medicaments that increase the blood flow.

3. *Question:* Would it make sense to continue with Ginkgo medication after the combined therapy if my tinnitus has not been improved?

   Answer: It is also possible to get relief after a longer period of drug therapy.

4. *Question:* Does the laser-Ginkgo therapy have any side effects?

   Answer: Caused by the Ginkgo medication, there might be some allergic reactions with known symptoms like skin reactions, for example. In this case, the therapy has to be stopped immediately.

5. *Question:* Is it possible that the laser causes skin damage?

   Answer: The energy of the laser is too weak to cause any skin reactions or other side effects. Nevertheless, your eyes should always be protected.

6. *Question:* If I get relief with this kind of treatment, how long will it last? Will I need repeated treatments?

   Answer: Patients often reported that relief occurring directly after the treatment did not last and that finally their tinnitus was as annoying as before. There are not any reasons against or in favor of a repeated application of the therapy.

7. *Question:* If the treatment makes my tinnitus worse, will that be permanent or temporary?

   Answer: There are also patients who reported that their tinnitus became worse during the treatment. But in most cases, this was temporary, and sooner or later the trouble was the same as before.

8. *Question:* For those patients who displayed an improvement on the VAS, was the loudness of their tinnitus comparably lowered? If so, was that effect temporary?

   Answer: The improvement on the VAS correlated very well with the decrease of the loudness of tinnitus. But there were only a few patients who were equally distributed within all four groups, so that the improvement has not occurred due to the laser-ginkgo-treatment but was a placebo effect. In those few cases with an improvement, it was only temporary.

10

Vitamin B$_{12}$ and the Treatment of Tinnitus
Review of the Israel Study

JACK VERNON, Ph.D.
Director, Oregon Hearing Research Center
Oregon Health Sciences University
Portland, Oregon

Many health care professionals have prescribed Vitamin B$_{12}$ for the relief of tinnitus, but in most cases knowledge about the effectiveness of B$_{12}$ or lack thereof as far as tinnitus is concerned was more a matter of faith and not knowledge. It is one of those calls dictated more by the vogue of the moment than by any hard knowledge.

Recently, however, a proper study was conducted concerning tinnitus and B$_{12}$ in noise-exposed patients. The study was conducted by Zecharia Shemesh, M.D., Joseph Attias, DSc., Michal Ornan, BA, Niva Shapira, Ph.D., and Ammon Shahar, M.D.; a group working in Israel.

They correctly point out that one of the most frequent causes of tinnitus in young people is *exposure to loud sounds.* They also correctly point out that there is a large variation in the amount of hearing loss and the incidence of tinnitus among those exposed to roughly the same kind and amount of traumatic noise. At this point they speculated that one of the determining factors is the condition of the neuronal pathways involved, and here they turn to studies of vitamin B$_{12}$ deficiency that have demonstrated deleterious effects upon sensory nerve fibers as well as increased central nerve conduction time. From all this they conclude that there may be a relationship between abnormal neuronal activity produced by vitamin B$_{12}$ deficiency and tinnitus. The study they established was unique and properly designed. They involved 113 army personnel, all of whom had been exposed to approximately the same amount and kind of military fire power noise and with an average age of 39 years. The subjects divided themselves into the following three groups:

Group One: Those with noise induced hearing loss (NIHL) and chronic tinnitus (57 subjects).

Group Two: Those with NIHL and no tinnitus (29 subjects).

Group Three: Those with no NIHL and no tinnitus (27 subjects).

The vitamin B$_{12}$ serum levels were measured in all subjects. A blood level of 250 pq per mL or greater was considered to be normal.

Notice that of the 113 subjects there were 86 (76%) who acquired noise induced hearing loss and 27 who did not. That indicates that 24 percent of their sample did not acquire hearing loss from the noise exposure. Of the 86 who did acquire hearing loss, only 57 also acquired tinnitus (66%). From these data we may conclude that noise exposure sufficient to cause hearing impairment does not necessarily also produce tinnitus. An even more conservative statement is that only 57 (50%) people out of 113 exposed to loud sounds developed tinnitus.

Results

In Group One, 47 percent of the subjects had a deficient B$_{12}$ plasma level of less than 250 pq per mL.

In Group Two, 27 percent had a deficient B$_{12}$ blood level.

In Group Three, 19 percent displayed a deficient B$_{12}$ level.

Interestingly enough they found that the tinnitus loudness measured at the frequency corresponding to the pitch of the tinnitus was greater for those patients with normal B$_{12}$ levels (average = 6.0 dB SL) than for those with B$_{12}$ deficiencies (average = 3.9 dB SL). These data may suggest that B$_{12}$ levels do not influence tinnitus loudness or even possibly that deficient B$_{12}$ levels reduced tinnitus loudness.

At this point these data begin to present an interesting picture. They seem to say there is a positive correlation between vitamin B$_{12}$ plasma levels and the results of exposure to excessive noise levels.

The next procedure was to replace the vitamin B$_{12}$ deficiency and measure changes in NIHL and tinnitus. That is to say, does restoring an appropriate B$_{12}$ level reduce tinnitus and/or hearing impairment produced by noise exposure? Twelve patients underwent B$_{12}$ therapy to see if the tinnitus was improved. The report is that some improvement was reported but measured loudness was not conducted or reported, which would have been the correct way to evaluate B$_{12}$ therapy. The authors point out that evaluation of B$_{12}$ therapy was not the purpose of the study, nevertheless, they recommend that tinnitus patients with noise induced tinnitus have their B_{12} plasma levels checked and, if deficient, initiate proper B_{12} therapy.

PATIENT'S QUESTIONS AND ANSWERS

1. *Question:*   The data seem impressive but should most tinnitus patients take vitamin B_{12} even if they do not have noise induced hearing loss?
   Answer: The study indicated an interaction between noise induced hearing loss and vitamin B_{12} deficiency and tinnitus. It seems safe to conclude that those patients who have no noise induced hearing loss would not benefit from vitamin B_{12} treatment.

2. *Question:*   If all these patients were exposed to the same noise levels, I don't understand why some incurred hearing loss as well as tinnitus, while others did not incur either.
   Answer: We, too, fail to understand. It is established that there are "tough ears" and "tender ears," but we do not know what causes either condition. From the vitamin B_{12} data it appears that vitamin B_{12} deficiency may be involved in this process. Of the 113 subjects studied, 86 (76%) developed hearing losses, thus it appears that "tough ears" are less common than those susceptible to noise damage. Of the 86 subjects who suffered noise induced hearing loss, 57 (66%) also acquired tinnitus. Thus we have to conclude that the presence of noise induced hearing loss alone is not sufficient to always produce tinnitus. Keep in mind that of the 57 subjects who developed both noise induced hearing loss and tinnitus only 26 (46%) were vitamin B_{12} deficient.

3. *Question:*   I am confused. Should vitamin B_{12} therapy be induced to treat tinnitus?
   Answer: If one has a measured deficiency in vitamin B_{12}, then such a therapy might be helpful. On the other hand, if the vitamin B_{12} deficiency and the tinnitus are present with normal hearing, vitamin B_{12} therapy may have no effect upon tinnitus.

Suppression of Tinnitus with Electrical Stimulation

STEVEN J. STALLER, Ph.D.
Clinical Studies Manager
Cochlear Corporation
Englewood, Colorado

INTRODUCTION

I am always surprised by the *magical* quality that surrounds the discussion of electricity in the treatment of medical problems. It is something akin to the mystery that, to this day, surrounds the application of computers to modern problems. Perhaps it is the nature of the "black box" phenomenon that most of us don't fully understand. Or perhaps it is the perceived danger posed by electricity that we have been warned about since childhood. In reality, the use of electricity is extremely common in diagnosis and treatment within modern medicine. Devices from heart (cardiac) pacemakers to ear (cochlear) implants are universally accepted as modern therapeutic marvels. There are electrical devices that, in some patients: (1) provide relief from chronic back pain (Transcutaneous Nerve Stimulators: TENS), (2) reduce intractable epileptic seizures, (3) restart failed hearts (implantable defibrillators), (4) allow paralyzed patients to void their bladders, and, some time in the not too distant future, to grasp with their hands, stand, and, hopefully, walk. There is even research underway attempting to electrically restore eyesight to the blind.

The fact that electricity can be used to affect bodily functions in so many ways actually is not surprising. Biological *electricity* is the motor that drives many of the basic functions of the body. Every cell in the human body controls the flow of bio-chemical electricity (positively and negatively charged particles known as ions) in order to receive nourishment, eliminate waste, and perform its biological functions. All sensory systems in the body, such as hearing, vision, and smell, have specialized cells known as "receptors" that convert energy from the outside world (e.g., light, sound, . . .) into biological electricity. This biological electricity is then passed from the receptor organs (e.g., eye, inner ear, . . .) to the brain, through a series of nerves, which conduct the electricity along wire-like projections known as "axons." The electrical impulses jump from nerve-to-nerve across small gaps known as "synapses" and eventually wind up in a specific portion of the brain where they are interpreted as sight or hearing.

Similarly, muscles use electricity to contract and release at the appropriate time. Some muscles, such as the heart, the diaphragm, and the walls of the intestines, con-tract rhythmically without conscious control and are known as autonomic muscles. These muscles perform life-sustaining functions that continue whether we are awake or asleep. Conversely, there are muscles that respond to electrical commands from the brain to initiate conscious muscular activities.

HISTORY OF ATTEMPTS TO ELECTRICALLY SUPPRESS TINNITUS

Since biological electricity drives so many bodily functions, the use of externally gen-erated electricity to influence these functions, was explored shortly after electricity was discovered. Only one year after Alexander Volta invented the battery (1801), which was at that time called the Voltaic Cell, a German physician named Grap-pengeiser hooked-up deaf patients with tinnitus to this new invention and, with more courage than insight, closed the switch. Although Grappengeiser's results were mixed, he succeeded in describing several phenomena that remain valid to this day. In order to suppress tinnitus, Grappengeiser found that, current had to flow with the positive terminal in proximity to the ear. If the current was reversed, the patients re-ported hearing a *rushing* sound and, in some cases, reported an increase in their tin-nitus. Grappengeiser also noted that any changes in tinnitus were present only while the electric current was turned on.

The first decades of the nineteenth century saw a number of experiments inves-tigating the use of electricity as a treatment for a variety of medical problems. In spite of this early enthusiasm, a number of leading physicians and scientists began to crit-icize the use of electricity for medical treatment, asserting that it was, at best, useless or perhaps even harmful.

Despite these criticisms, experiments in electrical stimulation of the ear contin-ued intermittently throughout the nineteenth century. With the invention of the induction coil by Faraday in 1831, a new form of electricity known as alternating current (AC) began to be explored. Alternating current, (the type of electricity found in virtually all wall outlets) flows from negative to positive and back again, rather than flowing in one direction. Direct current (DC), the type of electricity used by Grappengeiser, flows in one direction and is commonly found in automobile batteries. In 1855, Duchenne de Boulogne used Faraday's induction coil to deliver current to the ear through an electrode immersed in water in the external ear canal. Eight of the 10 patients treated were said to have been "cured" of their tinnitus, although little specific information is available.

In the latter half of the 19th century, various investigators *dabbled* in the treatment of tinnitus using both DC (voltaic) and AC (inductive) current with mixed reviews and little documentation of current specification, types of tinnitus that were treated effectively, and the influence of other confounding factors. Around the turn of the century, publication of work exploring electrical suppression of tinnitus essentially ceased, not to be "rediscovered" until the 1960s. At that time, electrical stimulation of the hearing and balance systems for other reasons once again refocused interest on the electrical suppression of tinnitus. It is interesting to note that many of the characteristics of electrical tinnitus suppression described in the 19th century were replicated in more recent controlled experiments.

MODERN HISTORY OF ELECTRICAL TINNITUS SUPPRESSION

In 1960, several American scientists (Hatton, Erulkar, & Rosenberg) were exploring the physiology of the balance (vestibular) system using electrical stimulation and noticed that almost half of their deaf patients (15 of 33) reported a reduction in their tinnitus during stimulation. This rediscovery of electrical tinnitus suppression first documented in the previous century, sparked a renewed interest in this area. From 1960 through the present, numerous articles and chapters describing the electrical suppression of tinnitus have appeared in the medical literature. In order to digest this *feast* of scientific information, without becoming completely confused, one must consider the various ways in which these experiments were conducted. The conclusions drawn from these studies range from negligible to almost universal success in electrically reducing tinnitus. The reason for these diverging conclusions may lie in the variability of experimental techniques, type of electricity used, types of subjects selected, and in the experimenters' definition of a "successful" outcome. Before summarizing the history of modern electrical tinnitus suppression, I would like to diverge for a moment to discuss these important differences.

Two critical differences among experiments are the type of electrical stimulation used and the location at which the stimulation is delivered to the patient. Since the days of Grappengiesser (1801), it has been known that voltaic or direct current (DC) was most effective in suppressing tinnitus, particularly if the positive terminal (electrode delivering the current) was close to the inner ear. Despite the promise of this technique, several problems limit its application in routine clinical practice. First, placing an electrode near the inner ear involves going through or under the ear drum, which can be done for short periods, but becomes less acceptable for chronic or take home use. Second, DC current is known to damage inner ear tissues and so cannot be used with patients who have any hearing whatsoever.

Another important difference across tinnitus experiments relates to the types of patients who were chosen to participate. A number of studies used deaf or severely hearing impaired patients, while others used patients with normal hearing or less than severe hearing impairments. The cause and severity of hearing loss was found to be related to the success of electrical tinnitus suppression in some studies while, in other studies, the type and severity of tinnitus was related to successful treatment. In other studies, neither factor related to the success of treatment.

Different experimenters defined "successful" treatment in many different ways. Reduction in tinnitus loudness generally was considered to be the criterion for success. However, experiments differed in how much, and for how long, loudness change was required to be considered successful. In addition, whether tinnitus reduction continued after the current was turned off, whether tinnitus reduction was consistently present, and whether the electrical stimulus could be heard by patients differed from study to study.

A final critical variable that is known to influence the results of experiments in electrical tinnitus suppression is something called a placebo effect. This does not mean that the patient is trying to deceive anyone but often occurs out of anticipation of improvement when an individual believes they are receiving effective treatment or from the desire to please the experimenter. To separate real improvement in medical conditions from placebo improvements, most medical experiments give a placebo treatment, as well as the "true" treatment, without telling patients which is which. As an example, patients might be given a medication during one phase of a study and a sugar pill during the second phase. Any improvement due to the medication should be greater than any perceived improvement during the placebo phase. Because electrical stimulation to suppress tinnitus is often detectable by the patient, the subtle influence of placebo effects can be extremely difficult to identify.

Having been warned of the pitfalls, let's discuss the modern era of electrical tinnitus suppression research. As mentioned previously, Hatton and his associates were pleasantly surprised at their success in electrically suppressing tinnitus in nearly half of their 33 patients in 1960. They found that positive (anodal) pulses of DC current delivered near the cheeks were most effective, particularly when the patients had severe hearing loss. In addition, tinnitus was suppressed in these patients only as long as the stimulation was present. They found that tinnitus could be completely suppressed when the current was presented just slightly above the patient's ability to detect it. In spite of their positive findings, Hatton and his associates concluded that electrical tinnitus therapy was not viable because of the damaging effects of DC current and because of the need to constantly stimulate the patients.

In the late 1970s, two groups of French researchers from Paris and Bordeaux, and a British group from London, began exploring electrical tinnitus suppression. All three of these groups believed that the secret to successful electrical tinnitus suppression laid in placing the stimulating electrode as close as possible to the inner ear. This was typically accomplished by placing an electrode against the bone of the middle ear (known as the cochlear "promontory") or against the membrane that separates the inner ear from the middle ear (known as the "round window"). Stimulation in either of these locations requires a minor surgical procedure. To stimulate the promontory a needle is placed through the ear drum, and to stimulate the round window the ear drum must be lifted and replaced.

In 1977, Graham & Hazell (London) found that by stimulating at the promontory with low frequency (10 to 30 cycles per second) AC sine waves, 2 of 13 patients (15%) reported tinnitus suppression, with one patient demonstrating continued relief following stimulation (residual inhibition) for four hours. This was the first reported case of residual inhibition due to electrical stimulation. Hazell published an additional study in 1983 reporting tinnitus relief in 7 of 12 deaf patients (58%) with a few demonstrating short term residual inhibition. Surprisingly, Hazell reported AC to be as effective as DC in these patients and found that 3 patients showed improvement to negative (cathodal) current.

The Bordeaux group led by Cazals, Portmann, Negrevergne, Aran, and Dauman published a series of studies beginning in 1978. Their initial study reported complete suppression when using pulsed DC stimulation at the round window and promontory in 12 of 15 patients (80%), all but one of whom were deaf. Tinnitus suppression always occurred on the side of stimulation and was effective if it was positive (anodal). Follow-up studies by this group confirmed their earlier findings, with tinnitus suppression in 47 of 78 patients (60%) when using positive (anodal) DC current. In this more recent study, the researchers found stimulation at the round window to be much more effective than at the promontory, which is logical if the inner ear was the source of tinnitus generation in these patients. In addition, these investigators felt that patients with greater hearing loss were more likely to be successfully suppressed with electrical stimulation. Little residual inhibition was noted, and the treatment was only effective if the tinnitus was localized within the ears (rather than in the head). After nearly a decade of research, Professor Portmann expressed disappointment in their results due to the inability to sustain tinnitus suppression and due to the necessity of using DC current, which by this time was well-known to cause damage to inner ear tissues.

At about the time of the Bordeaux group's initial explorations in this area, Chouard, Meyer, and Maridat were performing similar experiments in Paris. These investigators found that 30 of 64 patients (47%) experienced relief of their tinnitus following 20 minute sessions of stimulation with various currents at various stimulus locations. Some patients reported relief for days and even weeks after stimulation. As had been noted by other investigators, the Paris group found that positive (anodal) DC current produced the greatest benefit. However in contrast to the findings of the

Bordeaux group, Chouard reported that the greater the patients' hearing loss in the high frequencies, the less chance for a positive outcome.

With few exceptions, experiments during this decade found success in the use of DC current applied near the inner ear in patients with severe-to-profound hearing loss. Unfortunately, to this point, electrical stimulation offered little in the way of relief for tinnitus sufferers with usable hearing. During the mid 1980s to the early 1990s, three basic themes were followed in electrical tinnitus suppression research. The first direction of research during this period explored treatments using electrical stimulation in combination with sound or drug therapy. The second type of research focused on a wearable device known as the Audimax Theraband, which produced chronic low level electrical stimulation that was undetectable to the patient. The third, pursued by American, Japanese, European, and Australian researchers, extended the work pursued during the 1970s and 1980s in Europe. These experiments expanded the types of patients studied to include those with more residual hearing and explored more diverse types of electrical waveforms. I will discuss each of these research directions separately.

In the arena of combined treatment studies, one of the more unusual studies published by Morgan and his colleagues in 1985, explored the effectiveness of electrical tinnitus suppression presented with low frequency (144 cycles per second) sound. Using a commercial device called the Tinitop, patients underwent six, 45 minute sessions every 10 days, using pulsed electrical AC (sine wave) current in combination with the low frequency sound. Unlike previous studies the criterion for success was based on a sustained reduction in tinnitus loudness for a period of one week. Twenty-seven of the 50 patients (54%) reported reductions in their tinnitus loudness after one or more sessions. In spite of some initial success, I am unaware of any further published work with this device. Several other studies explored combined treatments of electrical stimulation with drug therapy. The drug lidocaine in combination with low level DC current in the ear canal, has been used for several decades to numb the eardrum. In 1985, Brusi and Loennecken used a combination of lidocaine and DC current on a daily basis in 50 tinnitus patients. Patients were given up to ten consecutive treatments and the investigators found at least partial relief in 31 (62%) of the patients. Ten patients (20%) experienced complete suppression, which in some cases did not return and in other cases returned at a lower level than before the treatments. It is unclear whether the reduction in tinnitus was induced by the lidocaine, the DC current, or the combination of the two.

The second focus of research during this period was the exploration of a device known as the Audimax Theraband. Initially described by Shulman in 1985, the Theraband was a wearable device that delivered undetectable, low level (amplitude modulated) AC current to the mastoid bone (behind the external ear) that systematically swept from low frequency (200 Hz) to high frequency (20,000 Hz). Patients began wearing the device for one hour on the first day and progressively increased their use to five hours per day. Patients wore the device home and filled out a daily log to track the loudness of their tinnitus. Shulman studied three groups of patients using the Theraband and reported that seven of the first 13 patients (54%) experienced decreased tinnitus and one patient (8%) got worse. A second group of 8 patients was tested and none of these patients received any tinnitus relief. This, subsequently, was attributed to hardware malfunction and a third group of 12 patients was studied. Six of these patients had been included in one of the two previous studies. Eight of these 12 patients (67%!) reported suppression with three of the subjects reporting complete suppression with residual inhibition. In spite of these initial promising results, several follow-up studies have failed to achieve this level of success with the device.

Because patients are unable to detect the Theraband stimulus, subsequent researchers were able to use very controlled experimental techniques to determine the true effectiveness of the device. The Theraband was worn at times turned on and at times turned off. Patients were asked to rate the loudness of their tinnitus on a daily basis without knowing whether they were receiving electrical stimulation. Thedinger and his colleagues studied 30 patients using this (double-blind) method and found that five patients reported improvement. Two patients improved with the device turned on and three improved with the device turned off. Two additional studies, by Dobie in 1986 and Vernon in 1987, found little if any benefit reported by patients using the Theraband. Dobie studied 20 patients with two reporting benefit with the device turned on and three reporting benefit with the device turned off. Vernon reported that none of his 16 patients experienced any tinnitus relief with the device.

More traditional forms of stimulation were the basis for continued electrical tinnitus suppression research in the 1980s and 1990s. The outcomes of these studies continued to be mixed. In 1985, Engleberg and Bauer stimulated 10 patients with a hand held probe at thirteen specific locations on and around the external ear. Each location was stimulated for up to two minutes with very low frequency pulses and patients received treatments up to three times per week for up to seventeen sessions. Although these investigators did not precisely define what they considered to be an improvement in tinnitus, they reported that 6 of the 10 subjects (60%) reported "improvements" in their tinnitus lasting from a few hours to several months. In some cases, patients reported a change in the frequency of their tinnitus and in some cases the effect was a reduction in tinnitus loudness. In a second more controlled experiment, these investigators split 20 subjects into two groups with one group receiving treatment and the other group receiving a placebo. Nine of the 10 subjects (90%) receiving treatment reported improvements in their tinnitus, while only one of the subjects in the nontreatment (placebo) group experienced an improvement. This remarkably high success rate may relate to the investigators' criterion for success, which included changes in tinnitus pitch rather than just loudness reduction.

A number of other studies were performed during this period with varying degrees of success. Investigators continued to be frustrated by the effectiveness of DC stimulation, which has long been known to cause damage. The use of safer AC current in various configurations, stimulation sites, and waveforms continued to be inconsistently successful. In 1985, Vernon and Fenwick repeated many of the earlier experiments of the Paris group. They used a variety of waveforms and stimulated in front of and behind the ear. Using a more rigorous criterion for success (a 40% reduction in tinnitus loudness after treatment), these investigators achieved little success with only five of their 23 subjects (22%) reporting benefit. Unlike Engleberg and Bauer, none of these subjects experienced any change in pitch of their tinnitus during or after stimulation. Of the few patients who experienced suppression of their tinnitus, typically only one waveform was effective for a given patient and most of the successfully treated patients experienced residual inhibition for only a few hours after treatment.

Among the other studies that have been reported since these experiments in the mid 1980s, Kuk and his colleagues from Iowa achieved a 50 percent success rate in reducing tinnitus loudness when using AC stimulation at the ear drum and, using the same technique, a Japanese group led by Okusa reported loudness reduction in 65 percent of 35 ears.

Other than the Theraband and the Tinnitop described above, little commercial interest has been shown in the area of electrical tinnitus suppression. In the early 1990s Cochlear Proprietary Limited, the manufacturer of the Nucleus Cochlear Implant, decided to explore this area and embarked on two large scale studies designed to clarify whether a commercial product was feasible for the treatment of tinnitus in patients with and without hearing. The first study, conducted by Ward and her colleagues at medical centers in Australia and the United States, was designed to validate electrical tinnitus suppression with AC current presented in the ear canal and, subsequently, using a needle through the eardrum to stimulate in the middle ear (promontory). Unlike most other studies, these patients were stimulated at levels approaching discomfort and then the stimulus was reduced to below their level of detection and left on for a period of five minutes. Success in this study required a 30 percent or greater reduction in tinnitus loudness after five minutes of stimulation. Twenty-eight percent of 79 subjects suppressed to ear canal stimulation and 50 percent of 64 subjects suppressed to stimulation at the promontory (middle ear). Sixty subjects underwent testing at both stimulation sites and 13 (22%) responded successfully to both locations of stimulation. These investigators attempted to identify patient factors that might predict success with electrical stimulation but were unable to find any. It was unclear whether the success noted in this study was related to the sustained stimulation below the patients' thresholds or to the intense short-term stimulation at the beginning of each trial. In order to clarify this and to determine whether any beneficial effects could be sustained over time, (which would be essential for any successful commercial tinnitus suppression device), a larger follow-up trial was begun.

In 1991, an international clinical trial began in eight hospitals in Australia, Sweden, Switzerland, the United Kingdom, and the United States. Wearable devices were built by Cochlear Proprietary Limited to allow patients to receive electrical stimulation over several weeks. Patients were stimulated initially in the ear canal and on the promontory (middle ear) with a variety of AC waveforms to determine their suitability for longer term stimulation. In order to be more conservative than the previous study, the criterion for success was a 40 percent reduction in tinnitus loudness. Ninety-one subjects received short-term ear canal stimulation and 65 patients were stimulated with a needle through the eardrum resting on the promontory in the middle ear. Only 18 percent of the patients tested suppressed to ear canal stimulation and 14 percent responded successfully at the promontory. Only one subject responded at both stimulation sites. Just over one-fourth (26%) of the patients responded at one of the two stimulation sites. In light of the earlier study, it was surprising that so few patients responded to electrical stimulation, especially since only a single waveform was used in the first study. The difference in results between the two studies may reflect the different criterion for success or some unknown differences in the two groups of patients. Because of the low success rate, the study was modified to include all willing patients in the wearable (long-term stimulation) phase of the experiment, rather than just those patients whose tinnitus was suppressed using stimulation in the ear canal or at the promontory. Twenty-three patients underwent a minor surgical procedure to allow placement of a small metal ball electrode under the eardrum to rest against the membrane (round window) separating the middle ear from the inner ear. This electrode was left in place for up to two weeks and patients kept a daily log describing their tinnitus and returned regularly to the clinics for evaluation and equipment maintenance. Just under one-third of the patients (30%) reported a significant reduction in tinnitus loudness; however, most found that the effect was not consistently present during the experiment. An additional 35 percent of the subjects reported changes in the pitch of their tinnitus or less than a 40 percent reduction in tinnitus loudness during stimulation. Nine percent of the patients reported a reduction in tinnitus even when the device was not turned on (without their knowledge) at the beginning of the study. A number of patient factors were reviewed in an attempt to identify certain patients who might be more likely to be successfully treated with electrical stimulation. The only characteristic that appeared to be meaningful was the duration of tinnitus. No patients who had experienced tinnitus for longer than thirty years reported any changes in tinnitus during electrical stimulation. Based on (1) the limited success of electrical stimulation in these patients, (2) the inability to consistently sustain reported benefits over time, and (3) the inability to predict which patients might be successfully treated, the company decided to discontinue efforts to produce a commercial tinnitus suppression device.

COCHLEAR IMPLANTS AND TINNITUS

Unlike the rather mixed bag of results described in the previous section, electrical stimulation for the restoration of hearing through a device known as a cochlear implant has been applied successfully in more than 14,000 patients worldwide. A cochlear implant is similar to a hearing aid, in that it receives sound through a microphone, converts it to an electrical signal, amplifies or processes that signal to enhance specific characteristics necessary for the hearing impaired user, and delivers the processed sound to the patient. Unlike a hearing aid, which converts the processed electrical signal back to sound, a cochlear implant delivers the direct electrical signal to the remaining hearing nerves of an individual with severe-to-profound hearing impairment through an electrode (or many electrodes) that is surgically placed in the inner ear. The external parts of a cochlear implant include a microphone that converts sound to electricity, a cable, and a speech processor about the size of a pack of cigarettes and a method of delivering the electrical signal to the internal electrode array. The speech processor recodes sound into a form that is interpretable by the brain and delivers it back up the cable to a small transmitter (shaped like a steering wheel). The transmitter is held in place on the skin behind the ear by a magnet that couples to a magnet in the internal implant. The electrical speech signal is sent across the skin by radio (frequency) waves to the surgically implanted receiver that rests just under the skin behind the ear. The receiver (similar to a transistor radio) receives the coded signal from the transmitter and passes it to the electrodes in the inner ear. This, in turn, stimulates the hearing nerve, resulting in the perception of sound by the patient. Early cochlear implants utilized in the late 1970s and early 1980s had only one electrode and provided detection of sound and assistance with lipreading. These "single channel" implants did not allow patients to understand speech without lipreading. In the mid 1980s, more sophisticated cochlear implants with up to 22 channels became available, which allowed patients to understand limited amounts of speech without lipreading. Since that time, cochlear implant technology has improved dramatically and the current generation of devices allows most patients to understand significant amounts of speech without lipreading in both quiet and noisy environments. Many patients are able to carry on conversations over the telephone.

One very positive side effect of electrical stimulation from cochlear implants has been the common report of reduced tinnitus in many patients. In the early 1980s, the single channel cochlear implant developed by the collaboration of the 3M Corporation and the House Ear Institute was the most widely used implant in the United States. Dr. John House noted reports of reduced tinnitus in some of his implanted patients and undertook a systematic study to better understand the phenomenon. Dr. House evaluated a series of 65 profoundly deaf patients who used the 3M/House device on a regular basis. Fifty-three percent of these patients reported a reduction in their tinnitus when wearing the device and 11 percent reported that their tinnitus became worse. Interestingly, there were reports of residual inhibition and also reports of suppression in the ear opposite from the cochlear implant. One year after the initial study, patients continued to experience tinnitus relief from their cochlear implants.

In a larger study, Ward and her colleagues surveyed 149 users of the Nucleus 22 Channel Cochlear Implant. In this unpublished survey, these investigators found that two-thirds of the profoundly deaf patients (66%) using the Nucleus device experienced relief from their tinnitus while using the implant. About 5 percent of the patients reported that their tinnitus was worse after implantation. Another study of Nucleus patients from the University of Michigan found that three quarters of their 33 patients (74%) experienced tinnitus relief when using the implant.

Although tinnitus relief is a very consistent, positive side effect of cochlear implantation, it is unclear whether the electrical stimulation from the implant is reducing tinnitus in these patients or whether listening to environmental sounds and speech is masking their tinnitus. One of the major stumbling blocks of this technology, as it might be applied to the majority of tinnitus sufferers, relates to the invasive nature of the procedure. Keep in mind that implant patients lose any residual hearing after surgery, which makes cochlear implants inappropriate for anyone with useful hearing. From numerous animal studies, as well as extensive clinical experience, it appears that the loss of hearing after implantation is related to damage to the inner ear hair cells from the insertion of the electrode array. An alternative to cochlear implants with electrode arrays inside the cochlea, are implants with an electrode that remains outside the cochlea (extracochlear). Some early cochlear implants used electrodes designed to rest against the round window membrane between the inner ear and the middle ear. Although this type of electrode is less traumatic to the inner ear and does not compromise residual hearing, it proved less effective at restoring hearing. However, as a tinnitus suppression device, an extracochlear implant may be an effective alternative for patients with hearing. In 1993 the London group of Hazell and colleagues explored extracochlear implantation of three patients who were deaf with severe tinnitus. They used very low frequency AC stimulation and were able to reduce tinnitus loudness in all of the patients for more than three years. As with many of the previous studies, treatment was restricted to patients with essentially no hearing. Suppression only occurred when the patients could detect the electrical stimulus. As is sometimes the case with acoustic maskers, this can be distracting to some patients. In addition, very low frequency stimulation, as was used in this study, can cause balance problems in some people.

A group from Toulouse France, headed by Professor Fraysse explored long term electrical suppression in 1983. Like the London group, these investigators placed an electrode on the round window membrane. Unlike the London group, they found that low frequency stimulation produced pain in most of their five patients who were deaf. Using positive pulses (DC) that varied in frequency from low (150 Hz) to high (1500 Hz), four of the five patients (80%) experienced relief of their tinnitus. Two patients experienced residual inhibition that ranged from one month to an amazing 18 months.

SUMMARY

Reviewing the history of two centuries of electrical tinnitus suppression presents a long and twisted (and exhausting) story! However, there are some conclusions that are clear.

1. Tinnitus can be relieved in some patients using electrical stimulation. Unfortunately, the most effective stimulus is DC current presented as close to the inner ear as possible. Because it is well known that DC is damaging, this can only be used in patients who are deaf and must be provided to patients on a continuous basis. This would involve surgical placement of an electrode in the middle or inner ear on a permanent basis.

2. Although some patients with hearing have been successfully treated with AC stimulation, the number of tinnitus sufferers who could be helped is unknown. In addition, we are unable to identify which individuals are likely to be successfully treated with electrical stimulation. AC stimulation is clearly less effective than DC stimulation. Unfortunately, DC stimulation creates tissue damage and therefore cannot be used in hearing patients. Success with AC stimulation has been extremely variable. We cannot currently identify who is likely to be successfully treated with AC stimulation, and we cannot predict what specific AC waveform might be most effective for a given individual. Therefore, the most logical approach must be to provide a variety of different waveforms if a reasonable level of success is to be achieved. It would also be helpful if a noninvasive screening test could be developed to decide who the best candidates for electrical tinnitus suppression might be.

3. Relief can rarely be achieved unless the electrical stimulus can be detected by the patient. The inability to truly "suppress" rather than "mask" tinnitus with electrical stimulation has been a disappointment. Although there is some debate that electrical masking is different than the masking produced by sound, the fact that patients must detect the stimulus will be distracting to some individuals.

4. Cochlear implants are successful in relieving tinnitus in a large proportion of individuals who are deaf. The relief experienced by these individuals is likely the result of several positive factors including masking, the positive effects of being reintroduced into the hearing world, and, possibly, the reduction of stress created by their improved ease of communication and improved sense of safety. Unfortunately, the few patients that I am aware of, who have been implanted specifically for tinnitus relief, have had very mixed results. It appears that listening to environmental sounds that mask tinnitus, without the desire to improve one's communication ability, is inadequate benefit for most individuals to be willing to undergo the costly and involved procedure.

Although the picture for electrical tinnitus suppression remains cloudy, much research continues in this area. Technology is changing at an extremely rapid rate and significant breakthroughs occur in medical science on almost a daily basis. What is today a dream, often becomes the reality of tomorrow. The most important fact that has been clearly established is that electrical tinnitus suppression is possible. The challenge for tomorrow is to turn that knowledge into a reality for the large population of tinnitus sufferers.

PATIENT'S QUESTIONS AND ANSWERS

1. *Question:*   Will the presence of electrical stimulation possibly damage the inner ear or reduce hearing ability?

Answer: The long-term effects of electrical stimulation to produce hearing or to potentially reduce tinnitus are currently unknown. If an electrical tinnitus suppression device is developed, it will have to undergo rigorous clinical trials under the guidance of the Food and Drug Administration to prove that it is both safe and effective before it is released to the public. To be safe, the device would need to use some type of "balanced (i.e., AC)" electrical current, and if used in hearing ears, would probably have a stimulating electrode near, but not in, the inner ear.

2. *Question:* Is electrical stimulation a viable treatment for tinnitus?
   Answer: No, current tests have revealed that electrical suppression works for some few patients, but it is not yet an acceptable treatment for tinnitus. I am convinced, however, that in the future it will become a viable treatment modality for tinnitus. At such a time, it should be one of many possible treatments.

3. *Question:* Has electrical suppression been tested in the presence of tinnitus suppressing drugs such as Xanax?
   Answer: No, it has not, but your suggestion is a good one. There is every reason to believe that treatment modalities might enhance each other when applied in concert, however, in general that sort of thing has not been investigated.

4. *Question:* If electrical suppression works initially, is there any reason to think that its effectiveness would decline with continued use?
   Answer: This possibility has not been adequately tested as yet. The results of TENS units, however, suggests that suppressive effects do not habituate and that its effectiveness will continue indefinitely. It is necessary, however, to keep in mind that for many patients the reduction of tinnitus was experienced only as long as the electrical current was flowing.

5. *Question:* How long would the batteries last?
   Answer: The length of time that batteries might last would depend on the type of current and level of current necessary to show a beneficial effect. The stimulation requirements would probably vary from patient to patient. A reasonable model might be the speech processor for the current Nucleus Cochlear Implant, which uses a single rechargeable AA battery that lasts up to 16 hours of continuous use.

6. *Question:* As I understand it, the cochlear implant utilizes electrical stimulation that causes the patients to hear things. Will the electrical stimulation for tinnitus cause the patient to hear things?
   Answer: In order for an electrical tinnitus suppression device to be acceptable to most patients, it would need to be inaudible. Unfortunately, this has been difficult to achieve in the experiments conducted to date. Finding an electrical waveform that suppresses tinnitus without producing sound or discomfort to the patient is the challenge that needs to be overcome before electrical tinnitus suppression becomes a viable clinical therapy.

7. *Question:*   Since the cochlear implant appears to have eliminated tinnitus for most of those patients, why not simply use the cochlear implant for tinnitus patients?

Answer: The vast majority of tinnitus patients have enough hearing so that they do not qualify for cochlear implantation. Cochlear implants are designed for patients whose hearing is so depressed that they derive little or no benefit from hearing aids. In addition, individuals who receive a cochlear implant typically lose all of their remaining hearing in the ear implanted. To my knowledge, the few individuals who have been implanted specifically to relieve tinnitus have typically had disappointing outcomes. The decision to receive a cochlear implant should be based on a desire to restore hearing in patients with severe-to-profound hearing losses, and any secondary benefits in the form of tinnitus masking should be considered "icing on the cake."

8. *Question:*   I am impressed by the results of the combined DC and lidocaine work by Brusi and Loennecken. Could you provide additional comment on their work?

Answer: They had a success rate of 62 percent in the 50 patients they treated. The procedure they used is that which is routinely used to painlessly anesthetize the ear drum. That they have not continued this type of work gives me pause to wonder. We might also question what they mean by *success*. Many tinnitus patients report that they feel better simply because they have had a professional take them seriously. It is for this reason that we feel it is important to measure the loudness of tinnitus and indicate success only when there has been a significant reduction in tinnitus loudness.

► 12

Suppression of Tinnitus by Cochlear Implant

JUICHI ITO, M.D.
Department of Otolaryngology,
Otsu Red Cross Hospital, Shiga

JUNJI SAKAKIHARA, M.D.
Department of Otolaryngology
Faculty of Medicine, Kyoto University, Sakyo-ku, Kyoto
Japan

It has been reported that 5 percent to 8 percent of all patients who visit otolaryngology clinics suffer from tinnitus and that 80 percent of all patients with ear disease have tinnitus. In the treatment of tinnitus, although blood vessel dilators, minor tranquilizers, and other drugs have been used, no effective therapeutic method has been confirmed. Transcutaneous and transpromontory electrical stimulation have been suggested for the treatment of tinnitus; recently, Chouard et al in France reported that transcutaneous electrical stimulation was effective in the relief of tinnitus in a third of patients with tinnitus. According to Hazell and co-workers, some patients carry a transcutaneous electrical stimulator and use it ten to thirty minutes per day to relieve tinnitus. Aran and Cazals reported that tinnitus was suppressed in 60 percent and 43 percent of patients with trans-round window and transpromontory electrical stimulation, respectively.

On the other hand, cochlear implantation has been used clinically to restore the hearing of severely hearing-impaired and totally deaf patients since the pioneer work of House and Urban in the 1970s. The multichannel cochlear implant device makes the discrimination of speech easier. In Japan the cochlear implant device has been used clinically for the last five or six years, and fairly good hearing results have been reported. Although it is known that patients experience relief of tinnitus after cochlear implant surgery, there are very few studies of this phenomenon. We consider it reasonable to assume that cochlear implant would be superior to transcutaneous or transpromontory electrical stimulation in relieving tinnitus, since the design of the cochlear implant is such that it stimulates the cochlear nerve directly. However, patients with cochlear implants are all either severely hearing impaired or totally deaf, and it is unknown whether the mechanism by which tinnitus is produced and that by which it is influenced by electrical stimulation are the same in these patients and in those with residual hearing. However, many physicians have experienced the suppression of tinnitus after cochlear implantation. Tinnitus is suppressed in 70 percent to 80 percent of cases after cochlear implant surgery. As did Brackmann and Doyle, two otologic surgeons in the United States, since 1987 we have performed cochlear implant surgery on 20 severely hearing impaired or totally deaf patients. Most had suffered from tinnitus before surgery, in the absence of any environmental sounds, which have been shown to suppress tinnitus. Like other investigators, we found tinnitus suppressed by the promontory stimulation test and after cochlear implantation. In the present study, we investigated the degree of tinnitus in cochlear implant candidates and the change in tinnitus at the time of promontory stimulation test and after cochlear implant surgery.

PATIENTS AND METHODS

Twenty patients who received cochlear implants since 1987, all of whom had been severely hearing impaired or totally deaf, were studied. Table 12–1 shows the clinical characteristics of the patients before cochlear implant surgery. The degree of tinnitus, classified as marked, slight, or absent, is shown in Table 12–2; 90 percent of the patients were suffering from tinnitus to some degree. The change in the degree of tinnitus on promontory stimulation test and after cochlear implant was investigated.

RESULTS

Prior to cochlear implant surgery, 5 patients (25%) had marked tinnitus, and 13 patients (65%) had slight tinnitus (Table 12–2). All patients except patients no. 6 and 18

TABLE 12–1   **Clinical Characteristics of 20 Cochlear Implant Surgery Patients**

Patient No.	Age/Sex	Cause of Deafness	Period of Deafness
1	55/M	Head injury	1 year, 6 months
2	50/M	Unknown	10 years
3	25/M	Head injury	5 months
4	62/M	Labyrinthitis	10 years
5	63/M	Head injury	2 years
6	38/M	Streptomycin	36 years
7	56/F	Sudden deafness	10 years
8	26/F	Unknown	2 years
9	58/M	Meniere's disease	7 years
10	21/F	Streptomycin	20 years
11	55/M	Meningitis	3 years
12	42/M	Head injury	1 year, 5 months
13	51/M	Labyrinthitis	1 year
14	59/F	Unknown	25 years
15	54/F	Meniere's disease	10 years
16	39/M	Meniere's disease	5 years
17	18/F	Meningitis	5 years
18	8/M	Meningitis	7 years
19	61/F	Unknown	16 years
20	39/M	Labyrinthitis	1 year

suffered from tinnitus to some degree. Table 12–3 shows the change in degree of tinnitus on promontory stimulation test in the 18 patients who suffered from tinnitus. As shown in Table 12–3, at the time of promontory stimulation test, tinnitus disappeared in 4 patients (22%), was suppressed in 9 patients (50%), and showed no change in 5 patients (28%). Tinnitus was not effectively relieved (abolished or suppressed) at the time of promontory stimulation test in 72 percent of patients with tinnitus.

Table 12–4 shows the change of degree of tinnitus after cochlear implant in the 18 patients with tinnitus. Tinnitus was abolished in 8 patients (44%), suppressed in 7 patients (39%), unchanged in 2 patients (11%), and aggravated in 1 patient (6%). Intracochlear electrical stimulation was effective in relieving tinnitus in 83 percent of patients with tinnitus who underwent cochlear implant surgery.

TABLE 12–2   **Tinnitus Status Before Cochlear Implantation**

Patient No.	Marked	Slight	None
1	X		
2		X	
3	X		
4		X	
5	X		
6			X
7		X	
8		X	
9		X	
10		X	
11		X	
12	X		
13	X		
14		X	
15		X	
16		X	
17		X	
18			X
19		X	
20		X	
Total (%)	5 (25)	13 (65)	2 (10)

DISCUSSION

There have been several reports that tinnitus is suppressed after cochlear implant surgery; we experienced the same phenomenon. However, the mechanism of tinnitus suppression is not clearly understood. A masker effect of sound stimulation is a possible explanation. It is well known that tinnitus is suppressed by environmental sounds, and this phenomenon is applied clinically. The physiologic basis for the mechanism of the masker effect, according to Vernon, is that environmental sounds vibrate the basilar membrane of the damaged site and suppress the abnormal activities in the hair cells in the inner ear that produce tinnitus, thus suppressing tinnitus. Some patients with cochlear implants experience residual suppressive effects of electrical stimulation of tinnitus, which continue after they switch off the cochlear im-

TABLE 12–3 **Tinnitus Status During Promontory Stimulation Test**

Patient No.	Disappeared	Suppressed	No Change	Aggravated
1	X			
2			X	
3		X		
4			X	
5		X		
7	X			
8		X		
9			X	
10		X		
11		X		
12	X			
13	X			
14		X		
15		X		
16		X		
17			X	
19			X	
20		X		
Total (%)	4 (22)	9 (50)	5 (28)	0

plant. They experience tinnitus again several hours later. The mechanism of this phenomenon is similar to the masker effect. However, in cochlear implant patients, the cochlea is functionally destroyed and the hair cells are no longer activated. After the insertion of electrodes, the basilar membrane is not vibrated. Therefore, the mechanism of tinnitus suppression of the cochlear implant is not exactly the same as that of the masker effect.

Another hypothesis accounting for tinnitus suppression by the cochlear implant is that the electrical stimulation from the implanted electrodes alter the activities of the cochlear nerve, which is, in this hypothesis, postulated to be the main cause of the tinnitus. In yet another explanation, the electrical stimulation from the implant device is thought to be transmitted to the cochlear nucleus and superior olive nucleus, and to directly inhibit the hair cells of the inner ear via the cochlear efferent nerves. The cochlear efferent nerves are reported to stimulate the outer hair cells of the inner ear; however, because these hair cells are no longer functionally activated in cochlear implant patients, this hypothesis is unlikely.

TABLE 12–4   **Tinnitus Status after Cochlear Implantation**

Patient No.	Disappeared	Suppressed	No Change	Aggravated
1	X			
2			X	
3		X		
4			X	
5		X		
7	X			
8		X		
9	X			
10		X		
11	X			
12	X			
13	X			
14		X		
15				X
16		X		
17		X		
19	X			
20	X			
Total (%)	8 (44)	7 (39)	2 (11)	1 (6)

In the present study, we found that 90 percent of cochlear implant candidates suffered from tinnitus, and that in 25 percent of them the tinnitus was very uncomfortable. Patient no. 12, who became deaf upon sustaining a head injury, had been receiving medication at the Department of Psychiatry for sudden deafness and severe tinnitus. This patient had expressed the hope that cochlear implantation would not only restore his hearing but also relieve the tinnitus. Fortunately, because the speech comprehension ability of this patient was fairly good and because the tinnitus completely disappeared, he was able to return to his previous job. As in this patient, tinnitus in some patients is suppressed after cochlear implant.

On the other hand, patient no. 15 complained of an uncomfortable feeling inside her head when using the cochlear implant. While it is unclear whether this sensation was, in fact, tinnitus, the sensation did annoy this patient. We are now controlling the electrical current from the implantable device in this patient and have instructed her to use the cochlear implant for a reduced number of hours every day to gradually become used to it.

Our results are based only upon the patient's subjective reports; the pitch-match test and loudness balance test could not be performed because of their deafness. However, the tinnitus of cochlear implant patients was, in most cases, suppressed. While the mechanism of this suppression remains uncertain, these results provide us with some valuable data that may be useful in the treatment of tinnitus.

PATIENT'S QUESTIONS AND ANSWERS

1. *Question:*   If tinnitus is present in both ears, will the cochlear implant in one ear relieve tinnitus in both ears?
   Answer: Most likely the relief will be restricted to the stimulated ear only. To date, no one has had a cochlear implant in both ears. It is important to realize, however, that in some few cases masking of one ear relieves tinnitus in both ears.

2. *Question:*   Would a cochlear implant be recommended for the relief of tinnitus in an ear with sufficient hearing as to not qualify for a cochlear implant?
   Answer: To our knowledge, such a procedure has been conducted on only one patient, and it did not relieve the tinnitus in that case. We would not recommend a cochlear implant for the sake of tinnitus alone. Remember, the act of implanting the electrode is very apt to destroy the inner ear mechanisms, and anything that reduces hearing ability usually increases tinnitus.

3. *Question:*   The data presented suggest that 72 percent of the patients with promontory stimulation got tinnitus relief. Is promontory stimulation dangerous to hearing?
   Answer: As a rule, promontory stimulation will not damage hearing unless applied at excessive intensities. An excessively intense stimulation will produce pain that most likely would prevent the subject from using that level of stimulation. Note that the cochlear implant was effective in more patients (83%) than was promontory stimulation (72%) . Nevertheless, promontory stimulation may be the answer for tinnitus patients who have hearing.

4. *Question:*   During promontory stimulation that causes tinnitus to disappear or to be suppressed, can the patient hear from that ear at the same time?
   Answer: In most cases, the electrical stimulation is at such a level as to not be heard, and, therefore, it does not interfere with speech intelligibility. Unlike the cochlear implant, promontory stimulation cannot be used to aid speech intelligibility.

5. *Question:*   In masking of tinnitus it appears that high frequency sound is necessary to be effective. Is it high frequency electrical stimuli that is required for electrical suppression of tinnitus?

Answer: The electrical stimulation used in the cochlear implant is the analog of speech and environmental sounds, therefore it would appear that high frequency stimuli are not required. In addition there is an investigator in London, Jonathan Hazell, who has found that very low frequency electrical stimuli are the most effective tinnitus suppressors. He used 30 or 40 Hz stimuli.

13

Psychological Treatments for Tinnitus

JANE L. HENRY, Ph.D.
University of New South Wales

PETER H. WILSON, Ph.D.
Flinders University of South Australia

ACKNOWLEDGEMENT

The authors would like to thank Dr. W. Hiller, Dr. G. Goebel, and Prof. Dr. M. Fichter of Klinik Roseneck, Prien am Chiemsee, Bundesrepublik Deutschland, for providing the opportunity and facilities that enabled portions of this chapter. We are also indebted to The University of New South Wales, The University of Sydney, and the Research Board of The Flinders University of South Australia for financial and practical support.

INTRODUCTION

Over the past ten years, there has been a very rich exchange of ideas about psychological aspects of tinnitus among a small, but active, group of researchers and clinicians on three continents. Over this period, there has been a considerable development of techniques that are aimed at reducing the distress experienced by many tinnitus sufferers. In this chapter, we provide an overview of the types of psychological thera-pies that have been used and developed in Australia by ourselves, in the United King-dom by Richard Hallam and Simon Jakes, in Sweden by Per Lindberg, Berit Scott, and their colleagues; in the United States by Robert Sweetow, and in the Federal Re-public of Germany by Gerhard Goebel and Wolfgang Hiller.

The work in Australia was carried out initially at The University of Sydney where over several hundred tinnitus patients were involved in self-management groups between 1983 and 1991. Over time, our treatment has evolved from a basic progressive muscular relaxation training and biofeedback approach to different types of cognitive therapy. Along the way, we have learned a great deal from listening to the patients talk about both their difficulties and their methods for coping with tinni-tus. Common reactions to tinnitus include depression, tension, irritability, and sleep problems. We take the view that many of these problems are a *reaction* to the tinni-tus, although in some cases, it is possible that tension or stress may itself exacerbate the tinnitus. Many tinnitus patients are initially somewhat skeptical about a referral to a psychologist, and may say; "My tinnitus is not in my head! I am not crazy! It is real!" It is important to realize that the psychologist will share your view that the tin-nitus is real rather than imaginary. A referral to a psychologist does not indicate that anyone thinks that you are crazy. It just means that there may be some ways to help in learning to live with the tinnitus, and a psychologist is in a good position to pro-vide that kind of help.

Psychological approaches emphasize that people can learn ways to cope with the tinnitus and with other life stresses. Indeed, we view tinnitus as a stressor in itself, rather like chronic pain or some other persistent aversive stimulus. Thus, tinnitus may have many consequences for the person's life, including an impact on family and so-cial relationships, engagement in work and leisure activities, in mood, life satisfac-tion, and psychological well-being.

The aim of psychological therapy is not to remove or even to reduce the tinnitus but to help people to cope better with the problem. The tinnitus will still be there, but the person can learn ways to react differently to it. The use of coping strategies will often assist the person to deal with difficult periods when the tinnitus is unusually loud or annoying, when sleep is severely disrupted, or when feeling depressed or un-able to concentrate or worried by the tinnitus. In the present chapter we will focus on describing a comprehensive approach in which relaxation training and several dif-ferent types of cognitive therapy are integrated into a single treatment program.

THINKING AND TINNITUS

One of the most important recent advances in the psychological approaches to tinni-tus is *cognitive therapy.* Cognitive therapy is a specific set of techniques that are aimed at helping an individual to change their way of thinking. Cognitive therapy is widely used in the treatment of depression, anxiety, chronic pain, and other problems.

In practice, several different forms of cognitive therapy exist, and we will refer to three of these: (1) cognitive restructuring, (2) attention diversion, and (3) imagery training.

In cognitive restructuring the therapist helps the person to identify the thoughts that go through their mind when they encounter a particular situation, such as tinnitus, and then to challenge the accuracy or usefulness of these ways of thinking.

Attention diversion involves helping people to learn ways to shift the focus of their attention away from the tinnitus and on to some other sensation or object.

Imagery training involves methods that harness the power of one's own imagination in order to evoke strong sensations that can compete with the tinnitus for attention.

WHY FOCUS ON THINKING?

This is an important question, so we will spend some time explaining the general principles involved here. During everyday activities, a person is exposed to a range of events and situations. The alarm bell goes off when

The telephone rings.

The coffee is cold.

The mail arrives.

The car will not start.

The car finally starts.

We get some good news.

We find a good book in the library.

We pass a friend who stops for a chat.

We have a pleasant lunch.

We return to the car to find a parking ticket on the windscreen, and so forth.

A micro analysis of any day, even when we stay at home, would consume many pages of this book. During the day, we also experience changes in our emotional state.

feeling angry

irritable

sad

happy

really down

anxious

elated

Of course, we often notice that there is a relationship between the events that occur and the emotions that we experience. However, these effects are sometimes quite subtle. We may experience the mood change, but we may not be able to identify the cause of that mood change. Most days are not full of significant events, such as a win in the lottery, or, fortunately, a parking ticket. Nevertheless, any event or situation that occurs during the day may trigger some change in one's emotional state. The event or situation may be something potentially negative, such as waiting for a friend who is late, failing a driving test, or losing some money. Other situations may be potentially positive, such as receiving a warm smile or hug from a friend, being paid a compliment, or having some success on a task. Many situations are somewhat ambiguous: neither clearly positive nor clearly negative—they may be open to interpretation. A person may, on some occasions, experience an emotional reaction to these otherwise neutral events, such as feeling of anxiety, depression, or anger. Of course, not everyone experiences the same reactions to the same events. Some people are not bothered at all by one situation but experience strong reactions to other situations. Likewise, a particular person may experience stronger reactions to a situation on one occasion compared with another time. How can we explain these variations?

One widely held view within psychology is referred to as the cognitive theory. The cognitive theory asserts that the influence of an event on the emotional state is through the way in which one thinks about each event or situation. That is, relatively spontaneous thoughts (self-statements, words, or sentences) or images (visual mental pictures) may influence our emotional state at the time. The thoughts may be either positive or negative in content. Thus, in response to an offer of assistance with the use of an automatic bank machine, a relatively ambiguous situation, the person might think something positive such as; "Oh, isn't it nice to know that there are helpful people around when I need them," or the person may think something negative, "I feel like such fool that I cannot use this machine. This person must think that I am really stupid. Everyone else can use these machines." Initial negative thoughts may give rise to other thoughts that may escalate in negativity, and a period of brooding over some past situation, or worrying about some future event, may be set in place. By this time, it may be very difficult to stop the thoughts, and the emotional state that is engendered by them may deepen. Of course, if the thoughts are positive, this persistence of thinking could be a good thing; but if they are negative, a depressive mood may be induced. The precise content of the thought is likely to be responsible for the different types of emotions, such as anxiety, depression, anger, happiness, confidence, and so forth. The main point here is that, according to the cognitive theory, the emotional response is the result of the content of the thoughts, *not the event itself.* The same event may occur to two different people, but one person may experience depression, while the other may experience a more neutral or even a positive mood. According to the cognitive theory, the emotion that is experienced will depend on the content of the thoughts, that is, how one interprets the events or situations.

Thus, we can distinguish between three aspects of our reaction to events that are commonly called A, B, and C.

A = the situation or event we experience.

B = our thoughts, beliefs, perceptions, and expectations about A.

C = our emotions and behaviors.

A-B-C Model : A General Example

A = The Situation or Event	B = Thoughts – Beliefs	C = Emotional Consequence
Offer of help with bank machine	Oh, isn't it nice to know that there are helpful people around when I need them.	Positive Feeling cared about
Offer of help with bank machine	I feel like such fool that I cannot use this machine. This person must think that I am really stupid. Everyone else can use these machines.	Depressed, Low self-esteem

WHAT ARE AUTOMATIC THOUGHTS?

We have previously used "automatic thought," which is a term used by Aaron T. Beck, the originator of the cognitive theory. The term conveys the general subjective experience of our thinking. That is, our thoughts seem to arise with little or no conscious effort, they are highly believable impressions, and they appear to be out of any direct control. The person is often unaware of the content unless there is an opportunity to stop and listen to the thoughts or self-statements. People usually believe their thoughts without questioning the basis or reason for those thoughts. However, it would be rather surprising if all our thoughts were correct or accurate perceptions of events! Sometimes, they are accurate, but on other occasions, they may be partly or wholly in error.

In the example concerning the bank machine, the individual who is having trouble with the machine probably has no real evidence that the person who has offered to help thinks that they are stupid. Nor is it likely to be true that all people can readily use the bank machines without assistance. Indeed, many people avoid these machines altogether because they fear making a mistake in front of other people. Thus, we have in this example two aspects of the thought (self-statement) that are probably erroneous. One is an example of reading another person's mind—thinking that you know accurately what another person in thinking, and the other error is an example of a false comparison—assuming that you are unique in not possessing certain skills. At a deeper level, these thoughts may also suggest a high degree of concern about what other people think about you or how important it is to be able to perform tasks correctly and independently. These concerns may give rise to similar automatic thoughts in many other situations.

TINNITUS AND THINKING

The explanation for the emotional reactions that we have outlined can be expanded to deal with the problem of tinnitus. Consider the way in which we think about *sounds* in general. Most of us hear sounds as part of our everyday routine, for example, the sound of an air conditioner, a train in a tunnel, the traffic in the street, and so on. We often do not notice the sounds until we focus on them. Perhaps our attention is drawn to them because they have changed a little, because someone mentions the sound, or because they have a special meaning for us (e.g., hearing our own name in a din of conversation at a party). Consider the following example: We may hear a sound in the night. The reaction to that sound depends upon the interpretation given to that sound. For example, we may experience anxiety or fear if we think that there is an intruder, but we may experience anger if we think that it is the wind banging a door that a neighbor forgot to lock. The precise reaction will depend on the content of our thoughts. So, for the same noise (banging), two different people may have quite different reactions: fear or anger. In one case, the person may be thinking; "What is that banging? There is an intruder in the house!! He might attack me," and this may lead to emotions of fear or anxiety. In the other instance, the person might think; "What is that banging? That careless neighbor left the door open again. Now I have to get up in the cold and close it. This really is a nuisance. Why does he do this to me all the time when he knows that I am a light sleeper," and this thought may lead to feelings of anger. We can draw up a list such as the following:

Sound	Thought	Reaction
Banging	There is an intruder in the house!! He might attack me.	Fear, Anxiety
Banging	That careless neighbor left the gate open again. Now I have to get up in the cold and close it. This really is a nuisance.	Anger

Any event or situation that we encounter, including a sound, may lead to some thought (self-statement) that, in turn, may lead to an emotional response. Tinnitus can also be viewed as a sound to which we can respond in different ways, especially when it varies in loudness or other characteristics. Thus, tinnitus can be regarded as an event (A) to which the person may respond with automatic thoughts (B) that, in turn, may lead to negative emotional states (C).

Let us now examine the types of thoughts that people commonly report when they notice that the tinnitus is bad. Some thought are seemingly negative, such as; "The tinnitus keeps on getting worse. It will eventually be so loud that I won't be able to cope," or "When I have tinnitus, it seems that the world is full of tinnitus."

Not all thoughts about tinnitus are negative. Examples of some positive, constructive thoughts include; "I think of the noise as being in the room," or "The tinnitus is part of me. It is ME—it is a part of me, and that is OK," or "I am going to conquer this." Thus, the A-B-C-Model, described above, can be applied to tinnitus. Here are some examples:

A = The Situation or Event	B = Thoughts – Beliefs	C = Emotional Consequence
Having Tinnitus	Why me? Why do I have to suffer ?	Frustration and despair
Having Tinnitus	This is not fair— it will drive me crazy!	Irritation Depression
Having Tinnitus	The noise is a nuisance, but there are so many good things in life I enjoy!	Optimism Acceptance
Being invited to a social function	I'll have to make up some excuse. I can never hear what's being said. I'll just end up making a fool of myself!	Frustration Tension
Being invited to a social function	Oh, good, when I'm out socially there are always too many distractions to be bothered by my tinnitus.	Excited Hopeful
Being invited to a social function	I know being in a noisy place makes my tinnitus a bit louder, but it will settle.	Reassured Positive

In the above tinnitus-specific examples, the situation remains identical, but depending on what the person is thinking to themselves, a differing emotional consequence is produced. What are some of the effects of negative styles of thinking? Given the strong association between thoughts and emotions, it is crucial for people to learn to think in a rational and coping-oriented manner. Let's consider the following set of negative thoughts in response to tinnitus:

Why me? Why do I have to suffer this noise?

Oh no ! I just can't cope with this noise!

The noise ruins everything for me!

This is not fair, the noise will drive me around the bend!

Before I developed tinnitus everything was fine but now things are terrible!

A person who consistently engages in such distressing thinking will most likely not be dealing very effectively with their tinnitus. They will just talk themselves into a more negative and distressed state! Negative thinking can have a powerful effect on your mood, emotions, and feelings; such thinking can make you feel a variety of negative emotional states including feeling low, depressed, anxious, upset, helpless, hopeless, frustrated, irritable, uptight, angry. Negative thinking can lead a person to being absorbed by the problem of having tinnitus. The more you think about the tinnitus, and the more you focus your attention on it, the more negative you may become. A vicious cycle begins: a person thinks negatively in reaction to their tinnitus; they focus on the tinnitus; they experience negative effects of their mood and emotions; they think more negatively; they focus more attention on their tinnitus; they feel more negative; and so on. Many people with tinnitus report that when their tinnitus is particularly bothersome, they find they are more aware of it, and they have difficulty directing their attention to anything else. Research on people with chronic pain indicates that focusing attention on pain heightens the pain and associated distress. This is also likely to be true with tinnitus.

Negative thinking can lead a person to avoid, or cancel, social and work commitments or other activities that might usually provide them a sense of fulfillment, achievement, and pleasure. This results in restrictions and disruptions to daily routine and lifestyle. It also allows for little opportunity to be distracted from the tinnitus.

How can a person overcome the negative consequences of tinnitus and improve their ability to cope?

COGNITIVE RESTRUCTURING

The aim of *cognitive restructuring* is to help people identify the content of their thoughts and to learn ways to challenge or control those thoughts that are either inaccurate or unhelpful. Thoughts only become controllable or open to analysis when we focus attention on them for a sufficient period to establish their content. We often are unaware of their content unless we stop and attend to ourselves. Often we are well aware of the response, such as feeling depressed or angry, without necessarily being aware of the content itself. As mentioned previously, one thought often triggers another, leading to a repetition of the same sequences on different occasions like a "tape recorder in the head." Cognitive restructuring involves learning how to press the *pause* button so that there is time to examine the accuracy of the thought and to effectively challenge unwanted thoughts. Of course, one does have a choice here: to either continue to dwell on the presumably unwanted thoughts or to take the opportunity to try to control these thoughts. It is not always easy, but it is certainly worth trying.

Psychological therapy for tinnitus is based upon the principles outlined above. The general principles of this approach are used in psychological treatments for various problems, and have been outlined by Beck, Meichenbaum, and others. The application of these ideas to tinnitus has been the result of work by the various groups of clinicians.

We begin the tinnitus treatment by going through examples such as those mentioned above. That is, we try to demonstrate the general principle that thoughts about specific events can influence emotions. It is often easier to grasp the principle involved by dealing with a stressor other than the tinnitus itself. So, we ask people to identify ordinary daily stressors, such as being delayed by a traffic jam, losing something that belongs to a friend, forgetting an appointment, or being criticized. Using a few examples of stressful situations (A), we identify the emotional response, such as guilt, depression, or irritability (C), and we ask people to identify the likely thought at *B* for each situation. We then try to find alternative ways of thinking about each event or situation.

Likewise, returning to tinnitus, we can let the tinnitus sound be the *A*, and we can identify the emotional responses as *C*. Then, we can begin to identify the thoughts (B) that may precede these emotional responses. As with the nontinnitus examples, we then try to find alternative ways of thinking about each tinnitus related situation. One aim of this technique is to learn to use more positive *B* thoughts when the patient notices the tinnitus, so that there may be a less negative emotional reaction to the tinnitus. The alternative, constructive thoughts ought to be brief, easily remembered, believable, realistic, and personally relevant. Thus, it is not simply a question of "positive thinking."

Based on the above ideas, we ask tinnitus patients to maintain and complete diaries each day between sessions, so that they can practice the techniques and learn more about the content of their thinking. We suggest that people record any events that may have led to an emotional reaction, such as depression, anxiety, anger, or irritability. We also ask them to do the same type of recording for situations related to their tinnitus. Examples of each of these thought listing diaries are presented at the end of this chapter. People gradually move from listing thoughts in their diaries to using this method spontaneously during everyday activities. Each session begins with a review of the previous week during which the therapist and other group members help to solve any problems that may arise in their use of the procedure. Incidentally, we also look for positive situations and good moods as well. The same principles apply to positive ones as well as negative ones. That is, happy moods may be the result of positive or constructive thoughts about daily events.

A patient's ability to cope with, or to tolerate tinnitus, in an adaptive fashion can be achieved by several methods. First, it is important to learn to adapt to the tinnitus; to take an active position in response to the tinnitus and to cultivate the attitude that you will not give in to the problem. This will allow for a greater sense of control and optimism, and will not allow the tinnitus to dictate or disrupt usual activities. Second, it is important to learn to reduce the emotional effects of having tinnitus by thinking in a rational, realistic, and constructive manner. It is also crucial to reduce the impact of tinnitus on lifestyle by taking an active role and seeking out activities for distraction and enjoyment purposes. Finally, you need to learn to be aware of stressful circumstances when your vulnerability to stress in general will be increased.

ATTENTION DIVERSION TECHNIQUES

Apart from cognitive restructuring, there are several other methods that some people find helpful in dealing with tinnitus. One such approach is referred to as attention diversion. The main aim of this approach is to introduce patients to the idea that the ability to divert attention from one stimulus (tinnitus) to another stimulus can be brought under self-control. The process of attention has several qualities that are significant for understanding its use in the management of tinnitus. A person is usually only capable of focusing totally on only one thing at a time. Various internal and external stimuli compete for our attention all of the time. Examples of internal stimuli include our thoughts, bodily sensations, pain, and tinnitus. External stimuli may include outside noises, light, temperature, or objects. We do have some control over the extent to which we allow our minds to stay focused on each stimulus. We can redirect our attention from one source of stimuli to another. This latter point is important since it is difficult, if not impossible, to stop paying attention to unpleasant sensations unless one refocuses their attention on to other things. Attention diversion refers to the ability to divert attention from one stimulus to another by self-control.

Part of the problem associated with tinnitus is the extent to which it grabs the attention of the person, but if you can control this attention, the tinnitus might be less distressing on some occasions. Through attention diversion exercises, a person can develop skill in refocusing their attention from their tinnitus on to other internal or external stimuli. Sensations can be brought into the foreground of your awareness or allowed to remain in the background. It is important to recognize that the idea is not so much to stop thinking about the tinnitus but to learn to direct attention both to and from the tinnitus.

As with the cognitive restructuring, the general principle of attention diversion can be illustrated before we move on to a tinnitus example. The main point to consider is that people can generally focus totally on only one thing at a time. Below are some attention diversion exercises for you to try. In the first exercise, we ask people to close their eyes and try the following procedure:

Exercise 1

Begin by focusing on your breathing, breathing in and out for a few minutes. Notice the different aspects of your breathing, for example, the *in* phase, the *out* phase, and the split second when the process reverses each time. Just try to pay attention to the point where the breathing changes direction, like the ebb and flow of water at the edge of the beach. Notice whether your *in* phase is longer or shorter than the *out* phase. While focusing on your breathing, you probably haven't been noticing the sensations that you can be aware of in your feet—just shift attention to your feet. Become aware of the sensations in your feet, first one foot, then the other. Try to identify each toe only by the sensations arising from them. Notice that while you pay attention to your feet, your breathing recedes into the background. Now open your eyes.

During a discussion after this exercise, we point out to patients that when they are paying attention to some other part of the body, other parts of the body can subside into the background. In other words, sensations can either be brought into the foreground or allowed to remain in the background.

We may then move through a number of examples until we reach a point where the tinnitus can be addressed more directly:

Exercise 2

Begin by focussing on your breathing, breathing in and out for a few minutes. Notice the *in* phase, the *out* phase, and the split second when the process reverses each time. Just try to pay attention to the point where the breathing changes direction, a bit like the ebb and flow of water at the edge of the beach. While focusing on your breathing, you probably haven't been noticing the sensations that you can be aware of in your feet—just shift attention to your feet. Become aware of the sensations in your feet, first one foot, then the other. Try to identify each toe only by the sensations arising from them. Notice that while you pay attention to your feet, your breathing recedes into the background. Pay attention to your awareness. Think of awareness as if it is a torch that you can use to highlight whatever sensation you wish. Allow your awareness to go back and forth from inside to out. Now inside . . . now outside. Continue to do that for a few moments. Notice that other objects and sensations fade in and out. Now listen for noises inside your head. Now notice the feelings in your feet. See how awareness can shift from one thing to another. Notice whatever thoughts and images come into your mind. See how these thoughts interfere with sensations and external sounds. Now pay attention to the noises again. Shift attention from internal to external again. Notice the air temperature, the sensations on the the palms of your hands. Notice that you can only focus on one thing at a time. Move freely back and forth between the noises and external stimulation.

We suggest that tinnitus patients spend about ten minutes each day practicing the technique, directing attention to and from the tinnitus. Once again, we emphasize that the idea is not so much to stop thinking about the tinnitus but instead to learn to direct attention *both to and from the tinnitus*. This idea is important because the concept of control over attention is what we wish to illustrate and achieve.

IMAGERY TRAINING

The main aim of this approach is to introduce tinnitus patients to the idea of imagery techniques that involve developing the ability to focus attention on sensory experiences in the mind. The mind may be directed to conjure up novel images or to recall places and events from past experience. In either case, the image can be strengthened by using all (or most) sensory capabilities, not just the visual mode. That is, when you use imagery it helps not only to visualize the scene but also to focus on what you can hear (e.g., birds, people speaking, waves crashing, wind, crackling fire, music); what you can smell (e.g., salt air, burning embers on a log fire, flowers, fish and chips, perfume); what you can feel and touch (e.g., warmth of sun, cool wind or breeze, cool water); and what you can taste (eg. refreshing drink, warm drink, delicious meal). The main use of such techniques is to provide a means of attention diversion that can be used in many different situations, such as when trying to fall asleep, while waiting for a bus, having a dental procedure, or thinking about your tinnitus.

An example of this type of exercise follows:

Exercise 3

Imagine that you are at the beach. It is early morning. Try to visualize the sand, the beach, and the sea. There is a wide sweep of fine, white, cool sand; there is a pale sky and the sun is just beginning to rise. Visualize the sea—notice how the waves form—they roll quietly in, curl over, and then break. Each wave washes up the sand. Notice the curves of soft creamy foam wash up the sand, and then recede. Keep the waves forming, rolling quietly in, curling, breaking, and washing up the beach in curves of soft creamy foam. They form, roll, curl and break, and wash up the beach. Notice the fresh, salty smells of the sea and the sand—the warmth from the golden glow of the sun as it begins to rise further. Now, let the images fade away . . . fade away completely.

After this scene, we ask patients a number of questions:

What did you like about it?

What did you dislike?

Could you imagine all the senses - sight, touch, smell, and hearing?

Could you see color?

Could you imagine movement?

Could you imagine closing your eyes?

From what vantage point did you initially imagine the scene; from above as a spectator, or as if you were lying on the ground, looking up?

It is important for patients to notice that when they are paying attention to a scene in imagination, other sensations will subside into the background. As mentioned earlier, part of the problem caused by tinnitus is the extent to which it grabs the attention of the patient, but if the patient can control this attention focus, the tinnitus might be less distressing on some occasions. This technique may be particularly useful for dealing with sleep difficulties.

We suggest a range of scenes that patients can imagine, such as sitting in front of a log fire. For the fire scene, we suggest that patients include images of warmth in different parts of the body, sounds of the crackling of the wood, views of the embers, and the smells of the wood burning. (Some people even imagine that they can smell the aroma of the glass of port that they are holding!)

The previous exercises have mostly involved practice in the general procedure. In the exercise that follows, tinnitus will be addressed more directly. One way in which tinnitus can be incorporated is to build a scene around the type of sound that is experienced by each patient. For example, a roaring sound may be rather like the sound of the sea, a waterfall, a fountain, or a stream. Other sounds may be like insects in the trees in summer, perhaps not especially enjoyable, but nevertheless a natural and familiar sound of summer. We ask each patient to describe their tinnitus sound and then to try to relate it to a natural, preferably pleasant, sound. In the subsequent exercise, we ask patients to imagine a situation in which the tinnitus sound is related to a sound in the environment. As with the other scenes, we suggest that patients add other sensory experiences to the scene, such as smell, sight, body sensations, and so on, so that it becomes more vivid and realistic.

We have had many interesting examples of sound matchings such as steak sizzling on a barbecue or cicadas in the trees. If the noise of your tinnitus sounds like an electric fan, imagine that is what it is. Imagine you are sitting in a comfortable chair, it is a warm summer day, the fan is on and is blowing a cool breeze on you. Study the shape of the fan. Notice how cool and pleasant you feel. Imagine that you reach out and pick up a cool refreshing drink, taste the drink, and sit back comfortably and enjoy the cool flow of air fanning your body! If the noise of your tinnitus sounds like a particular insect then imagine that is what it is. Imagine it is a perfect summer evening, you can see the sun low in the sky. It is warm but not too hot, and you can hear the insects, but what else can you hear? Imagine you can hear birds singing. You can see the leaves on the tree moving gently in the breeze, you can hear them gently rustling in the wind. What else can you see? What sensations can you feel on your skin?

We sometimes suggest that patients imagine some sound other than the sound of their tinnitus but that would be pleasant and could mask their own tinnitus sound. Indeed, this would be the preferred method if someone has a tinnitus to which no match can be readily made. Waterfalls or fountains are generally good examples of masking sounds, but some people prefer to imagine a particular piece of music and even to recall a location in which they may have heard the music. We suggest to tinnitus patients that they spend about ten minutes each day on the exercise above, possibly using the technique while trying to fall asleep.

The attention diversion and imagery training methods that we have described previously are adapted from techniques first described by Donald Meichenbaum, Dennis Turk, and Donald Bakal, who developed these approaches in the management of chronic pain and headaches. In fact, tinnitus has a great deal in common with chronic pain: it is not visible, it is generally persistent, it is perceived as unpleasant, and it may disrupt the person's lifestyle in comparable ways. Thus, it is not surprising that similar self-management techniques may be useful for pain *and* tinnitus.

RELAXATION TRAINING

Relaxation training may be included in the tinnitus treatment program, either in the early part of the therapy or after several sessions of the cognitive therapy. Many people with tinnitus report that there is a relationship between their tinnitus and stress. Some people comment that their tinnitus makes them nervous and tense; alternatively, others comment that their tinnitus becomes worse during periods of physical or emotional stress, or fatigue. It is possible that the presence of external stress may lead the person to view the tinnitus in a more negative manner, simply because stress makes everything seem worse (including the tinnitus). Relaxation methods may be helpful on these occasions. The technique that we have been using is referred to as Progressive Muscular Relaxation (PMR), which is a procedure that was originally developed by a physiologist named Edmund Jacobson in the 1930s and it has been modified in more recent years. PMR consists of learning to sequentially tense and then relax various groups of muscles throughout the body. The muscle groups include left and right hands, arms and biceps, jaw, forehead, neck, chest, shoulders, back and stomach, upper legs, lower legs and feet.

Learning relaxation is a skill. As with learning any skill (e.g., swimming, golfing, driving a car) relaxation requires regular practice in order to achieve maximum skill and benefit. In addition to regular home practice, learning to apply relaxation techniques in daily situations is crucial. Research suggests that substantial improvement will occur only if it is viewed as an active coping skill to be practiced and applied to daily life. Successful practice and training may result in increased control of one's reactions to stress and tension. Thus, relaxation involves the active participation of individuals in modifying their responses to stressful events. During relaxation there is a lowering of tension level and a slowing down of bodily processes; these physical effects are frequently accompanied by a change in direction of thought processes—there may be a feeling of calmness and a less critical or demanding attitude.

The goal of relaxation is to be deeply relaxed while remaining wide awake. A commonly reported problem concerns concentration difficulties. Clearly it is not possible to concentrate on relaxing for a long period of time. If there are intruding thoughts, it is important to refocus on relaxation as soon as you are aware your focus of attention has drifted. Of course, some people report that the tinnitus itself is more noticeable when they relax. However, the attention diversion techniques that we have already described can be used to try to deal with this problem.

An important aspect of relaxation involves learning to become more aware of particular tension areas; that is, those muscle groups in which you are prone to experiencing tension. Common areas include the neck and shoulders, the stomach, the jaw, and the forehead. We suggest that people do a spot check of their tension areas and deliberately relax them as soon as they notice any increase in tension. We also recommend that patients gradually move from relaxing in quiet, comfortable places to increasingly more difficult locations. For example, from a prone position one may move to relaxation practice on an upright chair in the living room, while typing in a study, eating in a cafeteria, standing in bedroom, waiting in a ticket line or for a train, and walking outside. Relaxation training is best undertaken with the assistance of a therapist who can adapt the approach to each patient's needs and who can advise on ways to maximize the effectiveness of the method. Although video tapes are available and may be helpful for some people, many people need the additional assistance that comes from professional training in this area.

SOME GENERAL COMMENTS

Successful coping with tinnitus may involve the use of several different techniques. We have described four methods: cognitive restructuring, attention diversion, imagery training, and relaxation training. The different methods may be helpful at different times and for coping with different types of situations. The important point is that, by experimenting with these methods, you may be able to identify the techniques that work best for you. Feelings of depression, anxiety or anger about tinnitus can be used as signals that you need to use one of these coping methods. You can use these feelings or the accompanying thoughts as a signal that you should engage in some specific activity. Time is needed to practice the techniques, so that they will become easier and more automatic. Progress is not necessarily continuously upwards, and there may be periods that are more or less difficult along the way. We encourage tinnitus patients to experiment with these ideas and to continue to employ the methods that produce the best results for them. Flexibility is needed in using each of these techniques at different times. For example, the attention diversion or imagery techniques might be very useful in assisting with sleep problems, relaxation training may be useful when daily life stressors are causing irritability or tension, and the cognitive restructuring may be most effective in dealing with anger, low mood, or depressive feelings.

We have been evaluating the effectiveness of these methods with tinnitus sufferers over a number of years. Although the precise methods have varied to some extent in each study, we can see that about 50 percent of people respond very well to at least one of these approaches. Relaxation training, or biofeedback, when used as the sole method of treatment, appears to be less beneficial than the cognitive methods. The overall success rate increases when several techniques are used together, presumably because the person has greater flexibility about the choice of techniques for different types of situations. We observe marked differences between people in their response to each individual component of the treatment. Therefore, we see it is important for tinnitus patients to try a number of different approaches. In our current programs, we include all the components described above in order to obtain the maximum benefits for each person. Unfortunately, some people seem to have difficulty continuing to use the techniques when therapy has ended, and it is important to realize that consistent and regular use of the techniques will be needed in order to maintain the early benefits. Most of this work has been conducted in small groups, but we now need to know if the effects are different when the same approaches are applied

Tinnitus Thought Recording Form

During the coming week, I would like you to keep a record of the thoughts that you notice having when the tinnitus is particularly loud or annoying. The first column is for recording the time/situation in which you noticed it. The second column is for recording any immediate or automatic thoughts that you noticed. The third column is for recording your attempt to challenge or change any negative thinking.

Time/Situation	Automatic Thought	Challenging Thought

General Thought Recording Form

During the coming week, I would like you to keep a record of the thoughts that you notice having when you are under stress or when something negative or unpleasant happens. The first column is for recording the time/situation in which you noticed it. The second column is for recording any immediate or automatic thoughts that you noticed. The third column is for recording your attempt to challenge or change any negative thinking.

Time/Situation	Automatic Thought	Challenging Thought

in individual sessions. It is quite likely that some people benefit more from the intensive contact with a therapist than they will from a group program. For many people, however, the group program is reported to be a very positive experience because it brings people together who have similar difficulties. In the groups, participants often find that they can share ideas and experiences in a constructive manner. For many people, it is also the first time that they have been exposed to methods that may help them to live with the tinnitus. This step often turns despair into hope and anguish into acceptance. Many patients report that, by using psychological techniques, they gain a sense of control over their reactions to the tinnitus. This sense of control may be the important factor in any successful efforts to reduce the distress caused by tinnitus. In this chapter, we have described several different methods by which this sense of control may be achieved. Like the patients themselves, we need to continue experimenting with these ideas in order to identify the most useful approaches for each person.

PATIENT'S QUESTIONS AND ANSWERS

1. *Question:*   You have mentioned a number of methods to change the way I think about my tinnitus. All seem to require the ability to focus attention at will. That is one of my problems. Because of the tinnitus, I seem unable to focus my attention on anything but my tinnitus.

   Answer: It is understandable that trying to get your attention away from your tinnitus is difficult to do. This is something that people often find is a problem at first. However, many people with tinnitus find it easier with more practice. The important thing is to keep working on this idea for long enough to be able to give it a reasonable try. The main thing is not to give up.

2. *Question:*   In your instruction for imagery training you indicate that we should direct our attention not only away from our tinnitus but also toward it. I should think it would be best to always direct our attention away from tinnitus.

   Answer: No, the purpose here is to establish control, and in order to have complete control, you must be able to direct your attention both to and from the tinnitus. Remember, it is much better for you to have control over your tinnitus rather than your tinnitus having control over you.

3. *Question:*   You have stated that the psychological approach to tinnitus is about 50 percent successful. Does that mean that it only works with certain kinds of tinnitus? For example, does it work for noise induced tinnitus but not for head trauma tinnitus?

   Answer: As far as we know now, psychological techniques are not restricted to any specific kind of tinnitus. In fact, one of the virtues of these techniques is that they are likely to be applicable across many different types of tinnitus. The aim of these techniques is not to cure tinnitus but to help people learn to cope with tinnitus itself. The kind of coping strategy used will probably depend very little on any knowledge about the cause of tinnitus. Perhaps when we know more, we may be better able to differentiate the kinds of techniques that work best for particular types of tinnitus.

14

Cognitive Therapy and Tinnitus: An Intensive Weekend Workshop Experience

DONNA S. WAYNER, Ph.D.
Director, Hearing Rehabilitation Center
Albany Medical Center Hospital
Albany, New York

Cognitive and behavioral interventions have been successfully used in the treatment of a variety of noxious conditions. When applied to the treatment of tinnitus, cognitive therapy deals with the psychological reaction to the experience of tinnitus. For many, it offers relief. Over the past ten years, cognitive and behavioral interventions have been successfully applied to the treatment of tinnitus. This approach is not intended to replace other treatments but rather to provide a supplementary method of assisting those who experience tinnitus with one more coping strategy.

The cognitive approach attempts to modify individuals' attitudes about the tinnitus by assisting them to adjust their reaction to it. It cannot and does not alleviate the experience of the tinnitus but has been useful in improving how persons perceive the tinnitus and in doing this provides relief. This rethinking process is facilitated by a systematic strategy. A change is effected by assisting the individual to directly reappraise situations that they have perceived as unmanageable, intolerably tension producing, and beyond their control.

Called by some "the thinking person's therapy," the cognitive approach provides a framework upon which to assist the individual to help themselves to realistically evaluate their experience of tinnitus. In the long run, it is important for the person with tinnitus to realize that this is not a cure, but a way by which they can better deal with their tinnitus on a daily basis. It is a means to change the way people think about their experience of tinnitus to help facilitate their improved tolerance of the problem.

From the psychological standpoint, it is not of particular importance how the tinnitus noises come about. It is important, however, to know how the individual interprets the cause of the tinnitus. Once the person has had a medical evaluation to rule out any malignant causes of the phenomenon of tinnitus, it is helpful for the "coping health" of the individual that support be available. This support can be facilitated with cognitive techniques.

Education through cognitive therapy enables people to modify their thoughts and behaviors and approach tinnitus in a positive rather than negative way. In such a learning environment, the participants can begin to take responsibility for their own education about tinnitus plus learn methods of coping with it more effectively. Having the opportunity to take action is, in and of itself, of value in the coping process. In such an atmosphere, the focus is directed toward the attitude about tinnitus rather than the tinnitus itself.

Basic to cognitive therapy is the idea that situations don't change one's moods but rather it is one's perception of them that does. In other words, the way one *thinks* has a profound effect on their physical and emotional health. Cognitive therapy guides participants to look realistically at their problem and replace negative thoughts, almost always containing gross distortions of reality, with positive ones. Cognitive intervention invites the participants to separate their thoughts into three distinct aspects: (1) what the situation is, (2) what they're feeling about it, and (3) what their thoughts are about it, that is, what they're saying to themselves. Then, it examines the available evidence or the basis for such thoughts. By putting the participants on the witness stand, so to speak, and confronting them with facts about tinnitus, the fallacy of negativity can be demonstrated and replaced with more positive attitudes.

It has been reported by Dr. Richard Hallam in his book *Living With Tinnitus* that over time there is a gradual transition from distress to tolerance and then to acceptance of tinnitus for most people; this process typically taking between three to eighteen months. It is important to note that the normal response to tinnitus is one of gradual tolerance and that after a period of distress, it is possible to come to terms with the noises and live with them. This is not to say that the tinnitus does not still inflict its presence on the individual but rather that it has become tolerable. This level of acceptance and tolerance of the tinnitus often comes only after effort and frustration, however, it does result in a *cure,* not in the medical sense, but in the psychological sense.

Dr. Hallam points out that some people reach this state of acceptance with much greater ease than others and proposes that it is the person who no longer pays attention to the noises who accomplishes such a psychological cure. His premise is that the noises become a frustration and problem when a person pays attention to them; and that based on the psychological process of attention, the person who experiences tinnitus can develop the ability to ignore the noises, making them emotionally neutral.

The method he proposes is the basis for the intensive cognitive therapy weekend workshops for people with tinnitus conducted in England and in the United States. While in England in 1987, I learned about the intensive weekend workshops for persons with tinnitus coordinated by Dr. Richard Hallam. Because of the clinical challenge often presented by patients with severe tinnitus when seen in my practice at the Hearing Rehabilitation Center at Albany Medical Center Hospital, I was intrigued to learn more about the intensive therapeutic approach used. We met and discussed the possibility of holding such a program in the United States, and with the support of the American Tinnitus Association, ran an intensive weekend workshop for persons with tinnitus April 6 to 8, 1990 in Albany, New York.

All group presentations and discussions that took place during the weekend were tape recorded and later transcribed. Specific dialogue that highlights the cognitive approach will be presented here as an example of the cognitive therapeutic method. Selections from the written transcript of the audio cassette recordings of this presentation about attention as related to accepting tinnitus follow. *F* stands for Facilitator (Drs. Richard Hallam, Robert Johnson, and Donna Wayner), *P* represents any one of the participants and in dialogue, *AP* stands for another participant.

Reactions were discussed regarding the concept that tinnitus would not be a problem if you did not pay attention to it. The concept that learning not to pay attention is a normal, involuntary, biological process and reaction was also discussed in the following dialogue.

F: *These are two very simple ideas: tinnitus would not be a problem if we did not pay attention to it and learning not to pay attention is a normal, involuntary, biological process. In other words, our brains can do it for us. We don't have to learn how to do it, because we do it all the time. For example, the sound of the overhead projector is going on, and if I don't think about it, my brain will switch off from it. That is really what we're aiming for in this psychological approach. We're not aiming to cure the tinnitus, i.e., to get rid of it, but to reach a point where you're not paying attention to it. If you can do it some of the time, why not more of the time? I'm suggesting to you that there is room to progress along the road toward not paying attention. Let me get your reactions to those basic ideas. What do you feel about that?*

P: *I think your example about the machine is an interesting one because I really had not heard the noise of that machine. But I have a computer near my desk that has a similar noise, and every once in a while I shut it off. Then you don't mind it, but when you hear nothing but that all day like the problem of tinnitus, it's different. In my case, it (the tinnitus) never goes away. I can substitute other things to try to forget about it, but I know that it doesn't go away. I can't, as with a machine, shut it off and that to me is the crux of the problem.*

F: *Right. The tinnitus doesn't go away, but you're saying there are times when you're not aware of it, though.*

P: *Absolutely.*

F: *So you accept that and if you accept that, would you also accept that the amount of time that you're not aware of it could be increased?*

P: *Yes.*

F: *That's what I'm claiming. I'm not saying that 100 percent of the time you won't be aware of your noises, but we're hoping to increase the time when you're not aware of it. I think it was interesting that a number of you said last night during our interviews that you became more aware of your noises when you started thinking about this weekend and coming here. That's a very common phenomenon which relates to the next set of ideas.*

The presentation continued with a consideration of the question: Why do we pay attention to noises; not just to tinnitus but to any noise? Dr. Hallam reviewed the four reasons: (1) intensity, (2) novelty, (3) unexpectedness, and (4) interest. See Table 14–1 for further detail.

These ideas were discussed by the group at length and the concept that our ability to attend can be distributed to many activities or concentrated into a few was described. An example was given to indicate that in some circumstances one's obsession with the experience of tinnitus could occupy the whole of one's attention. The importance of increasing the amount of time when interest is not given to tinnitus was discussed. After several examples were reviewed regarding how and why we discriminate sounds, Figure 14–1 was discussed.

TABLE 14–1 **Why Do We Pay Attention to Noises?**

REASONS INCLUDE:
Intensity
Loud sounds are more difficult to ignore than soft.
Novelty
Changing or different sounds are more noticeable.
Unexpectedness
Sudden sounds demand attention.
Interest
Attention is given to something we are interested in either positively or negatively.

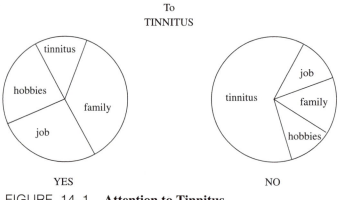

To
TINNITUS

YES   NO

FIGURE 14–1   **Attention to Tinnitus**

The following was said:

P: *Yes, the brain is constantly discriminating for all of our senses, and if we fill up the brain with enough things, it won't have any room to think about the tinnitus. Right?*

F: *That's one strategy, but the other is the brain will leave alone sounds that are boring, repetitive, and meaningless. If we can then neutralize the negative interest and meaning attributed to tinnitus, the brain will pay less attention to it. You can't do it by deciding not to pay attention. The brain has to allow this to happen spontaneously.*

P: *Isn't that what you really need to be able to do, keep tinnitus in the background?*

F: *Yes, That's right.*

P: *Otherwise, when the distraction is over, your brain will snap right back onto the tinnitus.*

F: *That's right. Of course you can tire yourself out with distractions. You busy yourself with so many activities that you get exhausted. So distraction alone is helpful up to a point.*

P: *You really need to combine those two ideas; first, giving tinnitus less meaning and then ignoring it by putting it on automatic.*

F: *It might seem too obvious to say that you pay attention to those events that are meaningful to you, but you have only an idea that something is important without knowing what it means or whether you'll be able to deal with it. You'll pay close attention to puzzling events in an attempt to make sense of them but once you are able to fit a puzzling event into a familiar framework, you're usually able to accept and ignore it. So, to accept tinnitus means making sense of it so you are satisfied that all of your important questions are settled. Then, it will be easier to ignore.*

A list of questions representing the "unfinished business" that needs tending before tinnitus can be ignored was presented for discussion and are listed in Table 14–2.

It was pointed out that these are all reasonable questions to ask about tinnitus, but to keep asking yourself these questions indefinitely is unreasonable, and as long as you keep asking them, the brain will find the tinnitus interesting. A good deal of discussion was generated by these questions and this segment of the workshop was drawn to conclusion with a consensus that at some point, in order to neutralize the meaning of the tinnitus, one must get the questions answered and then put them aside so they are no longer drawing attention to the tinnitus.

Building on the morning's discussion that (1) any belief that gives tinnitus meaning is likely to slow down the natural development of tolerance towards it, (2) we pay attention to sensations that have some significance for us, and (3) we stop paying attention to sensations that are repetitive, meaningless, and boring, the principles of cognitive therapy were introduced. It was pointed out that cognitive techniques have two purposes.

1. to help the participants to come to regard tinnitus noises as unworthy of attention since they are predictably familiar and without meaning
2. to help the participants become less distressed by tinnitus even when they do hear it

It was explained that since thoughts are caused by feelings and since the thinking process may be automatic and habitual, it is useful to investigate the thoughts that underlay the feelings of distress, identify these acute thoughts, dispute them, and replace them with positive, more constructive thoughts. Inconsistencies between what a person thinks and feels and how they act were examined. A series of questions to assist in this examination process, called challenges, are shown in Table 14–3.

TABLE 14–2 **Further Questions Participants Asked**

What exactly has caused this?

Why isn't there a cure?

Why did I get this? Why me?

Why can't I cope better?

When will it go away?

What if it gets worse?

How can I expect my family to put up with me?

What if I have a brain tumor?

What will happen in the future?

Will it ever get better?

TABLE 14–3   **Examples of Challenges to Irrational Thoughts**

1. What evidence do I have to support my thoughts?
2. How would someone else view my thoughts?
3. What is the effect of thinking the way I do?
4. Am I thinking in all-or-nothing terms?
5. Am I blaming myself for something which is not my fault?
6. Am I overestimating the chances of disaster?
7. Am I using a crystal ball to read the future?
8. Am I expecting myself to be perfect?

Examples were reviewed as the group considered various situations and the possible thoughts and feelings that could be associated with them. To facilitate this process, the use of a three-column listing was suggested, labeled with the abbreviations A, B, and C; with A being the Activating event or Antecedent, B standing for Beliefs; C referring to the Consequences, or one's feelings and actions. In this process, the automatic negative thoughts were disputed using the questions or challenges listed in Table 14–3. To avoid the feeling of a cross-examination, role playing was done once a participant described his or her feelings. A specific example provided by one of the participants as he viewed his tinnitus is shown in Table 14–4 and the associated interactive dialogue follows.

F: (to participant) *You brought up this morning that what bothered you about your tinnitus was what might happen. Is that right?*

P: *Yes.*

F: *Let's look at your concern from the point of view of A, B, C on the chart. What sort of feelings do those thoughts give you, or rather what is the feeling that you have predominantly about the tinnitus?*

TABLE 14–4   **Tinnitus Will Never Go Away**

A ANTECEDENT	B BELIEF	C CONSEQUENCE
At night alone	No escape	Panic
Worry the tinnitus	Can't get away	Anxiety
Will become too loud	Nothing I can do about it	Helplessness
	This will drive me mad	
	I might kill myself	
	If I take valium, I might	
	become addicted	

P: *In the context of it never going away, you mean?*

F: *Well, let's take that, yes.*

P: *All right. It's a feeling that might come most often, say during the night, when I'm alone with my thoughts, and there are very few distractions. If the tinnitus is at a high level of disturbance, I suddenly become aware of the fact that I can't escape from it, I can't get away from it. I'm using a claustrophobic analogy. It isn't as if I can walk out of a closed space and the claustrophobic feeling will stop. There's no way that I could ever get away from this, and that it's been there for so many years and from everything I seem to hear, it may not go away. So, there's absolutely nothing I can do to . . . (pause). It's a helplessness coupled with a certain anxiety of wanting, almost "a flee in panic" kind of feeling for a moment. Then, realizing that there's no place to flee to, that panic is all I can feel, all I'm left with.*

F: *So, some of those things you described are obviously feelings, panicky, like you feel helpless. And other things, there's no escape, I can't get away, there's nothing I can do . . . These are obviously thoughts, aren't they?*

P: *Right.*

F: *So, during this situation, at night and being alone, your tinnitus is probably higher than normal. Right? Now, I'm going to play naive here because that's the way we can understand these sort of thoughts. One way of doing this is to say, well, supposing there is no escape from the tinnitus. Just suppose that. What would be so bad about that?*

P: *Well, the level of distraction, I don't want to use annoyance because it's too mild a term in this context because it's a very hyper annoyance, will get, how can I say it? (pause) If I were up during the day, I could do something to try to distract myself, but during the night, I don't want to do that because I'm somehow trying to find some way to just quiet down and let this feeling pass, either by distracting myself or by taking valium.*

F: *Right. So distraction with cassettes and maybe taking a valium. Right?*

P: *Right.*

F: *Now I've written these feelings in this column (See Column C in Table 14–4). These are the consequences. So, these are things you do rather than things that you think. I mean, you think about how you might cope with it, but that doesn't quite answer the question here. You said something about your annoyance increasing. Is that right?*

P: *Yes, the level of annoyance is very hyper and that (pause) let me go back to the "not being able to flee" concept and that there is no way that I could ever end this, and, therefore, I am in a state of semipanic. I'm trying to equate it more to an emotional level now rather than to the thought process because the emotional level is one that I want to get away from. I want to get out of this feeling that "I can't." I'm stuck with it. I'm stuck with it forever and I don't know how to get away.*

F: *Right. I think people often are stuck with their feelings and it's very difficult to get beyond them. An important point of this sort of therapy is to try to see if we can get beyond the feelings and to what might be feeding that panic. Because, my hunch is that it may be possible to analyze this a bit further down the line. You said, there's no escape, you can't get away, there's nothing you can do. Now what I'm asking you is, what would be so bad about not getting away, not escaping?*

P: *That the constancy of the shrieking noise will drive me mad, and while I really am not a suicidal kind of person, the only way I can ever really escape it is to die. I don't know any other.*

F: *So, they are definitely thoughts* (while writing on board under Column B). *Maybe what is feeding that panic are some other thoughts, in the back of your mind. By saying this tinnitus is annoying me to such an extent that sometimes it might drive me mad and at that point, the only thing I might do is want to kill myself.*

P: *Yes, or even down to, well maybe if I take a valium, it will quiet things down, but then of course that brings up the concern, I don't want to become addicted, I don't want to become hooked on a narcotic or whatever. And, so I'm very, very selective about the times that I want to use them. I only use them at times when I just feel that it's particularly acute.*

F: *That's a normal thought* (writing in Column B). *You feel you might become addicted to tranquilizers, or something else if you have to resort to some other drug. So, now you see how the process works. It has worked out very well here.*
   I noticed your hesitancy to bring out these thoughts, which is natural, I mean, they are not the sort of thoughts that we like to have, you know, or even admit to. So, it's not surprising that not only do we not like to admit them here in this sort of group, but also you don't like to admit them to yourself. When you're alone at night you just want to shut those thoughts out, really, because they're much more terrifying when you're feeling panicky. I mean, you're not feeling panicky right at this moment, but in the middle of the night, those thoughts can be very terrifying.
   What we hope to do with these techniques is to find ways of seeing if these kinds of beliefs are reasonable; whether they're true; whether they make sense or not, whether it's likely that you will be driven mad; whether it's likely that you would kill yourself; whether it's likely you'll ever become addicted, right?

P: *Yes.*

F: *So, we're looking at the probability of these things happening, and whether they're likely to happen at all, and how bad they would be if they did happen. Now, of course, when I say how bad they would be, (pause) well, you might say it would be really bad if I was driven mad. But, the thing is that your idea of what being driven mad is, may not conform to reality. You may have a particular idea about madness which is not true, possibly. So, that's another way we can look at how rational these ideas are.*
   Now, the way we work on these sorts of beliefs is in very down to earth, common sense, straightforward style. It's the way we reason about everything in our lives. We

ask ourselves questions like, What evidence do I have to support my thoughts? In other words, What evidence do I have that this tinnitus will, in fact, drive me mad? Do I have the evidence from my past experience for that belief? Then, another helpful way of thinking about these beliefs is to say, How would someone else in the same situation view this? Would everybody in this room view this in the same way? And if not, why not? Just try to get a different perspective on it, you know?

Another thing we can do is to ask ourselves, What's the effect of thinking the way I do? Is it useful to think this kind of way about this particular situation? What am I getting out of it? Another thing that we can ask ourselves is are we actually thinking logically about it? Am I thinking in all or nothing terms? Now, that means, in black and white terms. Let's say you get distressed about tinnitus. People do get distressed, obviously. Now, does distress mean madness? In other words, are you thinking in black and white terms about this? People do get distressed, but that doesn't necessarily mean that distress equals madness. So this is something that may be useful to ask; Am I blaming myself for something which is not my fault? This is not particularly applicable to this situation, but it might be to other ones. Again, Am I overestimating the chances of disaster? You talked about the probability of this happening, you know. Am I accurately assessing the possibility?

Another thing you can ask yourself is, Am I using a crystal ball to read the future? Is this just pure guesswork on my part? What evidence do I really have? Am I just trying to foresee the future? On what basis?

Again, this is not particularly relevant here, but Am I expecting myself to be perfect? In other words, are the sort of standards that you are applying to yourself in a situation normal or everyday standards or are you expecting far more of yourself than anyone else would expect?

So, what we do is ask these sorts of questions in relation to beliefs creating a two-way dialogue. I have found the best way to do this is to role-play. Someone will play the part of you, having these beliefs and you could use these means of disputing them or we could have another participant (AP) and myself role-play this. We'll leave the overhead up so that we can refer to those thoughts and challenges.

Now, AP, do you want to do that? Shall I play the role of P, and do you want to use some of these challenges, or do you want to play the role of P?

AP: *Let me be P.*

F: *Right, you can be P. O.K., (to AP) you told me that sometimes you wake up in the middle of the night and the tinnitus seems to be really loud, is that right?*

AP as P: *It's true. It was terrible last night. I couldn't sleep at all.*

F: *How do you feel then?*

AP as P: *I was very, very distressed. I was very worried. I felt very panicked actually, as the night went on because I knew I wasn't going to be able to sleep and then I just got frightened inside of me.*

F: *Now, as you know, we are going to try to analyze the kinds of thoughts you're hav-*

ing when you're feeling panicky like that. What is it that comes to mind when you feel like that at night?

AP as P: *First, I get really worried that because I can't sleep, I won't be able to function when I get up in the morning or when the next day comes. So, I feel that threatens my ability to really make a living. That scares me, and it also frightens me that this is just going to get worse and worse and worse.*

F: *OK. What do you think would happen if it got worse? What sort of thoughts go through your mind when you think about that?*

AP as P: *I just don't think that I could stand it. I just don't think that I'd have the ability to do that* (pause) *to take it any more.*

F: *Let's work on that thought, that belief that you couldn't stand it any more. If you'd like, we'll look to see if that is a reasonable thought to have. Whether it makes sense. Whether you have any evidence for it. And, I'm going to use some of those challenges up here on the screen, and I'm going to ask you some questions about them. Now, what you're worried about is that it'll get too much for you. Is that right? What do you mean by too much? What exactly do you mean?*

AP as P: *That I just couldn't, I just wouldn't want to stand it any more, and I just would want to end my life.*

F: *Right, now let's ask some very naive questions about this. Have you in the past felt like that? Has it ever happened to you that the tinnitus has got too much where you've actually been tempted to take your life?*

AP as P: *Not really. I think I've felt that I might, but I've never felt that strong about it.*

F: *So, you never actually got to the point where you felt strongly that you might take your life.*

AP as P: *No, I think I'm worried that I might get to that point, but I have not.*

F: *OK. And when you have been in those difficult moments, what is it that has led you to feel that way? Was it just that the tinnitus was getting louder or was it other things as well?*

AP as P: *I think it was just that I was afraid. I think it was the fear that made me feel it more.*

F: *Yes. So, in fact, when you felt that way in the past it was times when you felt afraid that it's going to get worse. But, in fact, the tinnitus wasn't that much worse than it had been before, is that right?.*

AP as P: *I don't think so. It's hard to say, because I think the way I was frightened inside almost took over what I was really experiencing.*

F: *OK., before we go through this, I'm going to ask you to give me some probability estimates. What is the probability that you think you'd kill yourself?*

AP as P: *Really? Probably not very high.*

F: *OK. Now, in the past, when this happened, how did these thoughts go away, I mean, what happened? You've had this thought before, but the moment passed, presumably?*

AP as P: *I guess sometimes I was lucky, and I could fall asleep and that took it away. And then sometimes, I think I could just find something else that intrigued me and that helped to take it away.*

F: *So, when you've had these thoughts in the past, in some way that moment passed and you've survived them, and the next day presumably things looked a bit brighter, or you're coping better? So, over a number of occasions you've had these thoughts and you dealt with them. So the evidence we have then is that the tinnitus hasn't pushed you to this point?*

AP as P: *That's true.*

F: *So, on what basis do you predict that it could push you to this point?*

AP as P: *I don't think there is a basis.*

F: *Do you have any reason for thinking that if it got loud again in the future at night that you wouldn't be able to cope with it?*

AP as P: *I think I could cope, because I have before.*

F: *And you have means, if things get really bad, you do have means. You say you take some valium, or you don't like to take it and so you distract yourself with a cassette, or you use your maskers. Right? So, you do have some means of dealing with it if it gets really bad.*

AP as P: *Mm hmm. Yes.*

F: *Fine.*

P: *You did beautifully! You read my mind! You answered just as I would!* (Laughs of relief from group)

F: *I tried to use these challenges* (on overhead, Figure 5) *for the situation. I don't know how you felt when I was bringing up these challenges. Did you feel that it makes sense to you?*

AP: *Yes, I felt I went through a process, actually. I found it very interesting because initially I felt very uncomfortable and then as I addressed the circumstances and looked at myself, I came to a conclusion, which was a refreshing conclusion, and I liked that.*

F: *Now, if P was in that seat, he probably would have given me a tougher time, you know.*

P: *Well, I think she answered very accurately from the point of view of expressing my feelings and what I, as you would ask the questions, I thought of how I would answer them, and she answered very, very similarly to what I think I would have.*

Much discussion followed regarding the process observed by the group, and the participant whose issues were challenged continued with the following discussion.

P: *I can rationalize what you're saying, but that's not what I feel when I feel panicked. Logic doesn't always override the panic feeling. When you know that you're kidding yourself or you know that you're using a game to override the panic feeling and that's what you ultimately have to do because it's the only way and we always work our way out of it somehow. So that I agree with the conclusion, but I'm trying to deal with the panic. I'm trying to get to something perhaps that goes a step before where you're at that panic point and try to address that.*

AP: *What you're saying is, the panic destroys the logical thought process.*

P: *Yes, it overrides logic. Because, except for real things like a fire or something like that, most panic situations are not real fears, they are illogical fears, but they are very gripping and that's what I really need help with.*

F: *What I'm saying is that your panic is fed by those thoughts. So if you can be convinced that it is extremely unlikely that the tinnitus will get to a point that you feel you can't cope with it, you're less likely to get into a panic. So therefore, you don't have to have a panic attack which you rationalize out of because you don't get into the panic state in the first place if you're convinced of the invalidity of those assumptions you are making. You can convince yourself and then have the confidence that is true.*

The use of relaxation therapy was introduced using visualization and imagery techniques. Each participant was encouraged to choose an image to help them externalize their experience of tinnitus during the relaxation activity. By choosing an image, it was explained that it distanced a person from the noise, thereby making it more acceptable. Some examples of suggested images included (1) swimming away from it, (2) leaving the tinnitus on top of a mountain, or (3) selecting a positive image to replace the tinnitus such as the wind whooshing through the autumn leaves.

Dr. Hallam then led the group in a relaxation activity that proved to be refreshing to all of the participants, helping to create an even stronger bond in the group. Discussions regarding the experiences of the guided visualization and coping strategies for tinnitus continued late into the evening.

Participants were encouraged to practice applying the cognitive therapy approach to other life situations. Work related situations were of particular interest to members of the group. The group shared another guided visualization exercise so each could be relaxed for their journey home.

The experience of this directed group, applying cognitive therapy as yet another coping mechanism for people who experience tinnitus proved beneficial to all the participants. Their experiences were monitored with periodic questionnaires over a one year period following the workshop. A detailed description of the workshop and results obtained are available in a manual prepared by this author and a review of the methods used can be found in Chapters 5 and 6 in Hallam's book.

PATIENT'S QUESTIONS AND ANSWERS

1. *Question:* What is a brief description of cognitive therapy as it applies to tinnitus?
   Answer: The way you think about tinnitus can make a difference with how much it bothers you. It can affect how irritated, depressed, or worried you get about the noise. If you are upset by the tinnitus, you will notice it more. Cognitive therapy enables you to modify your behaviors in a positive way by helping to bring about a change in the way you think about tinnitus. By doing this, it can give you a more philosophical, accepting attitude that can help reduce your concerned mood. It can also help you to pay less attention to the noises so that you can better ignore them.

2. *Question:* Is it necessary to attend a group session to learn about cognitive therapy for people with tinnitus?
   Answer: The group experience can help bring about an exchange of information about tinnitus from which every participant can benefit, however, it is not the only way to learn the techniques of cognitive therapy. The book written by Richard Hallam, Ph.D. entitled, *Living With Tinnitus,* has information that can be a very helpful guide. In addition, consult your audiologist for a recommendation of a therapist or self-help group in your area.

3. *Question:* Is relaxation training something to consider to help with my tinnitus?
   Answer: Reducing stress and anxiety helps people to cope more effectively with tinnitus. Various relaxation techniques have been used, such as listening to favorite soothing music, use of taped relaxation and imagery exercises, breathing exercises, yoga, massage, heating pads, hot showers, and meditation. Any of these techniques may help an individual to relax, reducing tension and the effects of stress, that left unrelieved, can exacerbate tinnitus.

4. *Question:* I have heard that hypnosis might help me to cope with my tinnitus; is that so?
   Answer: Some individuals have found hypnosis to be helpful in reducing the effects of tinnitus. One form of hypnosis, self-hypnosis or autosuggestion, can also be useful. In this technique, the person who experiences tinnitus in effect hypnotizes him or herself and utilizes specific suggestions aimed at reducing the experience of tinnitus.

5. *Question:* Why does tinnitus become worse at night?
   Answer: Many who experience tinnitus feel that their tinnitus becomes worse at night. This may be due, in part, to the fact that at night our surroundings tend to be quieter, with less interfering noise. This may cause the tinnitus to sound accentuated. In addition, fatigue and stress have been shown to contribute to tinnitus. At the end of the day, we may have had to deal with stressors and tend to be more tired, which may contribute to the worsening of the tinnitus experience.

6. *Question:*   Is it common for pain to be associated with tinnitus?

   Answer: Some people who experience tinnitus, may suffer some pain as a result of tension in the muscles of the neck that, in turn, may cause tension headaches. It is important to seek medical advice about this so that other possible causes of the pain may be excluded and for advice about pain killers.

7. *Question:*   Will my tinnitus get worse? If it does, will it ever get better?

   Answer: Mild tinnitus has been shown to get worse in only about 5 percent of the cases. The level of tinnitus may fluctuate in relation to such things as stress, fatigue, diet, medication, or physical condition. Often an increase in the level of tinnitus may be offset by the use of techniques to reduce the tinnitus discussed above.

15

Biofeedback Training for Tinnitus Control

KAZUTOMO KITAJIMA, M.D., TAKAYO YAMANA, KAORU UCHIDA, and MASAAKI KITAHARA
Department of Otolaryngology
Shiga University of Medical Science
Seta, Otsu 520-21, Japan

STRESS MANAGEMENT IN TINNITUS CONTROL

Tinnitus is well known as a stress-related disorder. Once the patient notices tinnitus, the annoyance and life interference it causes create stress. The stress in turn boosts the degree of tinnitus by centering the patients' attention on the tinnitus. Thus a vicious circle is formed between tinnitus and stress. Stress control is, therefore, an essential element in the management of tinnitus regardless of its etiology.

BIOFEEDBACK TRAINING

In practice, however, obtaining objective and reliable information regarding the degree of stress is difficult. One method for obtaining this information is the EMG (electromyogram) biofeedback technique. Increases in stress raise anxiety levels and cause an actual contraction of the muscles. Conversely, when the muscles are in a state of complete relaxation, stress and stress-related complaints are alleviated. In EMG biofeedback equipment, myoelectric signals from the muscles are translated into easily understandable acoustic and visual signals. Patients are able to use these to judge their own degree of muscle relaxation and guide themselves in the proper direction, that is, for reducing stress.

Figures 15–1 and 15–2 show our biofeedback machine, which uses an EMG signal as a guide to relaxation. Three electrodes are placed on the forehead to record the activities of the frontal muscles. The subjects sit in a comfortable chair in a sound treated room. Feedback signals are both visual and acoustic. Visual signals are provided by green and red horizontal bars: the red bar extends to the right with increments in the EMG levels, and the green bar extends to the left with decrements in the degree of muscle tension. There is a yellow zone between the two bars. This zone is adjustable to the desired EMG level and shifted downward as the patient becomes increasingly proficient in the training. By observing this yellow zone and the two bars, the subject is able to see whether he or she is on the tension side (red) or on the relaxation side (green). Auditory signals are given by tone pips, which sound higher with rising EMG levels.

The following instructions and information are given to the patients.

1. There is no electric current flowing into your body through the electrode on your forehead. There is no pain or shock. The only role of these electrodes is to pick up EMG signals.

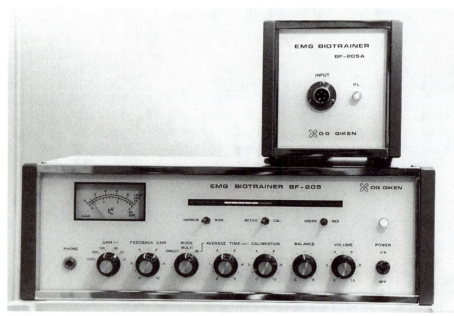

FIGURE 15–1   **EMG Biofeedback Trainer**

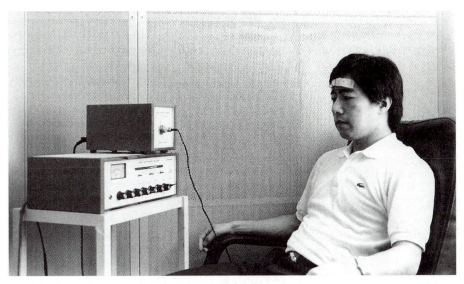

FIGURE 15–2   **Surface Electrodes Are Placed on the Forehead**

2. Wrinkle your brow strongly. You notice the red bar is extending to the right side, indicating that your muscle tension is becoming higher, and the tone pips sound higher. Then relax your brow. The red bar shrinks and the green bar is extended to the left side, indicating that you are in a quite relaxed condition, and the tone pips sound lower.

3. Breath calmly for five minutes. Do not breath deeply. After five minutes of calm respiration, the instructor records the EMG levels shown on the levelmeter. This level is used as baseline data. Then, the yellow zone is adjusted to the desired level of EMG in order that the green bar is extended and approximately one-third of the training period. This adjustment tells the patients that they are in a little bit of a tense condition, and the green bar encourages them, the tense condition is correctable. (If only the red bar is extended during the whole period of training, the patients would be disappointed with this training method.)

4. Try to shrink the red bar and extend the green bar. You don't need to think how to relax but just follow the color and length of the bars. You might feel heaviness, warmth of the extremities, or a sinking feeling of the whole body when the green bar is extended.

5. You may fall asleep. Falling asleep means that you are relaxed. However, it should be emphasized that the aim of biofeedback is to achieve this level of relaxation without falling asleep. Practice, when you are physically tired or immediately after a meal, should be avoided.

6. Practice for twenty minutes, twice a week, for at least four to eight weeks.

7. The last EMG level of your daily session can be read from the levelmeter. This will be the starting level of the next practice.

8. You might notice that the loudness of tinnitus is not reduced even after several trials. Don't be discouraged. The benefit of biofeedback training is not to reduce the loudness immediately but to achieve the ability to cope with the annoyance and life interference caused by tinnitus. These benefits may be obtained gradually.

9. We would advise practicing the relaxation exercises that you have experienced with the machine at home during your free time.

EFFECTIVENESS OF BIOFEEDBACK TRAINING

The effectiveness in 55 subjects are described in the present report. Most have had medical treatment in outpatient clinics without much benefit. The study consisted of more males than females (32 males and 23 females). The mean age was 59 years (ranging from 32 to 82 years).

We used Vernon's five level tinnitus grading scale shown in (Table 15–1) to describe the magnitude of loudness, annoyance, and interference with life activities (re-

TABLE 15–1 **The Tinnitus Grading Scale (Vernon, 1987)**

A. Loudness
1. Absent
2. Barely noticeable
3. Moderate
4. Very intense
5. Uncomfortably intense

B. Annoyance
1. Tinnitus is present if attended to but is not very irritating and can be ignored.
2. Tinnitus is often irritating but can be ignored much of the time.
3. Tinnitus is difficult to ignore even with effort.
4. Tinnitus is always present at an irritating level—often causing considerable distress.
5. Tinnitus is more than irritating, causes an overwhelming problem much or all of the time.

C. Interference with life activities
1. Tinnitus causes little or no interference with work or social activities.
2. Tinnitus causes some interference but can be lived with.
3. Due to the tinnitus, considerable effort is required to maintain normal work or social activities.
4. Tinnitus causes serious interference with normal living activities—only simple tasks are possible.
5. Tinnitus renders the patient unable to perform any work or social activities.

ferred to as "life interference" in the present study). The patients were then grouped into five tinnitus-type categories following Kodama's classification (see Table 15–2). Table 15–3 shows the results of classification. The percentage of Ann-Life type was 62 percent and much larger than that observed in Kodama's study (11%), which includes whole degrees of tinnitus treated in our clinic (346 patients). The patients in this study all failed to respond to such standard treatments as medication and maskers. As noticed from this comparison, the more difficult the case, the larger the percentage of subjects suffer from annoyance and life interference. The management of stress that would be caused by this annoyance and interference is important in tinnitus control.

The overall effectiveness of training is shown in Table 15–4. The effectiveness was evaluated in each of Vernon's categories. Training was judged effective when the scale was reduced by two or more in each category and was judged unchanged when the scale change was less than two. Subjects with one or two scales were excluded from the evaluations because their inclusion incorrectly lowered the apparent effectiveness. Biofeedback training reduced tinnitus annoyance in 65 percent of the patients, reduced life interference in 50 percent of the patients, and reduced loudness of tinnitus in 39 percent of the patients. These data indicate that biofeedback training is more beneficial in relieving the complications than in actual reduction of tinnitus loudness. In other words, biofeedback training is beneficial in helping patients cope or live with tinnitus. Table 15–5 shows the effects of age and gender on the results, indicating that these two factors did not affect the results. No patient showed an increase in scale (two or more) after training.

Before the training, each patient was given the Manifest Anxiety Scale (MAS) test, the SDS (Self-rating Depression Scale) test, and CMI (Cornell Medical Index)

TABLE 15–2 **Tinnitus-Type (Kodama, 1994)**

A. Average type (Avg-type)
B. High annoyance and life interference type (Ann-Life-type)
C. Annoyance predominant type (Ann-type)
D. Life interference predominant type (Life-type)
E. Low annoyance and life interference type (Mild-type)

Avg-type has scales of annoyance and life interference close to the *general group's average* for the particular degree of tinnitus loudness reported by the patient.

Ann-Life-type has higher-than-average annoyance scales and average or lower-than-average life interference scales.

Life-type has higher-than-average life interference scales and average or lower-than-average annoyance scales.

Mild-type has both annoyance and life interference scales lower than average.

TABLE 15–3   **Tinnitus-Type in the Present Study**

The digits show the number of patients as percentage of the total number (55). The digits on the bottom line show the percentage observed in 346 tinnitus subjects from our clinic who received medical treatment and maskers (Kodama, 1994).

	Avg-type	Ann-Life-type	Ann-type	Life-type	Mild-type
Present	3 (5%)	34 (62%)	16 (29%)	2 (4%)	0
Kodama	159 (46%)	39 (11%)	87 (25%)	26 (8%)	35 (10%)

TABLE 15–4   **Effectiveness of Biofeedback Training on Tinnitus**

Overall effectiveness of the biofeedback training is shown with percentages. The number of patients (*n*) in each category was different since those with scales 1 and 2 were excluded from the tables.

	Loudness	Annoyance	Life interference
	n = 38	*n = 46*	*n = 30*
Effective	15 (39%)	30 (65%)	15 (50%)
Unchanged	23 (61%)	16 (35%)	15 (50%)

test to determine the psychological states of the subjects. The psychological significance of these tests are listed in Table 15–6. Table 15–7 shows whether these psychological states have any influence on the effectiveness. The numbers of subjects who completed these psychological tests are different; 44 for MAS test, 55 for SDS test, and 54 for CMI test. The magnitude of MAS and of SDS influence the effectiveness of the training in any category, suggesting that effectiveness can be expected

TABLE 15–5   **The Effects of Age and Gender**

	Loudness *n = 38*		Annoyance *n = 46*		Interference *n = 30*	
age	*Effective*	*Unchanged*	*Effective*	*Unchanged*	*Effective*	*Unchanged*
greater than 60 years old	11	10	16	7	9	7
less than 60	4	13	14	9	6	8
gender						
Male	9	12	19	9	7	10
Female	6	11	11	7	8	5

TABLE 15–6   **The Significance of Psychological Tests**

MAS	greater than 23	Anxiety state
	less than 22	Normal
SDS	greater than 48	Neurotic or depressive state
	less than 47	Normal
CMI	Type I	Normal
	Type II	Autonomic imbalance
	Type III	Neurotic state
	Type IV	Psychosomatic disease

TABLE 15–7   **Effectiveness of Biofeedback Training in Relation to Psychological Tests**

The number of patients (*n*) in each category was different since those with scales 1 and 2 were excluded from the tables.

	Loudness *n* = 29		**Annoyance** *n* = 39		**Interference** *n* = 24	
MAS (n = 44)	*Effective*	*Unchanged*	*Effective*	*Unchanged*	*Effective*	*Unchanged*
greater than 23	5 (26%)	14	13 (57%)	10	8 (53%)	7
less than 22	6 (60%)	4	12 (75%)	4	3 (33%)	6

	Loudness *n* = 38		**Annoyance** *n* = 46		**Interference** *n* = 30	
SDS (n = 55)	*Effective*	*Unchanged*	*Effective*	*Unchanged*	*Effective*	*Unchanged*
greater than 48	5 (42%)	7	12 (63%)	7	7 (50%)	7
less than 47	10 (38%)	16	18 (67%)	9	8 (50%)	8

	Loudness *n* = 37		**Annoyance** *n* = 45		**Interference** *n* = 29	
CMI (n = 54)	*Effective*	*Unchanged*	*Effective*	*Unchanged*	*Effective*	*Unchanged*
Type I	3 (60%)	2	6 (86%)	1	0 (0%)	2
Type II	6 (38%)	10	12 (67%)	6	5 (42%)	7
Type III	2 (22%)	7	4 (36%)	7	4 (50%)	4
Type IV	3 (43%)	4	7 (78%)	2	5 (71%)	2

TABLE 15–8   **Effectiveness in Relation to EMG Levels**

Decrease of EMG Level	Loudness n = 38		Annoyance n = 46		Interference n = 30	
	Effective	*Unchanged*	*Effective*	*Unchanged*	*Effective*	*Unchanged*
greater than 0.6 microV	10 (38%)	16	18 (58%)	13	8 (44%)	10
less than 0.6 microV	5 (42%)	7	12 (80%)	3	7 (58%)	5

regardless of anxiety level, or neurosis or depression. There was no noticeable relationship between three categories and CMI types.

These results show that the psychological states have no effects on the results of biofeedback training. It should be stressed, however, that patients who do not understand the rationale of biofeedback training are not good candidates since these patients show a negative attitude toward the training. Thus, the subjects with psychopathological diseases are also not good candidates for this type of training.

We recorded the EMG levels before and after daily practice. The magnitude of decrease in EMG levels, however, showed no correlation with effectiveness as shown in Table 15–8. The patients should be informed of this observation if they are apt to give up the training because of their unchanged EMG levels.

Although not evaluated in this study, the types of ear lesions and time since onset of tinnitus had no influence on the effectiveness of training.

Biofeedback training has been applied to those patients who failed to respond to such standard treatments as medication and maskers. However, the demonstrated effectiveness of biofeedback in patients with various backgrounds makes it a good candidate as a standard treatment for tinnitus. It would not obstruct other forms of treatment, and its use might hasten the discontinuation of medication.

PATIENT'S QUESTIONS AND ANSWERS

1. *Question:*   You make it clear that stress and tension can increase the level of tinnitus but does it ever cause tinnitus?

   Answer: We never want to say never, but it is highly unlikely that stress or tension can actually be the cause of tinnitus. We know of several patients who make this claim, but we are inclined to believe that those patients simply had tinnitus occur and that occurrence happened to appear at a period of remarkable stress. The Tinnitus Data Registry at the Oregon Hearing Research Center indicates that 47 percent of their patients with severe tinnitus have the tinnitus for no discernible reason. If tinnitus can occur in the absence of the usual causes, then it is easily possible that one such occurrence could happen during any of a number of unrelated events that are then taken to be the cause.

2. *Question:* Is it correct to assume that all forms of stress are accompanied by actual muscle tension?

Answer: Yes, increases in stress raise the anxiety level that, in turn, produces contractions of muscles. Not infrequently, the muscles involved are those found in the head region.

3. *Question:* If muscle relaxation reduces the experienced stress, would not chemical muscle relaxants help tinnitus?

Answer: We are experimenting with muscle relaxants and preliminary results suggest that muscle relaxants do have a positive effect upon tinnitus. Our guess is the same as yours. Namely, that relaxing the muscles will reduce the tension and that reduction, in turn, will reduce the intensity level of the tinnitus. I hope you detect in all this that there is a great deal we do not know about tinnitus and that we have much to learn. The encouraging thing is that there are now professionals who are willing to investigate this perplexing problem.

4. *Question:* If relaxation helps tinnitus, one would then assume that in the morning, upon awakening, tinnitus should be at a low level? That is when my tinnitus is worse and then it gradually subsides a bit during the day.

Answer: Just because you are unconscious during sleep does not necessarily mean that all your muscles are relaxed. It is hard, however, to explain why your tinnitus should be worse immediately after sleep. If you take a short nap during the day, is the tinnitus worse upon awakening?

5. *Question:* It is not clear to me how hearing loss relates to the use of biofeedback for relief of tinnitus.

Answer: Hearing loss can be, and often is, very stressful in and of itself. It would simply be one more reason why biofeedback relaxation could be of benefit.

6. *Question:* Would tinnitus due to middle ear infection benefit from biofeedback training?

Answer: Remember, tinnitus of any cause can be stressful, and it is because of this imposed stress that biofeedback training would be of help.

7. *Question:* Once biofeedback training has reduced stress, is that reduction permanent?

Answer: No. The training effects can wear off and relaxation training must be reinstated. However, once established, additional biofeedback training is much more readily accomplished.

16

Psychological Treatments for Tinnitus

LAURENCE MCKENNA, M.D.
Consultant Clinical Psychologist
Royal National Throat, Nose and Ear Hospital
London, United Kingdom

WHAT HAS PSYCHOLOGY TO DO WITH TINNITUS?

Many people will find the idea of psychological treatment for tinnitus to be unlikely and possibly even offensive. I have frequently heard the tinnitus patient say, "I have come to the hospital about my ears; why have I been asked to see a psychologist?" The patient may go on to ask, "Does the doctor think I am mad or imagining my tinnitus?" The tinnitus patient is *not* thought to be mad or imagining the noises. Patients with tinnitus are asked to see a psychologist because it is recognized that tinnitus does cause many people a great deal of emotional distress and psychologists specialize in relieving such distress. The extent of psychological distress experienced by some people who suffer from tinnitus can be considerable. Several researchers have found a relationship between serious mood disturbance and tinnitus suffering.

There is a particular link between tinnitus suffering and depression and anxiety. It is generally accepted that emotional problems develop after the onset of tinnitus. It is, however, also the case that many people first notice their tinnitus during periods of high stress. Jonathan Hazell, a leading clinician and researcher in the tinnitus field, believes that it is possible that the stress is very important in the development of the tinnitus. He questions whether other people with similar dysfunction of the ear do not develop tinnitus because they have not suffered with stress to the same extent. There is no clear answer to this question, yet.

It seems to me that some people, patients, doctors, and others assume that tinnitus patients are somehow constitutionally very neurotic and that is why they have such a bad time. This idea is not only unhelpful but it is also *wrong*. The evidence available, however, does suggest that if you have suffered with depression in the past then there may be more of a struggle when you develop tinnitus. Clinical findings do indicate that the severity of tinnitus changes in synchrony with life stresses. However, the intermittent nature of most stresses may obscure this relationship.

Psychologists along with their medical colleagues believe that tinnitus is *real* and comes about because of a change in the state of a person's ears. A person's psychology is also intimately involved in the process. Psychology becomes involved from the beginning. Many people are reasonably content until they are told or realize that the noise is tinnitus. The first visit to the family doctor often brings with it the clearest demonstration of the importance of psychology. The patient is often very anxious and in need of reassurance. The doctor is quite likely to say that what the patient has is called tinnitus, that there is no "cure" and that the patient "must learn to live with it." Invariably, the doctor means well but the patient can be left with the impression that he or she must now go away and learn to live with feeling as bad as he or she does at that moment. The result can be that the patient feels much worse. At this point, the noise has not changed much but the psychological factors have. The reality of the situation is that it is very unlikely that the patient will have to go on feeling so bad forever. The outlook for the tinnitus patient is generally good.

Although an enormous number of people have tinnitus (as many as one in six people in the UK), it is a smaller number who *suffer* with tinnitus (one percent of people in the UK). Many who do suffer with tinnitus are skeptical about this point. They believe that it is not possible to have tinnitus and to not suffer. Even when they meet someone who has tinnitus and who is not suffering, they suppose that the nonsufferer must have quieter, or otherwise easier, tinnitus. The idea that the louder the tinnitus the more difficult it is to be tolerated certainly makes sense. The picture is, however, more complex than it might first seem. It is the case that people with quiet tinnitus can be very distressed; remarkable though it may seem, many people with loud tinnitus enjoy normal lives. Most people who are distressed by their tinnitus go on to become much less so. Such people may have good and bad periods with their noises, but the change in the distress generally happens without much fundamental change in the noise itself. The improvement comes about for other reasons

THE HABITUATION MODEL OF TINNITUS

Richard Hallam, a leading psychologist in the field, suggested that there is a natural history to tinnitus that is characterized by changes in the extent to which a person pays attention to the noise. At any one moment there are a great many things that you might be aware of and attend to; you could attend to information coming from any of the five senses or from movements of your body. Normally, a person attends to only one thing at a time. It is not possible to attend to all the information entering your system at once. Some information receives attention and the rest is filtered out or ignored. The information that gets attended to is usually that which is either surprising to you or in some other way important to you. Information that is very repetitive or meaningless, for example, the ticking of a clock, the hum of a refrigerator or traffic noise, will be filtered out of your attention and will not be reacted to. In addition, people perform many activities automatically, without much conscious attention or effort, for example, when riding a bicycle or driving a car you very often pedal, steer, or change gear, without having to think much about it. While learning to ride a bicycle or to drive, these activities take up an enormous amount of your attention, but once you are an experienced cyclist or driver, and the road is clear, they can happen while your attention lies elsewhere, for example, thinking about what you will do when you get to your destination. Information that is being processed automatically will receive your full attention if and when it becomes important to you.

Habituation is the process by which repetitive and unimportant information is no longer reacted to. The key to understanding this process lies in the first part of the word, "habit." Richard Hallam suggests that normally people habituate to tinnitus, that is, in time the person stops attending to the tinnitus and, therefore, stops reacting to it. The tinnitus becomes just another part of the person's life. Although the noise may remain physically present, it becomes less distressing. It becomes part of the background and has little importance. For the vast majority of people with tinnitus, this happens naturally and with little or no effort on their part.

Habituation to tinnitus follows the same rules as habituation to any other stimulus. A number of factors are likely to slow the process down. If there is a change in the tinnitus or if it becomes very unpredictable, then a person will go on reacting to it for longer. If the person is suffering from a high level of arousal, that is, is very *tense,* then he or she is likely to be more reactive to tinnitus. It may well be that the person feels tense because of the stress associated with the tinnitus, but tension may also result from other stresses. Many people become aware of their tinnitus for the first time during periods of high stress. Alternatively, an existing tinnitus may become worse at such times. If an emotional significance or meaning is attached to the tinnitus, then, again, it will go on provoking a reaction. Remember, you will tend to filter out noises that are repetitive and of no significance to you, for example, the noise from the air conditioning system. What distinguishes tinnitus from the air conditioning noise may not be its frequency or volume or other physical properties but its meaning. Tinnitus may be viewed as the thing that is interfering with or spoiling the things you want to do; the air conditioning noise is usually emotionally neutral. It follows from this that habituation to tinnitus will be facilitated by a reduction in a person's level of arousal by a change in the emotional significance or meaning of the tinnitus and possibly by a reduction in other stresses. Psychological treatment for tinnitus, therefore, tends to focus on lowering a person's level of arousal or tension through relaxation therapy and related techniques and on changing the person's attitude toward the tinnitus through the use of cognitive therapy. These approaches to tinnitus management will be discussed below.

PSYCHOLOGICAL TREATMENTS FOR TINNITUS PATIENTS

Relaxation Training

Relaxation training was described in the medical literature over fifty years ago. Jacobson, one of its main proponents, suggested that unpleasant emotional states such as anxiety cannot co-exist with deep relaxation, that is, you cannot be stressed and relaxed at the same time.

The rationale behind relaxation therapy merits some explanation. Some patients initially take the view that since the onset of tinnitus, they cannot relax and there is no point in trying. Relaxation therapy is not simply about putting your feet up or watching your favorite television program. Relaxation exercises seek to break into the cycle of tinnitus-tension-tinnitus. They are designed to reduce the level of arousal in the body; something that is of great importance if habituation is to take place.

Relaxation exercises have an effect upon the nervous system. The nervous system can be divided into two main parts; the voluntary nervous system (VNS) and the autonomic or automatic nervous system (ANS). The VNS is so-called because the things that go on within it do so because the person chooses to make them happen. For example, when a person decides to make a telephone call or make a cup of tea, the VNS is involved. The messages go from the brain to the spinal cord and on to the arms and so on until the actions are completed. These actions happen because the person remembers to make them happen. In contrast to this, many events and processes occur within the body without the person having to remember to make them happen. For example, you do not need to remember to keep your heart going, and you do not need to remember to make it beat faster when you run or to slow down when you rest; these thing happen automatically. A great many processes take place in this way including breathing, digestion, blood pressure control, temperature control, muscle tension, focusing of vision, and some functions of the ear.

There are two parts to the ANS; the sympathetic section and the parasympathetic section. The sympathetic section speeds the body up and uses energy, that is, it increases the level of arousal in the body. It speeds the body up in order to make it ready to deal with any threat or danger that is perceived. The threat may be a physical one or it may take the form of an emotional threat or worry. The body naturally seeks to deal with threats of any kind by either fighting the thing that is causing the problem or by running away from it. This way of responding was invaluable when people were living in wilder and more primitive circumstances. There is little else to be done, apart from fighting or running away, if confronted by a tiger in the wild. Today it is equally essential when facing a threat such as that posed by a street mugger; the sympathetic section of the ANS puts the body "in the right gear" to fight or take flight. If the threat is one that demands literally either fighting or fleeing (such as if really confronting a tiger) then the increased level of arousal in the body will not be disturbing. If, however, neither fighting nor running is appropriate then the increased activity in the system can be noticed as unpleasant symptoms.

Neither fighting nor running are particularly helpful if the threat takes the form of a worry. There are also physical events that are perceived as threatening but that are not helped by a fight or flight response; tinnitus certainly falls into this category. Unfortunately, the body very often does react as if tinnitus is a tiger or a mugger. The result can be continued orientation to tinnitus and the presence of other symptoms such as tight muscles, a pounding heart, sweating, and so on, or just a general feeling of *tension.* Although a lot of bodily energy is being used and the person may feel exhausted, high levels of arousal may make it difficult to sleep.

The *parasympathetic* section of the ANS works in the opposite direction from the *sympathetic* section. It slows the body and saves energy. The sympathetic and parasympathetic sections work together through a system of reciprocal inhibition, that is, an increase in activity in one will result in diminished activity in the other. Ordinarily, there is a balance between the activity of the two sections. This balance can be disturbed by the stress of tinnitus. Too much sympathetic ANS activity can be counteracted by increasing activity in the parasympathetic section. This is achieved by selecting a physiological process that is normally under ANS control and deliberately slowing it down. The easiest process to achieve this with is muscle tension. While muscle tension is normally regulated automatically, it can come under the control of the VNS. It is not necessary to consciously think about which muscles to tighten and contract when picking up a pen, but if you want to, you can change the tension in the muscles used to hold it. When one ANS process is slowed, the others may follow suit and the level of arousal in the whole body will be reduced.

All of this can be achieved by muscle relaxation exercises. These involve alternately contracting and relaxing selected muscles. The patient is asked to tighten up his or her muscles very tight and then to relax them completely. These tightening and relaxing exercises can induce states of deep relaxation. By concentrating on the sensations experienced during tightening and then during relaxing, the patient comes to learn the difference between the two states. Subsequently, patients are able to learn to induce the relaxation without tightening their muscles first. Once a patient is aware of the tension levels that he or she is producing in response to tinnitus, it should be possible for the patient to learn to produce a different response to the tinnitus. A person with tinnitus may typically respond to the intrusion of the noise with increased muscle tension and, as a result, a general feeling of being *up tight* or *tense.* Learning relaxation skills can help the person to reduce this tension. In time, the person will become aware of the build up of muscle tension earlier on or at lower levels of tension, and the relaxation can be employed sooner and usually more successfully. The person's response can change from the tinnitus-tension spiral to a more relaxed and controlled one.

It will normally take someone at least several weeks to master relaxation techniques. It may, however, take a number of months. This is not really a long time given the amount of time that people can suffer with tinnitus. It is also the case that some medicines take a number of weeks before they have a therapeutic effect. Learning relaxation skills is like learning any other skill, for example, learning to drive. It takes some time and practice. With a little application most people can succeed at it. Many people are introduced to relaxation therapy at a time of difficulty or crisis. There is a risk that once the crisis is over, the person then neglects the therapy. Unless practiced, the skills can become rusty just as would happen if once you passed your driving test, you did not drive for a long time. Relaxation skills need to be maintained and perhaps to become a way of life.

Biofeedback

Like the relaxation exercises described above, biofeedback seeks to reduce the level of sympathetic ANS activity. Biofeedback is about using physiological measurement instruments to assist the patient in obtaining voluntary control over ANS functions, such as heart rate, muscle tension, or the electrical resistance of the skin.

Information about the physiological process is feedback by the instrument giving a signal (usually audible or visual). For example, if heart rate is being monitored, then the instrument (an electrocardiogram) will emit an audible bleep the rate of which will change as the heart rate changes. It is thought that if a person can see or hear information that reflects a normally automatic physiological process, then the person may come to be able to control that process. People are often instructed to concentrate on changing the signal or information coming from the measuring device.

Biofeedback techniques have been used with considerable success in the treatment of many other symptoms, such as headaches and high blood pressure. It is not possible to monitor tinnitus levels in the same way as many other bodily activities, and, therefore, feedback cannot be provided about it. It is, therefore, necessary to measure and feed back information about the other physiological processes that are normally associated with emotional reactions. Typically, information will be provided about muscle tension or about galvanic skin resistance (GSR), that is, the level of electrical conductivity of the skin that increases at times of emotional distress.

Biofeedback offers the patient greater awareness of internal states and so may provide a method of exerting greater control over those states. There is, however, no clear evidence that biofeedback is generally more successful in the management of tinnitus than more straightforward relaxation techniques. It is likely to be particularly helpful to those patients who find it difficult to master traditional relaxation techniques; it may give such patients that extra help that they need. It is usual for patients to require six to eight sessions of biofeedback training before they are able to reduce stress levels. Sessions are normally attended on a weekly basis.

Cognitive Therapy

In the management of tinnitus cognitive therapy attempts to change the person's beliefs or attitude to tinnitus. Cognitive therapy is a widely practiced form of psychotherapy. The therapy aims to extend the discussion beyond *what* is happening to the person physically and on to what the person *thinks* about what is happening. It suggests that what the person thinks about what is happening may be more important than the actual event itself. Many tinnitus patients find this idea challenging and even somewhat threatening. It may sound as if the psychologist is saying that tinnitus is not important; its all in the patient's mind. That is to misrepresent the position. Remember that psychologists agree that tinnitus is real, however, examining what the patient thinks about it can shed great light on why it is a problem for one and not for another.

The point of cognitive therapy may best be illustrated by considering an example outside of the realm of tinnitus. Imagine that you are traveling on a tube (subway) train. It is rush hour and it is very crowded; you have to stand and to "strap hang." Someone pokes you in the back with an umbrella several times. How would you feel? Most people answer by saying that they would feel in some way unhappy about this, perhaps annoyed or angry, perhaps frightened. The next question is Why would you feel like that, or What is going through your mind about the person with the umbrella? The answer is likely to be that you think that person is being careless or possibly aggressive. If this is what you think then it follows logically that you will feel annoyed or frightened. If you now discover that the person with the umbrella is blind, how do you feel? Many people will say that they now feel less annoyed or that they feel some sympathy for the person. If so, why? Do you think something is different about the person? It is likely that you no longer think in terms of the person being careless or aggressive. Instead, you may believe the pokes in the back to be accidental. In summary, the physical event, that is, being poked in the back, remains constant. If that physical event is thought about one way, for example, this person is careless, then you will feel one sort of emotion, that is, annoyance. If thought about in another way, you will feel a different type of emotion. The point is that you will *feel* good or bad depending on what you *think* about an event rather than simply because the event happens. So your emotional well-being is determined by what you think. There is, however, a complication. What you think about the next thing that happens to you will, in part, depend on how you are already feeling. If you have been feeling depressed recently, then you are likely to think about the next event in a depressed sort of way. This will help to keep you feeling depressed. This vicious cycle leads to longer term changes in people's ways of thinking about life and in how they feel. Your thinking is likely to become more negative and unhappy. Many tinnitus patients will know what it is like to be awake in the middle of the night worrying about something. They will also know that whatever the nature of the problem, it seems different and a little more manageable by lunch time the next day. The vicious cycle I have described is very much like getting stuck with "middle of the night" type thinking.

One reason why tinnitus is a problem for some and not for others is because some apply "middle of the night" thinking and others apply "lunch time" thinking.

Commonly people think that tinnitus reflects some sinister illness, such as a brain tumor or impending total deafness. There is also the thought that it will get worse and that this will lead to a breakdown of some kind. A patient may say, "This tinnitus stops me from concentrating on anything; I will never be able to function properly as long as I have it." Alternatively, a patient may hold more subtle beliefs about the consequences of tinnitus, for example, "I can not enjoy life as long as I have tinnitus," or "I am not coping well with my tinnitus; I must be a very weak person." The contention is that the emotional turmoil results from such thoughts and not simply because the tinnitus is present.

It is all too easy to fall into the trap of "middle of the night" negative thinking. Many of our thoughts occur almost automatically, they are not always well formulated, and it is possible to develop a set of negative beliefs about something such as tinnitus without even realizing that you are doing so. Cognitive therapy aims to help the patient realize what his or her thoughts are about the tinnitus and then to see whether those thoughts are a reasonable reflection of the reality of the situation. More often than not, they are a poor reflection of the person's actual circumstances. This is not to deny that things may be difficult for a person, but, remember, a poor emotional state will cause a person to see things as much worse than they really are. Discussions with the therapist will help the patient to obtain a more accurate perspective on the situation. From this can come an improvement in the patient's emotional state.

Hypnosis

Hypnosis is commonly thought of as going into a trance or an altered state of consciousness in which extraordinary things can happen to you. There is, in fact, a long running debate about whether hypnosis does or does not represent a special state of consciousness; many researchers consider it to be no different from, say, being very relaxed. It is certainly the case that relaxation exercises are an integral part of most hypnotherapy. It is true, however, that interesting things can and do happen during hypnosis. When in a hypnotic trance, a person is more receptive to the voice of the hypnotist and ready to cooperate with the suggestions and ideas that the hypnotist puts forward. Hypnosis has been well recognized in the treatment of other physical sensations such as pain and nausea. There is also a long tradition of the use of hypnotherapy in the treatment of emotional distress. There have been a small number of papers in the medical literature reporting on the use of hypnosis in the treatment of tinnitus. More often than not, these are reports of particular cases on which the technique has been successful rather than systematic research studies. Often the hypnotherapy involves suggestions that allow the patient to relax more easily. Some of the studies have also sought to use hypnotic suggestion to change the patient's perception of the physical characteristics of the tinnitus, for example, to hear it as less loud. The aim is to directly reduce the tinnitus. Others have sought to change the emotional connotations of the tinnitus. This can be done by helping the patient to associate the noise with something pleasant, for example, Pooh Bear's happy hums, running water, or of the harmony of the heavenly spheres—images suggesting that all is well with the world. Alternatively, the patient is thought to associate the tinnitus noise with a state of deep relaxation so that when the noise becomes intrusive, it can act as a cue for the patient to relax. There is a sense in which these approaches represent a kind of synthesis between relaxation and cognitive therapy.

Some people may be apprehensive about losing control while being hypnotised. In reality, there is little to fear in this respect and hypnotherapy bears little resemblance to stage hypnosis. Essentially, people allow themselves to be hypnotised. It is a mistake to suppose that hypnosis is something that is done to the patient who can be simply passive and later "wake up" free from all problems. Like all other forms of psychological therapy, hypnosis requires hard work on the patient's part. It is likely that treatment sessions would be offered weekly over a period of six to ten weeks. Care should be taken that the hypnotherapist belongs to a nationally recognized professional organization.

Other Behavioral Techniques

A psychologist may be able to help a patient to become aware of patterns to his or her tinnitus and the distress associated with it. Most people with tinnitus are aware of fluctuations in their tinnitus. Some tinnitus patients will state emphatically that their tinnitus is constant and unchanging. On reflection, however, most of these people will agree that there are times when their tinnitus is worse; by implication there will, therefore, be times when it is better. Often the changes in a person's awareness of tinnitus are associated with doing different things or with different events. Discussions with a psychologist may help the patient realize which events or patterns of activity make it better and which ones make it worse. This insight may be therapeutic in itself, and it may lead to changes in the person's behavior.

Often people are all too aware of the circumstances that they find difficult. Sometimes, however, their attempts to change things can make the situation worse. Sleep disturbance, which is a very common problem associated with tinnitus, provides a useful example of this point. Many people who find it difficult to fall asleep may seek to physically exhaust themselves in the hope of going to sleep. This may help the person fall asleep in the first instance but may also lead to a poorer night's sleep overall. Others read, do crossword puzzles, write business reports, watch television, and follow a host of other activities in pursuit of sleep. Such behavior may help a person to escape from the distress of insomnia, but they are unlikely to promote sleep. Sleep is, to some extent, a habitual behavior and thrives on predictability. Many people in their quest for sleep begin to behave very unpredictably. An analysis of a person's behavior can help to reveal when things are going wrong and what needs to change. Psychologists may have other useful hints for the poor sleeper. For example, most people wake several times a night. Usually they return to sleep quickly and without any problems. This natural course of events is not so easy for many people who suffer with tinnitus. They may be kept awake listening to, and more importantly, thinking about the tinnitus, about the possible consequences of insomnia, or about any other stress in their lives. These thoughts may be addressed using a cognitive therapy approach, however, this may not be the easiest thing to do in the middle of the night. Instead, a person may benefit from learning articulatory suppression or thought stopping techniques that involve the repetition of simple words or phrases. Such techniques help to give a break from *snowballing* intrusive thoughts. With such a break a person can return to sleep.

It is well recognized that tinnitus can become more intrusive and more distressing at times of stress. A psychologist may help a person to examine how he or she is reacting to other stresses and, if necessary, to discuss alternative ways of responding. The cycle of tinnitus-stress-tinnitus-stress, and so on, is very familiar. It is all too easy to get lost in argument about which is the chicken and which the egg. It is, however, often more useful to address the stress reaction, and this is something that most psychologists, even those who are not familiar with tinnitus, are used to treating.

Counseling

The psychological treatments outlined so far have been formal ones that usually have specific goals associated with them. Many people benefit, however, from a less rigid approach. Much can be gained from talking to another person provided that other person knows how to listen. According to Carl Rogers, one of the most esteemed psychotherapists of modern times, listening is the single most important thing that a therapist can do for a patient. To be able to listen in a way that is likely to help a person in distress demands more than the ability to hear what is said. The listener, or counsellor, should have an appropriate professional background. Talking to another can help a person organize his or her thoughts in an otherwise bewildering situation. Talking to someone who is accepting of you and understands what is happening to you can provide much emotional relief. This can help a person with tinnitus to cope.

MEASURING SUCCESS IN THE TREATMENT OF TINNITUS

The problems associated with measuring tinnitus make it difficult to assess the effectiveness of any treatment approach. There are techniques available that allow the loudness of tinnitus to be estimated; the techniques involve matching the tinnitus noise to an external sound. Unfortunately, this is not the same thing as measuring how important the tinnitus is to a person or what impact the tinnitus is having on that person. To achieve this, it is usually necessary to rely on subjective measurement techniques. Patients taking part in psychological treatment approaches (and, indeed, most other approaches) may expect to make judgements about their tinnitus using numerical rating scales, scales using adjectives, or other devices such as the visual analogue scale (place a mark on a line to say how severe things are). Such methods may seem crude and may not inspire confidence in the psychologist or the treatment. In spite of their appearance, such measurement techniques have been the subject of a vast research effort and are widely accepted as appropriate in the assessment of subjective experiences such as tinnitus. Monitoring the progress of psychological treatment may also involve filling out questionnaire measures of emotional state. The questionnaires are usually published ones that have been thoroughly researched and have standards against which to gauge a person's responses. There are also a number of questionnaire measures of tinnitus complaint. Richard Hallam has devised one such questionnaire that allows the different ways in which tinnitus can affect a person, for example, emotional disturbance, insomnia, intrusion into quiet activity, to be assessed separately. This can be very useful for detecting change that is taking place in one aspect of tinnitus complaint but not in other aspects.

All of this recording and form filling can be time consuming. However, it can provide information on changes within the person; this is particularly useful if the changes are modest ones. The use of self-rating techniques has been criticized for focusing the patient's attention on the tinnitus when the aim of treatment is to reduce the attention paid to the tinnitus. On the face of it this seems a sensible criticism, however, it supposes that the patient would otherwise not be attending to the tinnitus very much. This is unlikely to be the case, and an argument could be made that self-report measures may, in fact, structure a patient's attention to tinnitus in a more constructive and useful way.

THE EFFECTIVENESS OF PSYCHOLOGICAL TREATMENTS

Most psychological treatment approaches have a common goal. This is not to cure the tinnitus (i.e., to physically remove it) but to relieve the emotional distress associated with the tinnitus.

The effectiveness of relaxation therapy, biofeedback, cognitive therapy, and to some extent hypnotherapy has been assessed in careful clinical trials. The results of these treatment trials have been mostly, but not universally, positive. While there has been considerable variation in the way that different trials have been conducted and in the exact nature of the treatments used, there appears to be some commonality to the results. It is rare, at least in the formal research trials that have been carried out to date, for patients to report a lessening of the noise by the end of the therapy. In some cases of hypnotherapy a lessening of the noise is reported by some patients during the hypnosis, but this does not appear to be a lasting effect. In spite of this, it is common for patients who have undergone one or another of these psychological therapies to report improvements in the unpleasant emotions associated with their tinnitus. Patients report an increase in their tolerance of tinnitus and a reduction in the annoyance associated with it. Patients regularly report that the beneficial effects of psychological treatment extend beyond tinnitus management and into other aspects of their lives. They often report being more relaxed, less irritable, less depressed and are experienced by other people as easier to live with. In the longer term, many patients who benefit in these ways go on to report that their tinnitus becomes less intrusive and that they are less aware of it.

Not everyone who takes part in a psychological treatment will experience improvements in their situation. No treatment approach will work for everyone, and this seems to be especially the case with tinnitus. Some people find that psychological treatment makes an enormous positive difference to their lives; they are virtually free from problems associated with the tinnitus and better able to deal with life generally. Many others state that they benefit considerably even though they continue to have some degree of difficulty with their noises. A few seem to obtain no benefit. It is surely the case that different people are better suited to different forms of treatment.

It is not always easy to know whether a person will benefit from a psychological approach. It is sometimes the case that a person regards tinnitus as a purely medical problem for which there can be only a medical solution. Superficially, this point of view may seem to have some validity, but a depth of understanding of tinnitus will reveal this to be an inaccurate and unhelpful approach. There may be many reasons why a person will hold on to this point of view including reasons connected with the way he or she has been treated in the past. It is a view that is held by many people who feel angry about some aspect of their medical care. A strongly held belief that tinnitus is a purely medical problem for which there can be only a medical (or surgical) solution may lead a person to reject a psychological approach or make it particularly difficult for that person to benefit from such an approach. Sometimes such people can benefit from meeting others who have had success with psychology or may be helped by seeing videos of such people giving an account of their history with tinnitus. If the person is to make progress in reducing the impact of tinnitus, then the hurdle of this belief in the exclusive nature of the medical approach will need to be overcome.

Some other people may feel overwhelmed by their emotional distress and as a result can find it difficult to engage and work with a psychologist. Time and patience will often reduce the divide. In some cases, however, the person seeking therapy may be helped by medicines designed to relieve emotional distress, that is, psychotropic medicines. Such medicines can help a person get to a position from which he or she can take advantage of psychological therapy. Psychological therapy, in turn, gives many people the resources to cope with their problems and so withdraw from their medicines. Psychotropic medicines, however, need to be used with care. Some, but by no means all, may bring about their own set of problems. All too often such medicines are inappropriately regarded as the treatment of first choice for people distressed by tinnitus. Many people who suffer with tinnitus are clearly helped by medicines such as tranquilizers, but an over readiness to prescribe such medicines brings with it a risk of perpetuating a myth that people who have a problem with tinnitus are simply neurotic.

All psychological treatments require a lot of hard work on the patient's part. Unlike some medical treatments, the patient cannot wait passively for the results to simply appear. The psychologist will not miraculously do something that will make the patient feel better. Patients must take some responsibility for their own emotional well-being. The work may even be emotionally painful at times. Acknowledging that you think certain things and feel unpleasant emotions can be challenging. It will also take time. I have already hinted that coming to grips with psychological treatment is like acquiring a skill, such as learning to drive. It will take commitment and practice before you are proficient. Some thought also needs to be given to the nature and extent of the treatment offered to a person. For many tinnitus patients it will be sufficient to offer relaxation or biofeedback training. For others, who have more far reaching psychological problems (even if these have begun since the tinnitus developed), the treatment approach will need to consider the wider issues that the person is confronting.

Psychological treatments compare favorably with other treatment approaches. This is true when the comparison is with other approaches (e.g. medication) in the treatment of emotional disorders such as anxiety or depression. It is also true when the comparison is with other methods (e.g., masking therapy) of treating tinnitus. It would not, however, be sensible to say that a certain percentage of patients will benefit from, say, cognitive therapy. Like many other studies, those that have sought to evaluate the effectiveness of psychological therapies have varied greatly in the types of patients they have used. It is sometimes the case that the studies have used patients who have not responded to other treatment approaches. It may well be that psychological treatments would benefit many people, including many to whom it is not routinely offered, because of scarce resources, uncertainty, or suspicion about psychology or for some other reason.

OTHER PSYCHOLOGICAL APPROACHES TO TINNITUS

Other psychologists have questioned whether the process of habituation and interference with that process offers a complete explanation of why people do or do not suffer with tinnitus. A swedish psychologist, Berit Scott, has questioned whether the natural history of tinnitus is quite as Richard Hallam and others have suggested. Two other Swedish psychologists, Soly Erlandsson and Sven Carlsson, experimentally tested the habituation hypothesis by measuring changes in the psychological responses of tinnitus patients to repeated external sounds. They did not find the types of changes in physiological responses that the theory would predict. Unfortunately, the experiment was a small scale one, and by itself this work does not refute Hallam's ideas. Erlandsson and Carlsson do, however, make an interesting suggestion. It may be that some people who suffer with tinnitus do so not simply because they have not managed to habituate to the noises, but they have actually become more sensitive to them. This idea does not lead to different treatment methods but suggests that different patients may be better suited to different treatments, for example, some to relieve anxiety and others to relieve low moods.

Jonathan Hazell and Pawel Jastreboff, working in Britain and the United States, have proposed a neurophysiological model of tinnitus. This model moves us away from the confines of the ear and highlights the importance of activity within the brain in the perception of tinnitus. Although it is referred to as neurophysiological, many of the ideas in this model are psychological ones.

In their model of tinnitus, Hazell and Jastreboff suggest that the cochlear may generate only a very weak signal and that it is psychological factors operating within the brain that makes the tinnitus very powerful. They point to the role that the brain plays in regulating whether a person attends to information from the sensory organs such as the ear. They point out that information from the ear arrives in the brain before it is consciously heard. Whether the person goes on to hear the information consciously or to disregard it will depend on what importance the brain gives that information. If the information is considered important by the brain, then its detection may be enhanced. This point may be illustrated by reference to the cocktail party effect. When at a party with many conversations are going on, it is possible for a person to attend to the discussion that she or he is actually involved in and to disregard the others. The mention of that person's name in another conversation, however, will easily draw the person's attention away. The mention of other names will not necessarily have this effect. Clearly, the person's brain has learned that one name is more important than others and detection of that name is especially easy for the brain even if it is uttered in whispered tones. Once the brain has recognized tinnitus as important, usually as a threat, the brain becomes more vigilant and increases its detection and reaction to it. Hazell and Jastreboff suggest that learning that tinnitus is important leads to the establishment of patterns of activity in the brain. These patterns of activity facilitate the detection of tinnitus signals coming from the ear. What started as a weak signal from the ear may end up as a powerful perception in the brain. Hazell suggests that tinnitus should be managed by using white noise to disrupt the patterns of activity in the brain that are associated with tinnitus and by counseling aimed at relieving the anxieties associated with the noises. He suggests a directive form of counseling aimed at tackling the most commonly held negative beliefs about tinnitus. He and his co-worker Catherine McKinney are currently evaluating the effectiveness of this approach. He suggests that in the long run this approach may be so successful that tinnitus is no longer perceived.

CONCLUDING REMARKS

Present day ideas about tinnitus are not entirely new. Alexander Kennedy, a psychiatrist writing in 1953, pointed out that although tinnitus is associated with deafness and other ear complaints, the factor of preoccupation plays an important role in the condition. He suggested that the important question is "How much of the experience is due to the cochlear factor and how much to the preoccupation factor?" In his view, the patient projected his or her own imaginations or ideas into the tinnitus sound. The continuity between this idea and those of today is striking. The overlap in the ideas of contemporary researchers, such as those of Hazell and Jastreboff and Hallam, is something from which tinnitus patients may take comfort. This consensus should lead to more consistent and more successful care. It is, again, interesting to reflect upon the words of an earlier author. Edmund Price Fowler, writing in 1944, stated that even if one fails to cure tinnitus, "it does not imply that one cannot handle it more intelligently." The psychological treatments outlined here do seem to offer an intelligent approach to the problem. They offer the patient the opportunity to put the need for a cure behind, and if Jonathan Hazell is proved right, we may even look forward to methods that train the brain not to perceive tinnitus.

PATIENT'S QUESTIONS AND ANSWERS

1. *Question:*   I have been asked to see a psychologist. Does the doctor think I am imagining my tinnitus?
   Answer: No. Tinnitus is real; people do not imagine it. Tinnitus can lead to distress and psychologists specialize in helping people to understand the causes of distress and to try to control those causes. If you have been asked to see a psychologist, it is not because your doctor does not believe you but because he or she is trying to help you in one of the best possible ways.

2. *Question:*   Are people who have a bad time with tinnitus simply more neurotic to begin with?
   Answer: No. There is no evidence to suggest that this is so. All types of people can be very distressed by tinnitus. It is not the case that those people are somehow "weaker" than other people. It may be, however, that if a person has suffered with depression in the past, then he or she may have more of a struggle with tinnitus. However, this does not happen to all people who have had depression and who get tinnitus.

3. *Question:*   Does tinnitus drive people mad?
   Answer: No. Clearly tinnitus can be a very distressing symptom. Many people with tinnitus do suffer from periods of depression or anxiety. This is also true for most other medical conditions. Having something wrong can result in considerable emotional upheaval. This is not, however, the same thing as going mad. The terms madness or insanity refer to very particular types of psychological changes that are often distinguished by the person losing touch with reality. This is certainly not characteristic of the changes that people with tinnitus experience. At times a person with tinnitus may feel *as if* he or she could get to a point where all reason is lost. Alternatively, the person may feel *as if* he or she will end up

completely unable to function. Many people experience the *as if* feeling at moments of great distress, but in reality, complete breakdown is very rare, and when it happens, it is usually because there are many other problems besides tinnitus. Most people with tinnitus will not suffer in this way.

Tinnitus is a very prevalent symptom. The psychological states that the term madness refers to are also quite common and inevitably some people will experience both. This does not mean that the two things are related or that one leads to the other.

4. *Question:* Does tinnitus lead people to commit suicide?
   Answer: No. The answer is similar to that for the previous question. The distress that some people with tinnitus experience leads them to feel *as if* they could kill themselves. Very few people with tinnitus actually do commit suicide. In recent studies on this subject, almost all of the people with tinnitus who did kill themselves were very high suicide risks, that is, they would have been at risk even if they had not had tinnitus. It may be that tinnitus represents an additional stress, but in this sense, it need not be thought of as different from other stresses. There is no automatic link with suicide.

5. *Question:* Can anything be done to ease the situation?
   Answer: Yes. Tinnitus is important not simply because it is there, it is important because it leads to certain changes in what you do and think and in how you feel. It may be difficult to physically remove the tinnitus, but it is certainly possible to do something about the changes in behaviors and mood that many people experience. By changing these consequences, it is possible to control the effects of tinnitus. This control may result in the tinnitus becoming less intrusive. Some researchers argue that if you gain sufficient control over the psychological changes, the tinnitus will no longer be perceived.

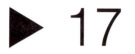

17

Treating Tinnitus as a Psychological Problem

BILL REID
Private Counseling Practice
Portland, Oregon

In the early 1980s tinnitus became my steadfast companion. In spite of the heroic efforts of Dr. Jack Vernon and Dr. Robert Johnson of the Oregon Health Sciences University, Oregon Hearing Research Center, I found no relief. I began working on a program for myself that, hopefully, would provide some amelioration. The result is the method presented here.

The target population of this treatment consists of those patients who have not responded well to other treatment and those who are emotionally distraught due to tinnitus. The Oregon Hearing Research Center, Oregon Health Sciences University, has referred some patients to me who do not respond to masking and are experiencing unusual stress due to their tinnitus.

For the purposes of this presentation, "tinnitus" may be interchanged with "pain." Tinnitus is the form of pain that we perceive as most associated with our center of consciousness. It is, therefore, the most difficult of all types of pain to separate from ourselves. I believe this explains the multitude of emotions and behaviors associated with acute tinnitus.

Prior to the beginning of treatment, questionnaires from the Oregon Hearing Research Center (see Chapter 17, Exhibit 1) are completed and evaluated. In addition to the questionnaires, a complete audiological workup must precede treatment.

With the information from the above sources, we are ready to begin treatment.

EVALUATION

A. Changes in the Patient Since Tinnitus Became a Conscious Problem.

Here we are searching for ways the patient's emotions and relations have changed since tinnitus became a problem. In our years of experience treating tinnitus patients, we have constantly seen the following conditions, either as new experiences or intensifications of preexisting experiences.

1. Depression is very common and can be clinical in severity. A significant percentage of these patients are suicidal.
2. Anxiety is an almost universal symptom among acute tinnitus patients.
3. Irritability and anger are very common and often directed toward family members and co-workers. These often lead to inappropriate behaviors in a variety of situations.
4. Often we see increased drinking and/or drug use since tinnitus began.
5. Social and familial difficulties are common and with respect to the spouse, difficulties may range from some discomfort to struggles leading to divorce.
6. Sleep difficulties are common and exacerbate all of the other problems.
7. Absenteeism may lead to the patient's giving up their work.

These emotions and behaviors are identified in talk therapy. A judgement is made as to how each change of this nature is directly affecting the patient and others in his life. Each of these changes will be treated as though tinnitus did not exist.

Those who suffer chronic pain (tinnitus) are often caught up in a cycle of emotional and physical responses, which may involve one or several of the above. In addition, they may suffer fatigue and loss of appetite, plunging them into a state of vitalization that affects every aspect of their being.

B. Evaluate Attitude

1. What is the patient's present attitude toward the problem?
2. What is the patient's attitude toward treatment?
3. What is the patient's attitude toward the purpose in living? This point becomes vital to the success of the treatment.

A young man, with his wife and their baby, came in for treatment of severe tinnitus. This patient owned and managed 5000 acres of farmland, a trucking firm, and other businesses and held a Ph.D. degree. A person who had *everything,* he had become almost non-functional. He did not tell me until after treatment that had we failed to help him, he had his death planned in detail because "life was not worth living."

In the course of treatment, we came to the "attitude toward life purpose" and, with intense exploration of the ultimate questions of life, this patient found all that was needed to bring his life back together. A year after he and his family returned to their home, we received a letter stating that he couldn't be happier and couldn't imagine living without the understanding he had come to in therapy concerning his purpose for living. This turning point in treatment paved the way for successful treatment of his specific tinnitus. These specifics are addressed in the next section.

C. Evaluate Obsession

Patients very often are obsessed with their tinnitus. It is essential that this condition be dealt with. Failure to do so will amount to failure in treating the patient. Every other effort in this treatment program might seem to be working for a time but without successfully addressing obsession, there is no long-term help.

An example illustrates this. A woman of about 60 years of age was referred to us by her otolaryngologist at the Oregon Health Sciences University. She presented herself well-composed. She seemed a pleasing affable person who, on the surface, simply wanted some help with her tinnitus problem. Shortly after I began to ask questions, she said she thought she could speed up the process by showing me some history of the problem. She reached in a briefcase and produced a number of diary-like volumes and presented one that dealt with a year of her life ten years ago. Every hour of the day and into the night she had recorded her codes indicating the intensity of her pain, her mood, and so on. This, it became clear, was her life. Total obsession. This illustrates an extreme, however, with any patient, a little bit of this poison can delay progress in treating the tinnitus.

TREATMENT

Particular personality traits make some patients more susceptible to the pain of tinnitus and less apt to experience success in treatment. The traits that we look out for are low self-esteem, poor self-image, negative sense of accomplishment, and dependency on others. These have to be addressed in order to pave the way for treatment success.

A. Alpha Awareness

Working with patients in an alpha level of consciousness facilitates treatment, allowing direct communication either in making suggestions or guiding visualization.

Briefly, I use a condensed form of progressive relaxation. The patient is asked to lie down and then asked to breathe deeply and slowly for several breaths. He is then asked to think of his feet relaxing to the point that they feel heavy and perhaps too heavy to lift. He is taken from the feet through the relaxation process with calves, thighs, lower back, upper back, shoulders, back of neck, muscles reaching up and over the head, temples, jaw, cheeks, eyes, and eye lids. At this point, count the patient down to even a deeper level from 25 to 0. The patient should be at an alpha level of awareness at the end of this process.

B. Treatment of Emotional Responses

All emotional responses are treated with cognitive therapy or guided visualization or both. The best guide to cognitive therapy is Aaron Beck's work presented so clearly by his astute pupil, David Burns, M.D., in *The Feeling Good Handbook* (Plume/Penguin).

Depression, anxiety, anger, irritability, drinking, relationship problems (at home or otherwise), sleep disorders, and absenteeism can all be treated with cognitive therapy. All of these symptoms must be treated as though tinnitus did not exist. After this treatment, movement to other aspects of the program is in order. In the treatment of these symptoms, the use of guided visualization when the patient is in an alpha level of awareness is beneficial.

An example: A man responsible for a division of a major corporation presented himself for treatment. He and his wife were childless, though his spouse wanted a child. Since the onset of his tinnitus, he had become hostile toward her; and it seemed that a separation was unavoidable. Using alpha awareness sessions, it became apparent that he loved his wife very much but was unsure about having a baby. The question of a baby was the center of his hostility toward his wife and this only after he developed tinnitus.

The three of us talked. He became angry when the subject of a baby was mentioned. Alone with him, I asked if he had always felt this way. He said no, and he agreed to explore, through alpha awareness, alternatives concerning a baby. I used guided visualizations; the first pictured him tenderly with his wife telling her he did not now, or ever, want a child. I asked him to tell her and deeply feel his emotions as a result. Then we changed the picture. He would tell her that he loved her and perhaps wanted to share parenthood with her. He was to feel deeply his emotions. Result: he chose to agree to and look forward to a baby. We were now ready to deal with tinnitus more clearly.

C. Treatment of Secondary Gain Behavior

Secondary gain is behaviors a tinnitus patient develops to compensate himself for having to suffer this injustice.

Some examples of secondary gain behaviors are control of family members or those in work environment; behaviors that elicit pity or sympathy; an excuse to withdraw from social situations; withdrawal from work; abdication of responsibilities, such as refusing any longer to write the checks, go to the grocery store, do household tasks, and so on; ordering the pattern for lovemaking to please only the patient; attending only the restaurants the patient chooses, only his choice of movies, and so on. All of this is done because, "I have tinnitus, so I can't do otherwise."

It is the role of the therapist to draw forth this behavior, examine it with the patient, and help the patient see what they are doing and why intensive talk therapy is required. Our goal is to help the patient understand what is occurring and then to help in reversing the behavior.

We use cognitive therapy and visualization constructed to change the obstructive patterns to positive and creative ones. This must always be done in partnership with the patient. Nothing here can be imposed.

D. Treatment in Relation to Choice and Attitude

Working with attitude comes at this point in the treatment because without the preceding work, we are not ready for this vital cornerstone to our success. We consider here two points: the power of choice and attitude.

Choice: The patient must become vividly aware that they have the power to choose any attitude they embrace, including the attitude toward tinnitus.

Choice is a fundamental of human life. Without this power of choice we are but robots, not human beings. The point we stress here is that the patient must become aware, acutely aware, that they are free to select any attitude toward tinnitus and that the attitude chosen will determine success or failure of treatment.

Attitude: The ideal attitude is, "Although I have tinnitus and am suffering, I will think and act in such a way that I will emerge as one greater than my affliction. I am more powerful and will overcome."

Other attitudes presented may be:

1. Nothing can really help.
2. Why me?
3. I deserve a pension because I can't be helped.
4. This is too much work, or too complicated, etc.

Assisting patients toward a positive attitude is fundamental to this method.

E. Treatment for Obsession of Tinnitus

We will discuss the phenomenon of obsession with the patient and provide an illustration such as the following:

You have a garden. You have it filled with the most valued of plants. You enjoy and love it. Then one morning you discover a large spreading weed right in the center of your garden. Now imagine that the only way to save your garden is to ignore the weed that could kill the garden. However, knowing this, you can't seem to help focusing on it, and as you do, the weed grows. Soon the beautiful plants are dying—this garden is in trouble.

Obsession, being fixed always on the tinnitus, produces the same effect. The more it is focused upon, the greater detriment it becomes to all emotions, social life, and general health. This complex situation is discussed and guided visualization is used to refocus the patient's attention.

F. Enhancing Techniques

The following techniques can be used indefinitely by the patient to enhance awareness bypass. We begin with (1) the switch-thought method.

The patient is taught to use this technique at any time he catches himself concentrating, even momentarily, on tinnitus. The key word is *switch*. You might visualize a train going down a straight track, then suddenly switching to another track that might be at a right angle to the track the train was on. This method is open-ended, with no preconceived notion of where the switch will lead. The only thing to remember is that (a) one sees the train going straight; this is the patient's thought when he discovers himself concentrating on tinnitus, (b) he sees the train switch, at which time he opens his mind to whatever he might see on the new track. He is, for a time, bypassing tinnitus.

We can also use (2) the stop-thought method. This technique differs from the switch-thought in that the patient knows where he is going prior to activating the method. The patient must first select four happy scenes of past experiences or imaginary scenes totally unrelated to the time of life after tinnitus. These scenes should be constructed in detail and these details should be written out.

A rubber band is put on a wrist. When the patient discovers himself focusing on tinnitus, he shouts STOP in a loud voice, then snaps the rubber band and immediately goes in his thoughts to one of the prearranged scenes.

If the patient is not in an environment for shouting, they can *shout* in silence, then snap the rubber band and go to the previously constructed scene. This technique changes the brain chemistry in such a way as to facilitate the move from obsessive concentration with tinnitus to one of the imagined scenes.

Note that one of the most successful ways to deal with phobias is to have the patient face the object feared in as close a proximity as possible without a break in concentration. What happens is that at some point the brain turns off; it will no longer cooperate and the patient cannot continue to feel fear.

Another technique we can use is (3) the keying method. This technique is akin to the previous method but there is a difference. Here we deal with one specific time in the life of the patient—a time before there was tinnitus. This time and place will be treated like a comfortable room, a place on the beach, a favorite time of day, sitting in a favorite chair, perhaps reading a choice book.

The place or time is real. It becomes a retreat to be used often. Once the patient has the place and by memory becomes warmly at home with it, the process is simple. Upon discovering any concentration on his tinnitus, the patient keys a transfer to this warm and comfortable, tinnitus-free place by touching thumb to index finger and momentarily pressing, thus, another awareness bypass.

Another technique is (4) the tracking method. This is an exercise that has proven most significant and useful with our patients seeking awareness bypass.

First, the patient is urged to become aware of the tinnitus. Just hold it in awareness. Listen to it. Second, the patient is asked to amplify the tinnitus. Feel the tinnitus. Focus intently on it. Experience all of it. Third, examine as an explorer the experience of this pain. Discover every part of it. Listen for heretofore unknown aspects of it. Does the tinnitus radiate? Does it circle? Does it touch your brain? Does it reach your jaw or cheek? Is it angry? In order to fully amplify the tinnitus try to objectively describe it to someone else in such detail that the person can experience what the patient is experiencing.

Fourth, the patient is asked to freeze the experience himself, tinnitus and all. See it as never before—as a new and unknown factor in the world. Fifth, the patient will reach a point where suddenly the mind switches tracks—where instantly the patient is hearing music or is out riding a horse. Awareness bypass is occurring but the patient has had to work at it. At this point, the patient is urged to concentrate on the experience of the moment, as they had previously done with the tinnitus. This procedure should be done at least three times a day. Soon awareness bypass becomes a subconscious experience and most of the patient's day will be free from tinnitus awareness.

PATIENT'S QUESTIONS AND ANSWERS

1. *Question:* How will you stop my tinnitus?
   Answer: I won't. Your tinnitus may last the rest of your life. This method of treatment is a process to help you permanently bypass awareness of tinnitus.

2. *Question:* What is your goal?
   Answer: To help you get to the place that you are unaware of your tinnitus 90 percent of the time.

3. *Question:* What is the determining factor that a patient must have for this program to work?
   Answer: An absolute desire to get better.

4. *Question:* Why do you say that depression, fear, anxiety, panic, anger, and social-domestic problems must be treated as though the tinnitus didn't exist?
   Answer: These problems are *pain* within themselves, and tinnitus seems to be the catalyst that brings them forth.

5. *Question:* You indicate that in some cases counseling such as you offer effects a lowering of the tinnitus. How can that be?
   Answer: The purpose of the counseling is to produce a better adjustment to the tinnitus. But in those patients for which there is a real reduction in the loudness of the tinnitus I have to guess that it is due to a reduction in stress. As you know stress and tension can increase tinnitus in some patients. In a sample of 1084 tinnitus patients 49 percent indicated that stress increased the loudness of their tin-

nitus. Most likely the counseling has reduced the stress of the tinnitus and that in turn has reduced the loudness of the tinnitus.

6. *Question:*   If counseling has a positive effect upon tinnitus, is it a permanent effect?

   Answer: In most cases it is a permanent effect. It is an approach to the adjustment to tinnitus, and, moreover, it is a way of adjustment that is often used to deal with other adversities.

7. *Question:*   What is the success rate?

   Answer: I figure my success rate, by follow-up of my patients, is 65 to 75 percent. Of the 25 to 35 percent who are not helped, the majority of these did not want to be helped. They use tinnitus to manipulate others.

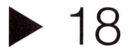

18

The Masking of Tinnitus

ROBERT M. JOHNSON, Ph.D.
Oregon Hearing Research Center
Oregon Health Sciences University
Portland, Oregon

The concept of masking tinnitus by the use of an external sound is certainly not new. This phenomenon was clearly alluded to by Hipprocates in 400 B.C. when he asked the question, "Why is it that the buzzing in the ear ceases if one makes a sound? Is it because the greater sound drives out the less?" The early literature is replete with descriptions of tinnitus-like sounds such as aural murmurs, roaring in the head, or that infernal racket in my ears. However, it was not until 1903 that a formal attempt was made to mask tinnitus with an external stimulus. At that time, a physician by the name of Spaulding used a piano keyboard to match the pitch of the patient's tinnitus. Having obtained a match, he would then produce the same note on a wind instrument so that it could be prolonged over time and would continue to increase the intensity of the sound until the tinnitus was inaudible. Spaulding also mentioned that, with certain patients, when the external sound was terminated the tinnitus disappeared.

In 1928, two clinicians by the name of Jones and Knudsen described two methods of treating tinnitus with external signals. The first method was to bombard the system with an objective sound that was similar to the tinnitus but louder. Upon removing the sound, they reported a lessening of the tinnitus that lasted for a short period of time. They also designed a large instrument that could be placed on a bedside stand for patients experiencing difficulty sleeping—thus was born the first bedside masker.

The first formal study involving tinnitus masking occurred in 1971 when a German investigator by the name of Feldmann used different sounds to try masking tinnitus. He discovered that for some patients the tinnitus could be masked with external sounds and oftentimes, when the noise was removed, the patient's tinnitus was inhibited (completely gone or substantially reduced in loudness). This phenomenon was later termed residual inhibition.

These early observations were important but were not clinically applicable for patients who suffered from this symptom. It was not until 1976 that Jack Vernon described a new tinnitus program at the Oregon Health Sciences University that involved the use of wearable masking devices. Since that time, masking of tinnitus has evolved as the most commonly used therapy for patients afflicted with this problem. This chapter is devoted to a discussion of the evaluation and treatment of tinnitus through a masking procedure.

EVALUATION OF THE TINNITUS PATIENT

The evaluation for tinnitus patients most generally consists of (1) a medical examination to rule out any medical problem that would exclude the patient from participating in the program, (2) a routine audiometric examination to determine the type and degree of hearing impairment, (3) a tinnitus evaluation, and (4) completion of the questionnaire included at the end of this chapter.

The Medical Examination

Most patients who are possible candidates for a tinnitus masking program are referred by physicians and have already undergone a medical examination. Some patients have seen numerous physicians and continue to search for relief from their tinnitus. A thorough examination, preferably by an otolaryngologist, is an essential first step in the process of evaluating and treating tinnitus patients. Tinnitus, like hearing loss, is a symptom of a medical disorder and any possible medical or surgical treatment for the problem should be ruled out prior to being fitted with any device. Furthermore, the physician is most often the entry-level professional who is responsible for determining which patients are experiencing enough difficulty coping with their problem to be referred for possible use of masking devices. As has been mentioned previously, there are millions of people who have some degree of tinnitus, many of whom are coping with the problem quite nicely without any form of treatment. It is an annoyance to them but is not really distressing. Therefore, it is important for the physician to identify those patients they feel need further help in adjusting to their problem and make the appropriate referral.

Another important aspect of the medical examination is to rule out an objective tinnitus, a condition that produces a sound in the patient's head that can often be perceived by the physician or clinician either by placing one's ear next to the patients or through the use of special equipment. This type of tinnitus can result from a constricted blood vessel or vein, an irregular contraction of one of the two muscles in the ear, a spasm of the soft palate, or a clicking sound in the ear due to a temporo-mandibular joint (TMJ) dysfunction.

Because tinnitus is, by definition, a spontaneous sound generated in the ears or head of a person in the absence of an external sound, many patients are seen at the Clinic who hear a pulsating sound that is synchronous with their heartbeat. This sound is generated by the vascular system and not by the auditory system. As such, these patients do not obtain relief from a masking program and should be referred back to their physician for further examination to determine the cause of the problem.

Likewise, some patients report hearing a synchronized clicking in their ear or ears due to an involuntary contraction of the soft palate. This condition, which is most often unilateral, is referred to as a palatal myoclonus and can be very loud and both-ersome to the patient. Again, this is a medical problem that can be treated by an oto-laryngologist.

A very common medical problem that induces tinnitus in a large number of patients results from a TMJ dysfunction. This problem will oftentimes follow a dental experience or a physical trauma from being hit on the head. It is also a very common symptom for individuals with improper alignment of their teeth. These patients will present to the Clinic complaining of pain or discomfort in the area of the joint, a pressure sensation in their ear, and sometimes a very pronounced clicking sound when they open or close their jaw. Tinnitus from a TMJ dysfunction is not an objective sound that another person can hear but is rather a subjective tinnitus that only they can perceive. However, there is a definite relationship between an abnormality of the temporomandibular joint and the onset of tinnitus; and, prior to fitting any patient with a masking device, it is important that they be seen by a proper professional to determine if orthodontic treatment can relieve the tinnitus. Tinnitus can be caused by a TMJ dysfunction but proper alignment of the teeth or jaw can also alleviate the problem for selected patients. If they do not obtain relief from their tinnitus with dental manipulation, many of these patients can be effectively masked.

The Audiometric Evaluation

The audiometric work-up for the tinnitus patient generally does not differ greatly from the typical audiometric assessment performed for diagnostic purposes or a hearing aid evaluation. This procedure includes pure tone testing, speech testing, tympanometry, and a test of the uncomfortable loudness level (UCL) for that individual. Many patients who have tinnitus and/or hearing loss also have a sensitivity problem that interferes with their ability to function in noisy environments, and it is important not to exceed their tolerance levels in fitting any instrument. Special auditory tests are performed only when additional diagnostic information is indicated.

In addition to providing diagnostic information with regard to the type of hearing loss the patient exhibits, the audiogram also aids in the selection of the appropriate masking device for a particular individual. Three different types of devices are used to offer relief for tinnitus patients: 1) tinnitus maskers, 2) tinnitus instruments, and 3) hearing aids. The selection of the unit will depend primarily on the amount of hearing loss the patient displays. The choice of instruments will be discussed under the management of the tinnitus patient.

The audiogram is also helpful in determining the loudness level of the tinnitus. Most measurements of the loudness of the tinnitus are based on the patient's threshold for a particular sound and how much above the threshold one has to make the sound so that it equals the loudness of the patient's tinnitus. This level, which is based on the patient's own threshold, is referred to as sensation level (SL). Again, this topic will be discussed more thoroughly later.

Finally, the audiogram restricts the use of masking devices for patients with extensive hearing losses. Although considerable effort has been made to design maskers whose output does not exceed the level at which sound is potentially dangerous to the ear, the clinician must always be aware that patients with severe to profound hearing levels could possibly lose some of their residual hearing if the masking sound is too loud.

The Tinnitus Evaluation

In an attempt to quantify the patient's tinnitus, an evaluation of the pitch of the tinnitus, the loudness of the tinnitus, the amount of sound needed to mask the tinnitus, the duration of residual inhibition if it is observed, and an actual trial procedure with wearable masking devices to determine whether the patient can benefit from a tinnitus masking program. These measurements can be made with a special tinnitus synthesizer, an audiometer, or several pieces of equipment cascaded together.

The pitch of the tinnitus for each patient is determined by a matching procedure. A reference signal is presented to the ear opposite to the side where the tinnitus is being measured. The reference sound might be a pure tone signal for those patients who complain of a ringing sound, a high-pitched band of noise for those who report hearing a hissing-like sound, a low-pitched noise band for patients who hear a roaring sound, or a combination of several sounds. Many patients report having several sounds in their ears or head. A large number of patients localize their tinnitus in the head rather than at the ears. Also, the tinnitus can be unilateral (one ear) or bilateral (both ears). Our ability to match the pitch of the patient's tinnitus is generally less accurate than for loudness or masking levels measures.

To measure loudness, a balance technique is used with the external signal generally presented to the opposite ear, where the tinnitus is being measured. Whatever sound was selected as the best pitch match for the patient is used as the referent signal to measure loudness. That signal is increased in the opposite ear until the patient first hears the sound. That is the threshold for that sound. Then the sound is increased until the patient indicates that it is equally "loud" to their tinnitus. The difference between threshold and when the external signal is equally loud to the tinnitus is the loudness of that patient's tinnitus. Unfortunately, the method that is used for making the loudness measurement is controversial and does not truly represent the magnitude of the tinnitus. In most cases, the level is 10 dB or less and is not indicative of the amount of distress that many patients exhibit.

After determining the pitch and loudness of the tinnitus, it is then important to ascertain the effectiveness of masking the tinnitus. Typically, masking is attempted with bands of noise that are fairly wide and the noise is presented to the same ear as the tinnitus. The effectiveness of the noise to mask the tinnitus is determined by first establishing the threshold of the masking stimulus and then increasing the noise until the tinnitus is just masked. This level is termed the "minimum masking level" and again is the difference between the threshold level for the noise and the amount of noise needed to mask the tinnitus.

The final measurement in the clinical evaluation of the tinnitus patient is to determine if the tinnitus is "inhibited" when the ear is continuously stimulated for a period of time. Often, upon removal of the noise, the patient will report a complete elimination or reduction of the tinnitus. This intriguing phenomenon has been coined "residual inhibition" and is generally measured by presenting a masking signal to the patient for one minute and upon removal of the noise observing the duration of the inhibition. Many patients report a reduction in their tinnitus that generally lasts for only a short time, but for some patients the duration of the residual inhibition can be quite lengthy.

Following the evaluation process with the synthesizer, ear level instruments are tried on each patient. The reason for this added procedure stems from the observation that the results obtained with the synthesizer or audiometer do not allow for an accurate prediction of the patient's ability to be masked with ear level instruments. Certainly, many patients who can be masked with the synthesizer or audiometer can also be masked with wearable units. Likewise, there are patients whose tinnitus is completely resistant to masking and who cannot obtain relief from this procedure. However, there are a number of patients who can be effectively masked with a synthesizer or an audiometer but not with ear level instruments. The opposite is also true. Some patients who cannot be masked with evaluation units can be easily masked with wearable devices. This trial period with wearable instruments adds about one-half hour to the evaluation process but has resulted in a much more effective method of determining if a masking program should be initiated.

MANAGEMENT OF THE TINNITUS PATIENT

Once the clinician has completed the tinnitus evaluation, that information along with the medical examination and the audiological assessment is used to properly manage the tinnitus patient. The management of the patient is very important and can be difficult and time consuming. Unlike the fitting of patients with hearing aids, most of whom respond very positively to amplification, tinnitus patients differ considerably in their ability to benefit from a masking program. Patients with similar etiologies and hearing losses will respond very differently to the masking stimulus. The interaction between the patient and the instrument is truly an individual matter and the degree and manner of relief will vary greatly from patient to patient. Therefore, the proper management depends not only on the clinician but also on the patient to experiment and establish a program that will offer him maximum relief from the tinnitus. This procedure may involve wearing the instrument full time or using it only for short periods of time.

Relief of tinnitus by masking can be accomplished in two ways. First, the external sound of the masker is generally a more acceptable sound than the patients tinnitus and can be substituted for the tinnitus. Secondly, a small number of patients can control their tinnitus through the extension of residual inhibition. These latter patients, upon removal of the masking stimulus, experience a period of time in which the tinnitus is either reduced or completely absent. The periods of "quiet" range in length from a few seconds to several days. Those patients who have long periods of quiet following stimulation will need to develop their own masking schedules since the clinician has no means of establishing a timetable for them. Some patients do not observe this phenomenon in any form.

It is also important to mention that many patients cannot benefit from a masking program, and it is the clinician's first responsibility to determine if the patient is or is not a candidate for a masking program. Sometimes this decision is very easy but other times it is extremely difficult. In some cases, the final judgment can only be made through the use of a trial period. Therefore, it is essential that the dispensation of masking devices be coupled to a trial period of a designated time.

If a positive decision is made to initiate a masking program for a patient, several important questions need immediate consideration. The initial consideration that is primary in managing the tinnitus patient relates to whether the patient also has a hearing loss. The clinician must decide if the patient's problem is related only to tinnitus or to a combination of tinnitus and a hearing loss. This decision will be foremost in selecting the proper instrument for that patient.

As mentioned previously, three types of instruments have been used for offering relief to tinnitus patients: (1) hearing aids, (2) tinnitus maskers, and (3) tinnitus instruments. Hearing aids have long been known to help selected patients who have both a hearing loss and tinnitus. When fitted with hearing aids, some patients will comment that not only do the hearing aids improve the patient's ability to understand conversational speech better but that it also either reduces or completely eliminates the patient's tinnitus.

Tinnitus maskers were first commercially introduced to the public in 1976 and consisted only of behind-the-ear (BTE) units. Two years later, amplification and masking were combined to produce the first tinnitus instrument. Since that time, many different hearing aid companies have designed and developed tinnitus maskers and tinnitus instruments. However, some companies have discontinued making these units because of a limited market for them. Later developments also included both in-the-ear (ITE) and canal maskers. The canal configuration is not large enough to accommodate both amplification and masking.

Recently, maskers that can be individually tuned by either the clinician or the patient have been designed. These new maskers allow for more flexibility for the patient in that the frequency can be varied to provide for more effective masking and a signal that is more acceptable for the patient in terms of listening to a substitute sound. These tunable maskers are available in both tinnitus maskers and tinnitus instruments.

Tinnitus maskers are recommended for patients who have normal or near normal hearing and do not need amplification. They are also used for patients who have a sensitivity problem and cannot tolerate loud sounds. Many of these patients could benefit from amplification but are unable to utilize it because of excessive tolerance problems.

If the patient has both a hearing loss and tinnitus, the clinician must decide whether to fit the patient with hearing aids or tinnitus instruments (a combination unit that contains both amplification and masking). Several factors are important in making this decision. If, during the trial period with wearable units, the patient's tinnitus is completely eliminated or is reduced significantly with just amplification, then consideration should be given to fitting the patient with a hearing aid because there is much greater flexibility when fitting patients with hearing aids as opposed to tinnitus instruments. However, if the patient is having a sleeping problem, it is imperative to use the combination unit so that the patient can turn off the amplification and use the masking sound at nighttime. Furthermore, the clinician must be aware that residual inhibition is not observed after the use of hearing aids. It appears that the constant stimulation of the masker is necessary to produce this very mysterious phenomenon. Thus, if hearing aids are recommended, one avenue of relief is probably precluded.

The final step in the tinnitus masking program is the dispensing of the instruments. As is true with hearing aids, tinnitus maskers and tinnitus instruments are dispensed on a trial basis. It is imperative that each patient be allowed a trial period following the dispensation of the instruments to determine the effectiveness of the device in relieving his or her tinnitus. Most dispensers automatically provide a month's trial period and many will allow additional time if needed. Unfortunately, the return rate of tinnitus maskers and instruments is considerably greater than for hearing aids. This procedure is advantageous for the patient but is costly for the manufacturer. Thus, it is important that the initial decision regarding equipment for tinnitus patients be made carefully.

Since the inception of the masking program at the Oregon Hearing Research Center in 1976, a number of follow-up studies have been conducted to determine the efficacy of the masking program. In 1982, a Tinnitus Data Registry was initiated that provides for a comprehensive method to follow patient progress (see Exhibit 18–1). Follow-up questionnaires are mailed to patients at six month and yearly intervals following their visit to the Tinnitus Clinic. Table 18–1 includes the latest follow-up data derived from the data registry. These data have remained fairly consistent over time.

For approximately 30 percent of the patients seen at the Tinnitus Clinic, no recommendations are made and approximately 10 percent are referred for medical treatment. All of the 370 patients included in Table 18–1 received recommendations for

TABLE 18–1   **Follow-Up Results of 370 Patients with Specific Equipment Recommendations**

	Hearing Aids (H/A)		Tinnitus Maskers (TM)		Tinnitus Instruments (TI)		HA and TM		TI and TM		Totals	
	No.	%	No.	%	No.	%	No.	%	No.	%	No.	%
Recommended for trial period	51		65		228		18		8		370	
Tried device but did not purchase	20	39	42	65	61	27	6	33	4	50	133	36
Purchased device	31	61	23	35	167	71	12	67	4	50	127	64

either hearing aids, tinnitus maskers, tinnitus instruments, or a combination of those units. It is immediately evident from this table that the majority of patients seen at the Clinic received recommendations to be fitted with tinnitus instruments. Only about 10 percent of the patients seen have normal hearing. Therefore, since tinnitus maskers are recommended only for patients who have normal or near normal hearing, the number of recommendations for patients to be fitted with tinnitus maskers is quite small. Furthermore, the success rate with tinnitus maskers (35%) is considerably poorer than for the tinnitus instrument.

Fortunately, the success ratio for the tinnitus instrument (71%) is much better since 62 percent of our patients are referred for these devices. Tinnitus instruments are the units of choice for several reasons. First, if the patient has both a hearing loss and tinnitus, the combination unit is more effective in treating both conditions. For most patients, the combination of amplification and masking is more effective in masking the tinnitus and also is more acceptable to the patient as a substitute for his or her tinnitus. Second, if the tinnitus can be masked or significantly reduced with only amplification, but the patient is experiencing difficulty sleeping, it is often beneficial to fit him or her with a combination unit that will allow the patient to use the masking feature during the night. Third, if a patient has a severe tinnitus problem and can initially be masked with a hearing aid but later needs masking, in most instances it cannot be added to his or her existing instrument. Our experience has been that only about one-half of the patients fitted with hearing aids get any relief from their tinnitus with amplification. Therefore, if there is any question regarding the need for masking, it is most cost effective to recommend the tinnitus instrument during the initial visit. The difference in cost between a hearing aid and a tinnitus instrument is minimal, and the patient always has the option of using either the amplification, the masking, or both, because the amplification and masking are adjusted with separate volume controls.

Although the results obtained with masking devices are not as positive as we had hoped, it is apparent that a large number of patients are benefitting from this program.

Fortunately, for those patients who cannot benefit from a masking program, other methods of treatment are also available and are discussed by other authors in this publication.

PATIENT'S QUESTIONS AND ANSWERS

1. *Question:*   What is the advantage of adding yet another noise to what I already hear?
   Answer: What you hear is an internal sound while masking is an external sound. We can easily ignore external sounds as long as they are constant, not too loud, and not interesting. We have had a lifetime of experience doing just that. Now if you ignore the sound that covers up your tinnitus, you will have automatically ignored your tinnitus. Masking provides control over your tinnitus rather than your tinnitus controlling you. Another advantage of masking is that the masking sound is more acceptable than the typical high pitched screech of tinnitus.

2. *Question:*   Why would I need two maskers? Why would not one suffice?
   Answer: For patients with tinnitus in both ears it is usually necessary to mask both ears although it is sometimes possible to mask both ears with only one masker. Only by actual testing is it possible to determine which situation works for each patient.

3. *Question:*   My tinnitus does not appear to be in my ears but rather to be located in my head? Does that signify a brain tumor that I have heard is a possible cause for tinnitus?
   Answer: Perceiving tinnitus as located in the head probably means that there is a neurological signal coming from each ear and that the two signals are exactly matched in loudness and phase relationship. It does not mean a brain tumor. For tinnitus located in the head it is usual that two masking devices are required if masking is to be effective.

4. *Question:*   Will my tinnitus get worse as I get older?
   Answer: We have no direct evidence on this topic. We have examined the tinnitus in a group of patients aged 65 or more as compared to a group aged 55 or less. In every dimension of tinnitus the older group was better. Their tinnitus was less loud, their tinnitus was maskable at a lower level, their residual inhibition lasted longer, and the average pitch of their tinnitus was lower. The only thing worse for the older group was that their hearing was not as good as the younger group. Since the older group had had their tinnitus longer than the younger group, I am inclined to say that there is no reason your tinnitus should get worse with time providing of course your do not expose your ears to loud sounds. That is the one guaranteed way to increase tinnitus.

5. *Question:*   Does the lack of residual inhibition mean that masking will not work?

   Answer: No. The purpose of masking is to effect relief while the masking sound is present and not necessarily to effect relief once the masking sound is turned off. If residual inhibition happens, it is a bonus; but it is not a test to determine the possibility for effective masking.

6. *Question:*   Will I have to wear maskers all the time? Even in sleep?

   Answer: No. One wears the maskers only when they wish to have relief of their tinnitus. Some patients wear them only when they are in the quiet. Others wear them during most of the day and there are some who wear them all the time including sleep. The in-the-ear maskers are suitable for use during sleep.

7. *Question:*   Will the masking sound interfere with my ability to hear and understand speech?

   Answer: Probably not and for this reason. Visualize a piano keyboard. The upper end (right-hand side) of the piano produces pitches at about 4000 Hz. Except for rare and exotic sounds almost all of our speech and environmental sounds are below 4000 Hz. Tinnitus on the other hand is high pitched, on average being matched at 7000 Hz. In order to mask tinnitus at such a high pitch it is necessary to use sounds in the same pitch region, which, as you can see, is at the wrong address to interfere with speech sounds. That is not to say that one could attend to the masking sound to the exclusion of speech sounds. But remember the natural tendency is to ignore the masking sound and not to attend to it.

8. *Question:*   You have indicated that the majority of tinnitus patients have a hearing loss of some sort. Does that mean that they would not be able to hear the masking sound and thus could not use masking to relieve their tinnitus?

   Answer: Remember there is the tinnitus instrument that is a combination of a hearing aid and a tinnitus masker with independent volume controls. This unit is specifically designed for tinnitus patients who have hearing impairment. When using the tinnitus instrument, it is important to always adjust the hearing aid portion of the unit first and after that to add in the amount of masking sound needed to effect relief.

9. *Question:*   Can the use of a tinnitus masker damage my hearing? Or make my tinnitus worse?

   Answer: The simple fact is that you would not tolerate a masking sound loud enough to either damage your hearing or make your tinnitus worse. The loudness of the tinnitus masking sound is under your control and you simply will not accept masking that is too loud or uncomfortably loud. Remember the measure loudness of tinnitus averages 7.5 dB, which is a very weak sound.

10. *Question:*   I have trouble believing that tinnitus is such a weak sound. Mine seems to be screaming at full volume.

   Answer: I think there is a difference between loudness and distinctiveness. The tinnitus sound is very distinctive for the simple reason that it is so high pitched as to be very distinctive from other environmental sounds. And, that distinctiveness is what makes tinnitus appear so obvious. But it is not loud.

11. *Question:*   You caution that tinnitus patients must avoid loud sounds. What is loud?
    Answer: Any time it is necessary for you to raise the loudness of your voice in order to be heard, that situation is too loud for your tinnitus. I admit that this is a conservative estimate, but I would rather you be safe than sorry.

12. *Question:*   It is not easily possible for me to get to your tinnitus clinic. Is there any way I can determine whether masking would work for me?
    Answer: Yes. If you have a compact disk (CD) player you can request a Moses/Lang CD masking recording from the Oregon Hearing Research Center (530-494-8032). That disk has seven different brands of masking sounds and if any one of them relieves your tinnitus it is then highly likely that wearable tinnitus maskers would work for you. If you do not have a CD player then do the "Faucet Test." Stand near the kitchen sink with the water running full force. If the sound of that running water makes it impossible for you to hear your tinnitus it is then likely that wearable tinnitus maskers would work for you. If the sound of the running water does not cover your tinnitus, it may be due to a hearing loss that would mean that the tinnitus instrument would be required to relieve your tinnitus.

13. *Question:*   Where does one obtain tinnitus maskers or tinnitus instruments?
    Answer: From any hearing aid dispenser. These units are made by the Starkey Hearing Aid Co., and any hearing aid dispenser can order them for you. It is important that you know that tinnitus maskers and tinnitus instruments are sold on a 30-day money back guarantee. If you have tried maskers in the distant past that failed for you, you should know that the present day units are superior in that they provide a masking sound at higher pitches. In the not too distant future maskers will have the advantage of digital processing, which will allow for much more precise designation of the masking composition.

EXHIBIT 18-1

TINNITUS HISTORY

Appointment

Name_____Age_____   Date:_____ Time_____

Address_____

Birthdate _____   Phone (____)_____-_____   (____)_____-_____
　　　　　Month/ Day/ Year   *Home*   *Work*

Male ☐   Female ☐   Eye Color:_____   Your Preferred Hand: Right ☐   Left ☐   Unsure ☐

Referred to Tinnitus Clinic by:_____

---

2. About how long have you been aware of having tinnitus?
   1 .... Less than 1 yr   4 .... 6 - 10 years
   2 .... 1 - 2 years   5 .... 11 - 20 years
   3 .... 3 - 5 years   6 .... 20+ years

3. Some people know the date when their tinnitus started. *YY/MM/DD if known*:_____

4. Did you become aware of your tinnitus suddenly or more gradually?
   Suddenly (1 week or less) 1
   More gradually................................. 2
   Do not know 3

5. Were illness, accident or other special circumstances associated with the onset of your present tinnitus? *(Please describe briefly)*

   _____
   _____

5a. Before that did you experience any episodes of temporary or milder tinnitus?
   No 1
   Yes.. 2

5b. If **YES**, circle all that apply

   After exposure to loud sound 1
   Associated with colds, flu, or allergies 2
   Any other time(s): _____

   _____

6. Since it started, has there been any change in the **amount of time** you are aware of hearing tinnitus?
   No, there has been no change 1
   Yes, I now hear tinnitus **more**
   of the time...................................... 2
   Yes, I now hear tinnitus **less**
   of the time...................................... 3
   I am not sure if the amount of
   time I hear it has changed 4

7. Which **one** of the statements below best describes your current tinnitus?

   Tinnitus usually lasts a few
   minutes at most 1
   Tinnitus usually lasts up to
   several hours 2
   Tinnitus usually lasts up to
   several days 3
   Tinnitus is always there 4

8. If your tinnitus is **not** present all the time, about how much of the time does it seem to be present?

   Less than half the time 1
   Half the time or more 2

9. How **much** of a **problem** is your tinnitus?
   Not a problem 1
   A small problem............................... 2
   A moderate problem 3
   A big problem 4
   A very big problem 5

9a. If tinnitus **is** a problem, about **how long** has your tinnitus been a problem?
   1 year or less .... 1 *(Go on to Q.10)*
   More than 1 year 2

9b. If more than 1 year, about **how many** years?
   _____years

10. Which is **more** of a problem for you, **hearing difficulty**...or...**tinnitus**?

   Hearing difficulty is worse problem... 1
   Tinnitus is worse problem 2
   They are equally bothersome 3
   Not sure 4
   Neither one is a problem 5

Adapted from Meikle, Griest & Press (1986)   11.10.94

11. Where does your tinnitus appear to be located?

    A. **Left** ear .... No   Yes

    B. **Right** ear........................... No   Yes

    C. **Both** ears........................... No   Yes

    D. **In head**, on **left** side .... No   Yes

    E. **In head**, on **right** side .... No   Yes

    F. **Fills head** .... No   Yes

    G. Other location .... No   Yes

    _____

             (Please describe)

12. If your tinnitus is in more than one location, where is it **worst**?

    (**CIRCLE** only **One** answer below)

    Left ear worst 1

    Right ear worst 2

    Both ears **equal** 3

    In head, left side worst..................... 4

    In head, right side worst 5

    Fills head 6

    Other location 7

    _____

             (Please describe)

13. Since it started, has the **location** of your tinnitus changed?

    No change 1

    Started in 1 ear, now in both 2

    Started in both ears,

        now in 1 ear................................ 3

    Other 4

    _____

         (Please describe changes)

14. Do you feel that tinnitus makes it more difficult to hear clearly?

    No .... 1 *(Go on to Q.15)*

    Sometimes 2

    Often........................ 3

    Unsure 4

14a. If tinnitus does make it more difficult to hear, in what situations does tinnitus interfere with your hearing?

    _____

    _____

    _____

             (Please describe)

15. Does your tinnitus seem to be one sound or more than one sound?

    1 sound................................. 1

    2 sounds 2

    3 or more sounds 3

    Unsure 4

16. In the list below, please choose the sound or sounds that most closely resemble your tinnitus.

    A. Ringing .... No   Yes

    B. Clear tone .... No   Yes

    C. More than one tone .... No   Yes

    D. Whistle .... No   Yes

    E. Hissing .... No   Yes

    F. Buzzing .... No   Yes

    G. Hum .... No   Yes

    H. Music .... No   Yes

    I. Sizzling .... No   Yes

    J. Transformer noise............... No   Yes

    K. High tension wire .... No   Yes

    L. Crickets, insects .... No   Yes

    M. Pulsating............................ No   Yes

    N. Pounding............................ No   Yes

    O. Ocean roar......................... No   Yes

    P. Clicking .... No   Yes

    Q. Other: _____

    _____

17. From the list above, or in your own words, please LIST your tinnitus sound(s) starting with the sound that bothers you the most:

          Sounds like: Location:

    1. _____ is in: _____

    2. _____ is in: _____

    3. _____ is in: _____

    4. _____ is in: _____

18. Besides the sounds that you listed above, do you hear any additional tinnitus sounds?

    No, I don't ever hear any

        other tinnitus sounds 1

    Yes, I sometimes hear other

        tinnitus sounds 2

    Yes, I hear additional sounds

        most or all of the time 3

19. On the scale below please (CIRCLE) the number that best describes the loudness of your **usual** tinnitus:

1	2	3	4	5	6	7	8	9	10
Very quiet				Intermediate					Very loud

20. Since it started has your tinnitus grown **louder** than when you first noticed it?

　　No change in loudness 1
　　Tinnitus has grown louder 2
　　Tinnitus has grown softer 3
　　Both types of change have
　　　occurred 4
　　Not sure if loudness of tinnitus
　　　has changed 5

21. Does the **loudness** of your tinnitus tend to fluctuate up and down?

　　Loudness rarely or never
　　　fluctuates 1
　　Loudness fluctuates several times
　　　per month 2
　　Loudness fluctuates several times
　　　per week 3
　　Loudness fluctuates daily 4

21a. If your tinnitus shows **loudness fluctuations**, how large are the changes usually?

　　Barely noticeable 1
　　Moderate 2
　　Very marked 3
　　Variable in size 4

22. Have you noticed an increase in tinnitus **loudness** caused by any of the following?

　　A. Noise exposure .... No　　Yes
　　B. Stress or fatigue .... No　　Yes
　　C. Colds, sinus, hayfever .... No　　Yes
　　D. Tobacco use .... No　　Yes
　　E. Alcohol use .... No　　Yes
　　F. Aspirin or other pain
　　　　medication .... No　　Yes
　　G. Head or neck injury .... No　　Yes

22a. Anything else that has caused changes in your tinnitus? (Please indicate whether tinnitus became louder or softer)

_____

23. Does your tinnitus interfere with sleep?
　　　　No .... 1 *(Go on to Q.24)*
　　　　Yes, sometimes 2
　　　　Yes, often 3

　　23a. If tinnitus does cause you sleep
　　　　problems, how severe is the problem?
　　　　Mild problem 1
　　　　Moderate problem 2
　　　　Severe problem 3

　　23b. Have you found anything that helps you
　　　　sleep?

　　　_____
　　　_____
　　　　　　　　(Please describe)

24. How much of an effort is it for you to **ignore** tinnitus when it is present?
　　　　Can easily ignore it 1
　　　　Can ignore it with some effort 2
　　　　It takes considerable effort 3
　　　　Can never ignore it 4

25. How much **discomfort** do you usually experience when your tinnitus is present?
　　　　No discomfort 1
　　　　Mild discomfort 2
　　　　Moderate discomfort......................... 3
　　　　A great deal of discomfort 4

26. Have you changed jobs because of tinnitus?
　　　　No, tinnitus has not caused job
　　　　　change(s) 1
　　┌─Yes 2

　_____

　　　　(Please describe job changes)

27. Have you made other changes in your lifestyle because of tinnitus?
　　　　No, tinnitus has not caused
　　　　　lifestyle change(s) 1
　　┌─Yes 2

　_____

　　　　(Please describe lifestyle changes)

Adapted from Meikle, Griest & Press (1986)　　　　　　　　　　11.10.94

PROBLEMS CAUSED BY HEARING DIFFICULTIES OR TINNITUS

The problems listed below are sometimes reported by people with hearing difficulties or tinnitus or both. How often have hearing difficulties or tinnitus caused you to have the problems listed below?

CIRCLE the number that best describes you

	Never	Rarely	Sometimes	Usually	Always
Have hearing difficulties or tinnitus . . .					
1. Made it uncomfortable to be in a quiet room?	1	2	3	4	5
2. Made it uncomfortable to be in a noisy environment?	1	2	3	4	5
3. Made you feel irritable or nervous?	1	2	3	4	5
4. Made you feel tired or stressed?	1	2	3	4	5
5. Made it difficult for you to relax?	1	2	3	4	5
6. Made it difficult to concentrate?	1	2	3	4	5
7. Made it harder to interact pleasantly with others?	1	2	3	4	5
Do hearing difficulties or tinnitus . . .					
8. Interfere with your social activities or other things you do in your <u>leisure time</u>?	1	2	3	4	5
9. Interfere with your <u>required</u> activities (work, home care, other types of responsibilities)?	1	2	3	4	5
10. Interfere with things you need or want to do with your family?	1	2	3	4	5
Have hearing difficulties or tinnitus caused you . . .					
11. To feel left out of conversations?	1	2	3	4	5
12. To feel frustrated or angry?	1	2	3	4	5
13. To get discouraged?	1	2	3	4	5
Do hearing difficulties or tinnitus . . .					
14. Cause you to feel embarassed at times?	1	2	3	4	5
15. Interfere with your overall enjoyment of life?	1	2	3	4	5
16. Cause you to feel depressed?	1	2	3	4	5

1-10,15: Adapted from Meikle, Griest & Press (1986); 11,13,14,16: Adapted from Demorest & Erdman (1987); 12: Adapted from Wilson, Henry, Bowen & Haralambous (1991) and Demorest & Erdman (1987)

11.10.94

HEARING HISTORY

Name_____ Birthdate _____
        Last   *First*   *Initial*   *Month/ Day/ Year*

DIRECTIONS: For all questions, fill in the blank or (CIRCLE) the answer that best describes you.
Have you had any difficulties hearing speech or other sounds?

		NO	YES, sometimes	YES, often
1.	Difficulty hearing speech when there is noise 1		2	3
2.	Trouble hearing soft or weak sounds 1		2	3
3.	Trouble hearing high-pitched sounds 1		2	3
4.	Difficulty hearing the words people are speaking.......................... 1		2	3
5.	Any other types of hearing difficulty 1		2	3
	(Please describe) _____			

> **If you DO HAVE difficulties hearing speech or other types of sound,
> please answer Questions 6, 7, and 8. If NO difficulty hearing, go on to Question 9.**

6. Which ear(s) are affected:
    LEFT ear 1
    RIGHT ear 2
    BOTH ears 3
    Unsure 4

7. When did you first notice difficulties with your hearing?
    19____

8. Were the hearing difficulties associated with an illness, accident or any other special circumstances?
    _____
    _____

9. Have you ever worn a hearing aid?
    No....................................... 1 *(Go on to Q.10)*
    Yes 2

9a. Which ear(s)?
    Left ear 1
    Right ear............................. 2
    Both ears 3

9b. Do you still use hearing aid(s)? No___Yes ___

9c. When did you first get hearing aid(s)?
    19____

9d. How much help have you received from using hearing aid(s)?
    No help 1
    A little help 2
    Some help 3
    A lot of help 4

9e. Make and Model currently worn: _____
    _____

10. Do you find loud sounds more unpleasant than you used to?
    No .... 1 *(Go on to Q.11)*
    Yes 2
    Unsure 3

10a. Please indicate how often you are bothered by loud sounds:
    Occasionally bothered 1
    Bothered fairly often 2
    Bothered all the time 3

11. Overall, how much of a problem are you having with your hearing?
    No problem 1
    Mild problem 2
    Moderate problem 3
    Big problem 4
    Very big problem 5

Adapted from Meikle, Griest & Press (1986)   11.10.94

OREGON HEARING RESEARCH CENTER   Hearing History, Page 6

HEARING DIFFICULTIES

In the list below we have described situations that sometimes cause people to have trouble hearing. Please indicate how much of the time you are having these types of hearing difficulties.
(If you normally wear a hearing aid or aids, answer each question as though you were wearing your aid(s). If you use a hearing aid only part of the time, use your own judgment in deciding how to answer).

(CIRCLE) the number that best describes you

Do you have any difficulty hearing . . .	Never	Rarely	Sometimes	Usually	Always
12. When someone talks to you while you are travelling in a car?	1	2	3	4	5
13. When you are at a social gathering with music, lots of people talking, or other background noise?	1	2	3	4	5
14. When you are carrying on a conversation with several other people in a fairly quiet location?	1	2	3	4	5
15. When someone is talking to you from another room?	1	2	3	4	5
16. When you are using the telephone?	1	2	3	4	5
17. When you are listening to TV, movies, or radio?	1	2	3	4	5
18. When you are travelling and you have to listen for information in an airline, rail, or bus terminal?	1	2	3	4	5
19. When you are in a store and you need to discuss something with the clerk?	1	2	3	4	5
20. When you are listening to a speaker addressing a large group (such as church, lecture, stage play, or other public event)?	1	2	3	4	5
21. In a restaurant when you need to discuss your order for food or drinks?	1	2	3	4	5
22. When you are listening for sounds that you <u>need</u> to hear at work, school, or other required activities (alarms, whistles, machine noise, etc.)?	1	2	3	4	5
23. When you are listening for sounds that you <u>need</u> to hear at home (doorbell, telephone, timers, kettle boiling, household appliances, etc.)?	1	2	3	4	5
24. When you are listening to things you would <u>like</u> to hear at home (children or grandchildren talking, family time together, etc.)?	1	2	3	4	5

25. Are there other situations where your hearing creates difficulties for you? Please tell us about **ANY OTHER HEARING PROBLEMS** you may have. _____
_____
_____

12-21 Adapted from: High, Fairbanks & Glorig (1964) and Demorest and Erdman (1987)   11.10.94

26. Do you ever feel dizzy?
　　Never .... 1 *(Go on to Q.27)*
　　Rarely 2
　　Sometimes 3
↓　Most of the time 4
　　Always 5

26a. What type of dizziness?
　　1) Turning or spinning sensations .... No　Yes
　　2) Faintness or light-headedness .... No　Yes
　　3) Loss of balance, feel you may fall .... No　Yes

26b. Age when you first noticed dizziness: ____years

27. Do you ever experience pain in the ear?
　　Never .... 1 *(Go on to Q.28)*
　　Rarely 2
　　Sometimes 3
↓　Most of the time 4
　　Always 5

27a. In which ear(s)?
　　Left 1
　　Right 2
　　Both 3
　　Varies.............................. 4

27b. Age when you first noticed ear pain: ____years

28. Do you ever have feelings of "fullness",
　　"plugging", or "pressure" in your ears?
　　Never .... 1 *(Go on to Q.29)*
　　Rarely 2
　　Sometimes 3
↓　Most of the time 4
　　Always 5

28a. In which ear(s)?
　　Left 1
　　Right 2
　　Both 3
　　Varies.............................. 4

28b. Age when you first noticed "fullness": ____years

29. Have you had frequent or repeated earaches or
　　ear infections?
　　No .... 1 *(Go on to Q.30)*
　　Yes 2

29a. Age at first earache:　　　　____years

29b. Age at most recent earache:　　　____years

29c. About how many times each year:

_____

30. Have you ever been diagnosed as having any
　　of the following ear diseases:

			Age at onset
1) Meniere's disease	No	Yes	____years
2) Otosclerosis	No	Yes	____years
3) Facial pain, numbness or paralysis.................	No	Yes	____years
4) Mastoiditis	No	Yes	____years
5) Labyrinthitis..................	No	Yes	____years
6) Cholesteatoma.............	No	Yes	____years

31. Have you had **other** ear problems or ear injury?
　　No .... 1 *(Go on to Q.32)*
　　Yes 2

_____

_____

_____

(Describe, give approximate age)

32. Have you had significant injury to your head or
　　neck?
　　No .... 1 *(Go on to next page)*
　　Yes...................... 2

32a. How **many** times did you injure your head or
　　your neck? _____

32b. About what year(s): _____

32c. Location(s) of injury:
　　Head 1
　　Neck 2
　　Both 3
　　Unsure 4

32d. Did injury cause any of the following?

1) Concussion	No	Yes
2) Skull fracture	No	Yes
3) Dizziness	No	Yes
4) Unconsciousness	No	Yes
5) Vertebral fracture	No	Yes
6) Whiplash	No	Yes
7) Tinnitus	No	Yes

Adapted from Meikle, Griest & Press (1986)

11.10.94

NOISE EXPOSURE HISTORY

We need to know about noise exposure in your past, even as a child. An example of loud noise is noise that makes it hard to talk to or hear another person, or makes your ears ring after exposure.

NOISE AT YOUR WORK

1. Have you worked in any of these noisy jobs?			Date Started	Date Ended	How often did you use hearing protection?		
					Never	Sometimes	Always
A. Cannery	No	Yes	19____	19____	1	2	3
B. Construction	No	Yes	19____	19____	1	2	3
C. Factory:_____ *(Type of factory)*	No	Yes	19____	19____	1	2	3
D. Farming	No	Yes	19____	19____	1	2	3
E. Logging, lumber industry	No	Yes	19____	19____	1	2	3
F. Loud music (performing/ working around)	No	Yes	19____	19____	1	2	3
G. Mining	No	Yes	19____	19____	1	2	3
H. Police, Fire Dept.	No	Yes	19____	19____	1	2	3
I. Printing	No	Yes	19____	19____	1	2	3
J. Transportation (truck, boat, plane, etc.)	No	Yes	19____	19____	1	2	3
K. Any other types of noisy jobs	No	Yes	19____	19____	1	2	3

Describe: _____

NOISE DURING MILITARY SERVICE

2. Were you exposed to noise during military service (including basic training and reserves)?			Date Started	Date Ended	How often did you use hearing protection?		
					Never	Sometimes	Always
A. Artillery	No	Yes	19____	19____	1	2	3
B. Explosion	No	Yes	19____	19____	1	2	3
C. Planes, helicopters	No	Yes	19____	19____	1	2	3
D. Small arms	No	Yes	19____	19____	1	2	3
E. Tanks, other heavy equipment	No	Yes	19____	19____	1	2	3
F. Other types of noise:_____ *(Describe)*	No	Yes	19____	19____	1	2	3

NOISE DURING RECREATION

3. Have you been exposed to noise during recreational or leisure-time activities?			Starting Age	Length of Time	How often did you use hearing protection?		
					Never	Sometimes	Always
A. Gunfire	No	Yes	____	____	1	2	3
B. Loud engines (boat, auto, plane, motorcycle, skimobile)	No	Yes	____	____	1	2	3
C. Loud music	No	Yes	____	____	1	2	3
D. Power tools	No	Yes	____	____	1	2	3
E. Other:_____ *(Describe)*	No	Yes	____	____	1	2	3

4. Have you undergone any accidental exposure to sudden, intense noise?

No........1 *(Go on to next page)*

Yes.......2

4a. Type of noise: _____

4b. Your age then: _____ years

4c. Which ear or side?

LEFT ear 1
RIGHT ear 2
BOTH ears 3
Not sure 4

Adapted from Meikle, Griest & Press (1986)   11.10.94

MEDICAL HISTORY

Name: _____   Birthdate: _____

　　　　Last　　　　　　First　　　　　　Initial　　　　　　　　Month/ Day/ Year

1. Have you had any of the medical problems listed below? If you have not had the problem, CIRCLE (No). If you have had the problem CIRCLE (Yes). Please fill in the blank showing how old you were when the problem began. Also, indicate whether you have the problem now.

Have you had...		About how old were you when problem began?	Do you have this problem now?	
Heart disease ....No	Yes	_____years old	No	Yes
High blood pressure ....No	Yes	_____years old	No	Yes
Hardening of arteries.........................No (arteriosclerosis)	Yes	_____years old	No	Yes
Varicose veins, phlebitis ....No	Yes	_____years old	No	Yes
Stroke ....No	Yes	_____years old	No	Yes
Emphysema, asthma ....No	Yes	_____years old	No	Yes
Arthritis or rheumatism ....No	Yes	_____years old	No	Yes
Diabetes ....No	Yes	_____years old	No	Yes
Thyroid problem ....No	Yes	_____years old	No	Yes
Kidney disease ....No	Yes	_____years old	No	Yes
Cancer..No	Yes	_____years old	No	Yes
Depression ....No	Yes	_____years old	No	Yes

Do you have **other** significant health problems?　No .... 1　　Yes 2
IF **YES**: Please list problems below:

_____	_____years old	No	Yes
_____	_____years old	No	Yes
_____	_____years old	No	Yes
_____	_____years old	No	Yes

(Please use an extra sheet of paper if you need more space for any questions on this page.)

2. What medications are you taking currently?

Medication name:	Taken for what condition:	Started about when:
_____	_____	_____ years old
_____	_____	_____ years old
_____	_____	_____ years old
_____	_____	_____ years old

3. Have you had surgery for any reason?　　No........1　　Yes........2

Surgery #1: _____ at about _____years old

Surgery #2: _____ at about _____years old

Surgery #3: _____ at about _____years old

4. Have you been hospitalized for severe burn, wound, or other serious medical problems? No......1 Yes......2

Problem #1: _____ at about _____years old

Problem #2: _____ at about _____years old

Adapted from Meikle, Griest & Press (1986)　　　　　　　　　　　　　　　　　　11.10.94

OREGON HEARING RESEARCH CENTER   Medical History, Page 10

5. How often do you take over-the-counter medications for pain, headache or arthritis?	Never or almost never	Once a week or less	Several days each week	Once a day	More than once each day
A. Aspirin (Anacin, Excedrin, Empirin, Ascriptin) 1	2	3	4	5
B. Ibuprofen (Advil, Nuprin, Motrin) 1	2	3	4	5
C. Acetaminophen (Tylenol, Datril) 1	2	3	4	5
D. Other pain medication: _____ 1	2	3	4	5
E. Other pain medication: _____ 1	2	3	4	5

(Name of medication)

6. If you have tinnitus, have any medications caused your tinnitus to change in any way?
   No 1
   Yes 2
   Do not have tinnitus 3

   If **YES**, list medications that caused tinnitus changes and describe how tinnitus changed:
   _____
   _____
   _____

7. How often do you get headaches?
   Rarely 1
   Several per month 2
   Several per week 3
   Daily 4

8. Are headaches a significant problem for you?
   Not a problem 1
   Small problem 2
   Moderate problem 3
   Big problem 4
   Very big problem 5

9. Have you had any problems with your teeth or jaw?
   No .... 1 *(Go on to Q.10)*
   Yes 2

   9a. Pain or discomfort of jaw .... No   Yes
   9b. Incorrect bite or other
       misalignment .... No   Yes
   9c. Jaw injury, surgery, infection .... No   Yes
   9d. Clicking or other noise in jaw .... No   Yes

   9e. When did you **start** having problems with
       your teeth or jaw? _____ years old

   9f. Are you currently having problems with your
       teeth or jaw? .... No   Yes

10. If you have tinnitus, does it **change** when you move your jaw or clench your teeth?
    No change 1
    Tinnitus gets louder 2
    Tinnitus gets softer 3
    Tinnitus changes in other way(s) 4
    Do not have tinnitus 5

11. How often have you needed medical care during the past 6 months? For each question, please CIRCLE the answer that best describes you:	Never	Once	Two-three times	More than three times
During the past 6 months...				
A. How many times were **you** admitted as a patient in a **hospital**? 1	2	3	4
B. How many times did **you** receive treatment at an **emergency room or urgent care center**? 1	2	3	4
C. How many separate times did **you** need to visit a **medical doctor or clinic** (not counting hospital, emergency room or urgent care)? 1	2	3	4

5-10: Adapted from Meikle, Griest & Press (1986); 11: Adapted from Kaiser Permanente, NW Region (undated)   11.10.94

OREGON HEARING RESEARCH CENTER   Medical History, Page 11

HEALTH AND DAILY LIFE

Because of a physical or health problem, do you have any difficulty when you do the following activities by yourself and without using special equipment?	HOW MUCH DIFFICULTY?			
	NO DIFFICULTY	SOME	A LOT	UNABLE TO DO IT
1. Preparing your own meals 1		2	3	4
2. Shopping for personal items (such as toilet items or medicines) 1		2	3	4
3. Managing your money (such as keeping track of expenses, or paying bills) 1		2	3	4
4. Using the telephone 1		2	3	4
5. Doing heavy housework (like scrubbing floors, or washing windows) 1		2	3	4
6. Doing light housework (like dishes, straightening up, or light cleaning) 1		2	3	4

People sometimes have problems doing their normal daily activities if they have chronic, long lasting health problems of any type, including hearing problems or tinnitus.

When you think back over the past 6 months, have you had any trouble doing your work or other regular daily activities, as a result of problems with your hearing, or tinnitus, or your overall health?

In the past 6 months, have you found that you...

7. Had to take **frequent rests** when doing work or other activities .... No   Yes

8. Cut down the **amount of time** you spent on work or other activities .... No   Yes

9. **Accomplished less** than you would like .... No   Yes

10. Did not do work or other activities as **carefully** as usual .... No   Yes

11. Were limited in the **kind** of work or other activities .... No   Yes

12. Had **difficulty** performing work or other activities (for example, it took extra effort) .... No   Yes

13. Required **special assistance** (the assistance of others, or special devices) .... No   Yes

14. Are you currently employed?
    YES,
        Employed full-time 1
        Employed part-time or on-call 2

    NO,
        Retired 3
        Looking for employment 4
        Unemployed because of health 5
        Other reason: 6
        _____
        (Please describe)

15. What kind of work have you done most of your working life?_____
    _____

16. What is your current marital status?
        Married, living with spouse 1
        Married, separated 2
        Widowed... 3
        Divorced 4
        Never married.................................... 5

17. Compared to other persons your age, would you say that your health is:
        Excellent 1
        Very good 2
        Good............................... 3
        Fair 4
        Poor 5

1-6: Adapted from 1984 National Health Interview Survey, Supplement on Aging; 7-13,17:Adapted from RAND (1986);14:Adapted from Neal (1990);15&16:Stewart & Archibold (1994)   11.10.94

The following questionnaire lists some problems people sometimes have, particularly if they have any type of chronic health condition. Even if you do not have any chronic health conditions, it would help us to know which of these problems might apply to you.

When trying to decide whether a statement applies to you, THINK BACK OVER THE PAST 6 MONTHS. If the statement is true for you, CIRCLE one of the numbers on that same line, to indicate the correct description. If it does not apply to you over the past 6 months, select "1" (to indicate "not at all").

HOW MUCH DOES THE STATEMENT APPLY TO YOU?	NOT AT ALL	A LITTLE	A MODERATE AMOUNT	QUITE A BIT	VERY MUCH
1. I have difficulty falling asleep	1	2	3	4	5
2. I have difficulty staying asleep	1	2	3	4	5
3. My appetitite is poor	1	2	3	4	5
4. I am not able to work	1	2	3	4	5
5. I lose too much work time because of health problems	1	2	3	4	5
6. I am not able to perform all of my duties at home or at work because of health problems	1	2	3	4	5
7. I have difficulty concentrating	1	2	3	4	5
8. I have difficulty remembering	1	2	3	4	5
9. I have difficulty thinking clearly	1	2	3	4	5
10. I have difficulty doing household chores	1	2	3	4	5
11. I have difficulty with transportation	1	2	3	4	5
12. It is hard for me to get out of the house very much	1	2	3	4	5
13. I am sitting or lying down most of the day	1	2	3	4	5
14. I have difficulty enjoying time with relatives and/or friends	1	2	3	4	5
15. I have problems in planning social activities because I do not know how I will feel	1	2	3	4	5
16. I have difficulty going out to dinner, movies and other activities	1	2	3	4	5
17. Family or friends do not come over to visit often	1	2	3	4	5
18. I do not get along well with my family	1	2	3	4	5
19. It has been difficult to maintain old friendships	1	2	3	4	5
20. I find it difficult to meet new friends	1	2	3	4	5
21. My family expects me to do more than I am capable of doing	1	2	3	4	5
22. I have difficulty relaxing	1	2	3	4	5
23. I feel irritated or nervous quite often	1	2	3	4	5

Adapted from Kames, Naliboff, Heinrich & Schag (1984)

11.10.94

19

Tinnitus Masking with Tinnitus–Maskers and Hearing Aids

A Longitudinal Study of Efficacy From 1987 to 1993

PROF. DR. HASSO VON WEDEL

ULLA–CHRISTIANE VON WEDEL

DR. RER.NAT. MARTIN WALGER
Universitäts–Hals–Nasen–Ohrenklinik Köln
(Direktor: Prof. Dr. E. Stennert)
Köln, Germany

RESULTS OF THE STUDY

This paper reports the results of the acoustical therapy with tinnitus maskers (TM) and with hearing aids (HA) for patients with severe disabling chronic tinnitus from May 1987 to April 1993. This longitudinal study covers the results of 792 patients over a period of two years visiting our tinnitus clinic at the ENT department of the University Clinic of Cologne. To compare the benefits of hearing aids or tinnitus maskers over a period of at least one year the patients were examined for the features of tinnitus, masking effects during use, residual inhibition effects after use, and subjective scaling of the therapeutic efficiency.

In 62.7 percent of the patients a partial masking via environmental noises could be produced by hearing aids, in 18.5 percent by tinnitus masker. Complete masking was reported by 17.3 percent of the patients using a hearing aid and 76.9 percent using a tinnitus masker. After a trial instrumentation over a period of at least four to six weeks, 18.7 percent (on rental base) purchased a hearing aid and 5.6 percent a tinnitus masker. After one year the return rate was 7.4 percent for the hearing aid instrumentation and 19.8 percent for the tinnitus masker. The return rate of the devices increased to 9.6 percent for the hearing aids and 24.7 percent for the tinnitus masker after two years. The results were completed by investigations of residual inhibition effects after the rental trial. About 94.7 percent of the hearing aid users reported a partial or complete residual inhibition lasting less than thirty seconds and 0.3 percent lasting about sixty seconds. The occurrence of total residual inhibition for less than thirty seconds was found in 71.3 percent of the patients with tinnitus maskers. 15.7 percent reported one minute lasting residual inhibition effects and 13 percent lasting up to 2 to 3 hours. Our results confirm earlier investigations of our working group showing a stable benefit for more than 90 percent for those patients wearing hearing aids and about 75 percent using tinnitus maskers.

INTRODUCTION

Besides therapeutic electrical auditory stimulation via iontophoreres or directly at the promontory, acupuncture, neural therapy, psychotherapy, biofeedback, combination of low power laser and ginkgo, hyperbasic oxygenation and different medial treatments have been tried in tinnitus therapy. Tinnitus devices like hearing aids, tinnitus maskers, and tinnitus instruments have met ongoing interest in Germany since the Third International Tinnitus Seminar in 1987. Tinnitus masking provides control over the tinnitus that affords significant benefit for those suffering from severe chronic tinnitus. Hearing aids or tinnitus maskers may provide partial or complete masking accompanied by residual inhibition after use lasting normally for at least thirty to sixty seconds and occasionally up to several hours. The limitations and possibilities of these devices have been tested in a variety of locations. Examinations with regard to longitudinal effects, however, are rare and very controversial.

Other investigators using masking devices such as the tinnitus clinic in Oregon report success between 58 percent and 65 percent for several thousand patients based upon two–year follow ups. Von Wedel and Opitz, working in Germany, reviewed 34 patients for a follow–up period of more than one year, differentiating between daily and occasional use. A total of 18 (53%) were using their device daily while the remainder resorted to occasional use as need directed. Shulman and Goldstein reported a positive tinnitus control for about 22 percent of their patients who had used their tinnitus maskers for several years. Von Wedel could show a stable benefit for 80 percent wearing hearing aids and 65 percent using tinnitus maskers over a test period of more than three years. To compare the benefit of hearing aids and tinnitus maskers over a utilization period of one to three, years 792 patients with severe disabling chronic tinnitus were examined for the features of tinnitus, degree of masking during use, residual inhibition after use, and subjective scaling as to the therapeutic efficiency.

THE STUDY

All patients completed a medical audiological evaluation consisting of a complete neuro–otological examination including a cochleo–vestibular evaluation, tinnitus evaluation within a complete audiological examination (tinnitus frequency and intensity, masking curves, tinnitus threshold shift of masking intensity, measurement of residual inhibition), selection of appropriate instrumentation based on the audiological and tinnitus evaluation results, first trial in the clinic with hearing aids and/or tinnitus maskers, a trial period of at least two to four weeks, and follow–up visits after purchase over a period of up to three years.

In cases of normal audiogram or mild hearing loss, a tinnitus masker (Starkey TNS/TN5) was tested, in cases of moderate to severe hearing loss, especially in high frequency losses with tinnitus, a hearing aid alone was chosen. The goal of the use of the tinnitus masker is to establish a comfortable masking level for partial or complete tinnitus masking effects. The use of the hearing aid should include training with respect to masking influences by environmental noises. The patients were free to control frequency, duration, and time of use of the instrumentation.

The result of instrumentation for May 1987 to April 1993 included 792 patients. All patients performed a short trial with hearing aids ($n = 472$) and/or tinnitus maskers ($n = 648$) during their investigations at our clinic (Table 19–1). Of this number 472 (60%) were recommended hearing aids and 648 (82%) were recommended tinnitus maskers for a rental trial of a device via a hearing aid acoustician. Of those who followed through with a rental trial 88 (19%) purchased the hearing aids and 36 (6%) purchased the tinnitus masker. After one year 8 (9%) returned hearing aids and 6 (17%) returned tinnitus maskers. After two years 9 (10%) returned hearing aids and 8 (22%) returned tinnitus maskers. Objections to the devices have included less suffering from tinnitus without the device (a reduction in the intensity of the tinnitus), negative cosmetic aspects of the devices (maskers look exactly like hearing aids), more and effec-

TABLE 19–1   **Hearing Aid and Tinnitus Masker (1987–1993)**

Type of Device	Rental Trial	Purchase	Return after 1 year	Return after 2 years
HEARING AID	**472** (59.6%)	**88** (18.6%)	**8** (9.1%)	**9** (10.2%)
TINNITUS MASKER	**648** (81.8%)	**36** (5.6%)	**6** (16.7%)	**8** (22.2%)

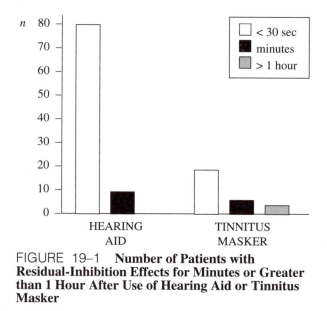

FIGURE 19–1   **Number of Patients with Residual-Inhibition Effects for Minutes or Greater than 1 Hour After Use of Hearing Aid or Tinnitus Masker**

tive use of external noise sources, lack of a complete masking effect, no, or too short, occurrence of residual inhibition and no long lasting "cure" of tinnitus.

Residual inhibition with a duration of some minutes were reported by 9 patients with hearing aids and 7 patients with tinnitus maskers after one year of utilization. More than one hour of residual inhibition, up to three hours in three cases, was displayed by no patients with hearing aids and six patients with tinnitus maskers (see Figure 19–1).

When scaling the efficiency of tinnitus therapy by hearing aids or tinnitus maskers using a scale from 0 to 6 with 0 being the lowest rating, the results correlated with the time the devices were used (Figure 19–2). In no case was there a loss of hearing or a persistent increased intensity of tinnitus following the use of instrumentation.

CONCLUSION

The ability to mask tinnitus in the frequency range of 2 to 6 kHz by hearing aids or tinnitus maskers gives important relief to those patients suffering from severe chronic tinnitus. The reported results of two therapeutic strategies (hearing aids and tinnitus maskers) over a period of at least one year of use show a stable benefit for most of the patients. Because some other therapeutic concepts like the low power laser in combination with ginkgo have not yielded the often reported claims, the approaches described in this paper are still of utmost importance in combating tinnitus. With regard to the use of tinnitus maskers to produce long lasting residual inhibition, no pos-

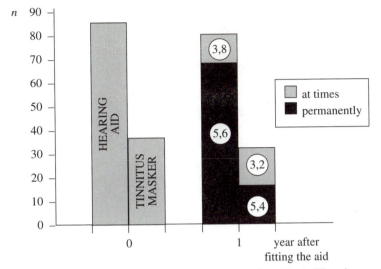

FIGURE 19–2 **Number of Patients Wearing Their Hearing Aid or Tinnitus Masker Permanently or at Times After One Year of Use; From the Scale of 1 to 6 with Regard to the Subjective Success of the Therapy, the Mean Values Are Placed in Circles Inside Each Column**

itive claims can be reported from our study and possibly for the reason that the tinnitus masker intensities were fixed at a level to just mask the tinnitus either partially or completely and not to a level 10 dB above the minimal masking level.

PATIENT'S QUESTIONS AND ANSWERS

1. *Question:* In your introduction you mentioned hearing aids, tinnitus maskers, and tinnitus instruments as devices that were receiving attention. In your presentation you compared hearing aids and tinnitus maskers. What are tinnitus instruments and should they have also been compared?
   Answer: Tinnitus instruments are combination units that include a hearing aid and a tinnitus masker in a single case but with separate volume controls. The tinnitus instrument is much like the simultaneous use of a hearing aid and a masker. And, yes, we should have also compared the use of tinnitus instruments.

2. *Question:* I think I understand the use of a tinnitus masker, but I fail to understand how a hearing aid can relieve tinnitus?
   Answer: The hearing aid amplifies environmental sounds and speech sounds that are relatively low pitched sounds. If the patient has a hearing loss for the low

pitches and also has low pitched tinnitus then the hearing aid has an excellent chance of masking the tinnitus with the improved hearing for low pitched environmental sounds.

3. *Question:*   How would I know whether I should try a hearing aid or a tinnitus masker?

   Answer: As a general rule, if you have hearing loss of any type, trying the hearing aid is recommended to see if it can not only improve your hearing ability but if it will also mask your tinnitus. You have mentioned the key word; you said "try" and that is the main thing. You should try the hearing aid, and you should try the tinnitus masker and then select the one that works best. The interesting thing is that you will know almost immediately if the unit will produce relief for you.

4. *Question:*   If I am fitted with a tinnitus masker, do I wear it all the time or intermittently?

   Answer: No, you only use the tinnitus masker when you feel you need relief from your tinnitus. Some patients wear maskers twenty-four hours a day and some only use them occasionally. You determine when you need masking and when you do not need masking. Do you see that with masking you are in control of the tinnitus rather than the tinnitus controlling you? When masking works, you can determine when you will and when you will not hear your tinnitus.

5. *Question:*   What do tinnitus maskers look like?

   Answer: They look exactly like a hearing aid. Indeed, they are encased in hearing aid cases, and they can be obtained as an in–the–ear or a behind–the–ear unit.

20

The Role of High Frequency Audiometry in the Evaluation of the Tinnitus Patient

J. DOMÈNECH, M.D.
Dept. of ORL, Hospital Clínic, Faculty of Medicine
University of Barcelona
Barcelona, Spain

When a patient complains to his physician about a noise in his or her ear, the first test that is prescribed is usually a tonal audiometry. This test has really nothing to do with the tinnitus but it tells us something very important: the current status of the different mechanisms that form the hearing apparatus.

Hearing loss is a common finding in tinnitus patients, and we can assume that, in most cases, these two symptoms are both caused by a single disease, which is the one we want to diagnose. The type of the hearing loss (conductive or sensorineural) and its severity, together with several other factors, tell us a lot about what is happening inside the ear. For these reasons, tonal audiometry is the most important audiological test.

However, in this test we do not really assess the whole of the frequency range of human hearing because of physical restrictions. Our hearing extends from about 20 Hz, in the low tones, to about 20,000 Hz, which is the highest frequency that a young person can hear. I want to stress the word *young,* because the upper limit of the frequency range decreases slowly with advancing age, at a predictable rate in the absence of any ear disease.

Current clinical audiometers can only assess hearing thresholds up to 8000 Hz by air conduction, and up to 4000 to 6000 kHz by bone conduction. This suffices largely when we want to evaluate hearing thresholds for other reasons, such as before and after operations, because the important hearing frequencies are between 125 and 4000 Hz. These two values are the limits of the so-called conversational frequencies, which are just that: the tones which matter for understanding speech and for human relationship.

But frequencies above 8000 Hz are also interesting from several points of view. We know that most diseases of the inner ear impair hearing first in these high tones, extending to middle and low frequencies as the disease advances. For example, the effects of drugs and medications that are toxic for the inner ear appear primarily in the frequencies above 8000 Hz, and for this reason these effects are not detected until hearing in this frequency begins to deteriorate. Similarly, noise-induced hearing loss damages primarily the inner ear cells in the basal turn of the cochlea, the ones responsible for hearing the highest frequencies.

The technique of tinnitus matching, or comparing the tinnitus to an external generator of tones (usually, an audiometer) to know its frequency and intensity, requires that the audiometer be capable of generating all the auditory frequencies. If this is not the case, any tinnitus above 8000 Hz will be impossible to match. Finally, the audiological assessment of a patient is not complete without the evaluation of hearing thresholds in all the frequencies that the patient can hear.

The meaning of all this is that it is important to assess hearing thresholds in the complete frequency range of human hearing and to match all the possible frequencies of the tinnitus. These results can be of help in the diagnosis and management of this elusive symptom. The following is a report of a study whose purpose was to assess patients with tinnitus with conventional audiometry (CA) and high-frequency audiometry (HFA), in order to know the differences that exist between the two types of auditory evaluation and to find out exactly the incidence of hearing loss among tinnitus patients.

Fifty-eight patients with subjective tinnitus and without conductive hearing loss were studied with CA and HFA. CA thresholds were considered normal if no frequency was below 25 dB. HFA was performed with an Audimax 500 electro-stimulation audiometer, which overcomes several of the limitations of current clinical audiometers by using mild electrical currents to elicit auditory sensations within the cochlea. It is also possible to assess high frequencies by air conduction; in fact, it is easier by this approach, as there are several commercially available audiometers able to generate high-frequency tones through ceramic earphones.

As high-frequency hearing thresholds depend on the age of the subject, the results of the tests in this study were compared against reference values established previously from 300 normal subjects, distributed in several age groups. These reference values are only valid for this kind of audiometer and should not be used for air-conduction tests. The results were considered "normal," "within one SD of normal," and "beyond one SD," according to how these results compared against reference values.

When CA results were considered, 19 patients (27.1%) had hearing thresholds within normal limits. However, when HFA was performed, only 5 patients (7.1%) had their thresholds within one SD of mean reference values for their age group. The 14 additional patients found to be outside normal limits were considered completely normal on the basis of CA results.

In other words, about 73 percent of the patients with tinnitus show some degree of hearing loss on CA, which is perfectly unremarkable. However, there is about a quarter of tinnitus patients with apparently "normal" hearing thresholds, which is not easy to understand. However, when all the auditory frequencies are assessed, the patients with hypoacusia are now 93 percent of the total, because in 20 percent of them the shift is above the frequency limit of conventional audiometers (and has not been noticed in CA tests).

I am still surprised because some patients have both tinnitus and normal high-frequency hearing thresholds, as 7 percent of the patients show; as tinnitus is, or should be, a symptom of a disorder in the auditory sensorineural pathways, this 7 percent of normal-hearing patients is a challenge. By the way, these patients also show normal results on BERA tests (which evaluate the progress of auditory neural signals through the lower central nervous system).

Tinnitus is a symptom that usually means some kind of disturbance in the sensorineural hearing pathway. As such, it should be associated to some degree of hearing loss. As most sensorineural hearing impairments show only in the uppermost frequencies that a patient can hear, it is evident that some of these impairments will not be detected if HFA is not performed.

HFA has other uses in these patients. One of them is that with high-frequency data it is possible to make some kind of prognosis about how the hearing thresholds of a patient will evolve in the future. One of the worries of someone who has tinnitus is what will happen to his or her hearing, a question we are sometimes not able to answer. As HFA allows us to see what happens in the upper frequency limit, and this is the place where the first changes usually take place, we have a greater scope to deduce if hearing thresholds will or will not worsen in the near future.

In subsequent controls of the patient, HFA is a more discriminating tool than CA to discover small changes in hearing levels. In this way, even if this technique does not help us directly to trace the origin of tinnitus, it is a very useful addition to our test battery to increase our knowledge about what causes this irritating auditory symptom and how to control it.

PATIENT'S QUESTIONS AND ANSWERS

1. *Question:* Is it the case that many tinnitus patients suffer with high pitched tonal type of tinnitus?
Answer: Yes, the data from the Tinnitus Data Registry compiled at the Oregon Hearing Research Center indicates that in a sample of 1544 patients with severe

tinnitus, 1217 (79%) have tonal tinnitus while 327 (21%) have a noise type tinnitus. Tonal tinnitus is similar to the sound produced by hitting one key on a piano while noise type tinnitus is composed of many tones such as a hissing or a humming sound. Of those with tonal tinnitus, the average pitch match is 6000 Hz. To orient you, the highest note on the grand piano is slightly above 4000 Hz. Of the patients with tonal tinnitus, 90 percent had a pitch match between 3000 and 12,000 Hz. One of the disturbing features of tinnitus is its high pitched screeching quality.

2. *Question:*   Does knowledge of the pitch of my tinnitus help you in relieving it?
   Answer: Yes. If we attempt to mask your tinnitus with an applied sound, it is important to know which pitches the masking noise must include. It is also important for those cases that are above the capability of the present day masking devices. For example, we have seen a few patients with tinnitus pitched higher than 18,000 Hz, and there is no masking equipment currently capable of producing such high pitched sounds.

3. *Question:*   If high frequency audiometry reveals that a patient has high frequency hearing loss, will hearing aids help with their tinnitus?
   Answer: There are cases for which hearing aids have relieved tinnitus, but usually those patients have a relatively low pitched tinnitus accompanied with hearing loss which extends down into the low frequencies. Patients who have both high pitched tinnitus and high frequency hearing loss utilize tinnitus instruments for relief. See the section on Masking.

4. *Question:*   If my tinnitus is so high pitched as to be unmaskable, is there any other treatment to try?
   Answer: Yes, and the answer is to try the drug Xanax, which has been demonstrated to be effective against most forms of tinnitus. Whether it will work for a given case can only be determined by an actual trial test with it.

5. *Question:*   My tinnitus is in a dead ear, thus audiometry of any sort is impossible. Does that also mean that there are no treatments available for me?
   Answer: No, there are two possibilities to try with patients such as you. First of all, however, one would want to check to insure that your ear is truly dead. Often, if the hearing is sufficiently depressed as to prevent benefit in understanding speech with hearing aids, it is considered to be totally deaf when, in fact, there may be sufficient hearing with which to effect masking of the tinnitus. If the tinnitus ear is truly and totally deaf, then the first thing to try is contralateral masking, that is, masking delivered to the opposite and good ear. Sometimes that works, and we can only know if it will work by trying it. If contralateral masking does not work, then we would recommend a trial with the drug Xanax indicated above.

▶ 21

Tinnitus and the Jaw Joint (TMJ)

DOUGLAS MORGAN, D.D.S.
La Crescenta, California

In 1959 I was working with another oral surgeon doing surgery for ankylosis. This is a condition in which there is fusion of the hard and/or soft tissue of the jaw joint. This condition is obvious as the patient is able to open the mouth no more than a quarter of an inch, or in some cases, not at all. We would surgically free the bony or fibrous union, and then place a metal Vitallium implant that would prevent refusion of the bone.

Some of these patients afterwards mentioned to me they not only could open their mouths better, but they no longer had headaches or neck aches. Also, they stated the ringing sound in their ears was better or eliminated entirely. Some stated their hearing was improved, and sensitivity to loud sounds reduced. Others said their dizziness or nausea was better.

I asked them why they had not mentioned these symptoms to me before. They stated, "I told my doctor about them. Why would I mention them to you, a dentist?" I understood their reasoning. However, I was intrigued by their multiple symptom reduction after TMJ ankylosis surgery.

The only thing I learned about TMJ as an undergraduate student at USC Dental School was that there was a jaw joint called the temporomandibular joint. It was variously misspelled and mispronounced.

My early works on TMJ were published more than twenty years ago. One article published in the Southern California State Dental Association Journal in 1971 discussed five patients with TMJ disorders. Three of these people had tinnitus along with their other symptoms. In all three cases, there was a reduction or elimination of the tinnitus as a secondary effect of TMJ surgery using a Vitallium articular eminence prosthesis.

Three more patients with tinnitus were discussed in a 1973 article. Two of the three patients had tinnitus before surgery and no tinnitus after TMJ surgery. In this article, for the first time I discussed the work of Doctors Olympio Pinto and David Goodfriend. Dr. Pinto came from Brazil to the United States to get his master's degree from the Georgetown University School of Medicine. In his anatomic research, which was encouraged by Dr. Goodfriend, he discovered a tiny structure missing from textbooks on anatomy at that time. The significance of this research was the establishment of a structural link between the ear and the jaw. Dr. Pinto's description of his work includes this statement: "A tiny ligament was found connecting the neck of the anterior process of the malleus to the medio posterior-superior part of the capsule, the interarticular disc, and this sphenomandibular ligament. This fibrous layer of the tympanic membrane seemed to be continuous with the structure. The tiny ligament has an embryological origin common with that of the malleus and incus."

I have called TMJ disease "The Great Impostor," because TMJ disorder mimics so many different disorders and seemingly unrelated symptoms. Doctors Bernstein, Mohl, and Spiller have stated, "Perhaps the most important idea to convey is that this syndrome of pain and dysfunction can masquerade as acute or chronic disease of the ear, nose, and throat." TMJ dysfunction produces symptoms initially diagnosed as migraine, ear and mastoid pain, vertigo, eustachian tube malfunction or secretary otitis media, pain in the zygomatic arch and fullness in the cheek, acute sinusitis, or pain in the preauricular area and gonial angle, as well as paratitis.

In 1976, in an article that appeared in the *Journal of the American Medical Association*, I commented that tinnitus can be one of the many symptoms caused by a disorder of the temporomandibular joint (TMJ).

More recently, an article in the ear-nose-and-throat journal, *The Laryngoscope,* details a fourteen-year study of the results of TMJ implant surgery using Vitallium articular eminence devices. This unique longitudinal study utilized a questionnaire in which the patient was sent details of his original TMJ questionnaire along with a new questionnaire asking him to indicate whether these original pain and dysfunction symptoms had improved, not changed, or were worse. Additional data was collected on nonpain symptoms, such as ringing in the ears, dizziness, and nausea. Data was collected by an independent research group, The Orthopedic Research Division of the 3-M Company, Minneapolis-St. Paul, Minnesota, and entered into a computer. The fourteen-year study results showed that of those who reported tinnitus, 21.7 percent had total elimination of that symptom, 17.1 percent had improvement, 19.4 percent had no change, and 6.2 percent were worse. These patients who had surgery were individuals who generally had already undergone nonsurgical TMJ therapy without results. There was organic disease in the jaw joints, usually an osteoarthritis. It is not difficult to extrapolate similar or better results might be obtained from nonsurgical treatment as well, if the problem is recognized early on. It is my considerate opinion of over thirty years of seeing and treating TMJ patients that a significant percentage of people with tinnitus symptoms may be suffering from one of the many manifestations of TMJ disorders.

Recently, a 1983 study sponsored by the American Tinnitus Association showed an important relationship between TMJ disorders and tinnitus. Twenty individuals were selected, whose primary symptom was ringing in the ears. They had all been to ear specialists to rule out organic ear disease or trauma, or other causes that might account for the symptom. They were not known to be TMJ patients. They did not have pain and/or dysfunction that could be related to the TMJ. Eight separate tests were done on each person, X-Ray studies, clinical examination, electromyographic tests (EMG), jaw tracking studies by computerized mandibular scans (CMS), jaw joint sounds, and so on. It was discovered, on analyzing these tests, that 19 of the 20 patients studied had at least one positive test for organic TMJ disease. Ten of the 20 people had tested positive on all eight tests for a TMJ disorder.

In 1992, Dr. Richard Chole, writing in the ENT literature, did a study on over 1000 patients. Over 300 had temporomandibular disorder (TMD), and nearly 700 people served as two age-matched control groups. He found tinnitus and vertigo were significantly more prevalent in the temporomandibular disorders group than in either of the control groups. Dr. Chole further stated, "The mechanism of the association of TMD and otological symptoms is unknown."

It had been postulated that Pinto's ligament, also called the disco-malleolar ligament, or anterior malleolar ligament, was the connection between the jaw joint and the ear. Our clinical experience through thirty years showed that when a TMJ patient who has ear symptoms such as tinnitus is treated for pain and/or dysfunction, the ear symptoms are often reduced or eliminated. Common sense told us there had to be some relationship between the ear and TMJ that would account for these symptoms. However, animal research was not possible. In animal experimentation, the subjects cannot respond and say their ears do not ring, or they are no longer dizzy, or they hear more clearly, and so on.

There is an old saying, "It is an ill wind that does not blow someone good." There was a company, Vitek, now out of business, that made TMJ Teflon-Proplast implants that covered the entire upper part of the jaw joint, (the socket). They did not understand the anatomy of the fossa (socket) and the importance of the opening (fissure) in the back portion of the jaw joint socket. Another company still manufactures an implant that covers this same opening. In fact, in the out-of-date patent, it purposely covers this opening (fissure) to prevent ankylosis (joint fusion). They are now using this implant for other purposes than bone and/or tissue fusions. In any event, when these implants are placed over this fissure, they can interfere with not only the anterior malleolar ligament, or Pinto's ligament, but with a nerve that goes to the tongue (chorda tympany) and the anterior tympanic artery that goes to the tissues surrounding the ear drum. After these implant surgeries, the patient can now have ringing in the ears, dizziness (vertigo), subjective hearing loss, super acute hearing (hyperacusis), and even tongue pain. They did not have these symptoms before implant surgery.

When these implants are removed and a metal implant we have designed that does not cover this fissure is placed, the ear symptoms are eliminated or greatly reduced. I and a number of other surgeons have experienced this same reaction. An article has been published on this discovery in the scientific literature. We can say unequivocally that anything that interferes with these structures in the TMJ can cause ear and other ear-related symptoms. Anyone with tinnitus should have the temporomandibular apparatus carefully checked by someone who understands this joint.

For a period of time, it may be difficult to find these people. It will take a number of years to convince, educate, and then train the ENT specialist and dental practitioners on how to diagnose and treat the TMJ with related ear symptoms.

PATIENT'S QUESTIONS AND ANSWERS

1. *Question:*   My tinnitus was initiated by exposure to fire crackers that went off very near my ear about ten years ago. Is it possible that, in the meantime, I could have developed a TMJ problem that has gradually exacerbated my tinnitus?
    Answer: That possibility is greatly enhanced if you are displaying any of the other TMJ signs, such as jaw pain, alteration of tinnitus upon jaw movement, and so on.

2. *Question:*   I gather that tinnitus can be caused by or exacerbated by TMJ dysfunction. Does it follow then that the presence of tinnitus may indicate TMJ dysfunction?
    Answer: Yes, it is possible. A recently published study of 20 people who had tinnitus and no TMJ symptoms was done. Eight separate tests for TMJ disorders were done. Nineteen of the 20 people had at least one positive test for TMJ. Half of these 20 had all eight signs of a TMJ disorder.

3. *Question:*   If I have a TMJ problem and tinnitus, how is it treated?
    Answer: Most people, 90 percent, will be treated nonsurgically. This involves such treatments as a neuro-muscular orthotic, a bite altering device, physical therapy, muscle T.P. (trigger point) injections, calcium supplements, papaya enzymes, orthodontics, and other modalities. Ten percent may require some form of surgery. Arthroscopic procedures may help in early stages of disc dysfunction. In cases of a torn disc and bony damage (osteoarthritis), an alloplastic implant (metal) over the temporal bone eminence may help.

4. *Question:*   Is there a jaw joint-ear connection?
    Answer: Yes, with recent anatomic research, we now feel confident a ligament from the malleous in the middle ear connects to the jaw joint. Movement of the capsule and disc of the TMJ moves this ligament and can cause inner ear and other symptoms.

▶ # 22

Treatment of Tinnitus Based on a Neurophysiological Model

PAWEL J. JASTREBOFF, Ph.D.
University of Maryland School of Medicine
Baltimore, Maryland

JONATHAN W.P. HAZELL, Ph.D.
RNID Medical Research Unit, ILO with the Ferens, University College
London, England

WHY IS TINNITUS SO HARD TO TREAT?

Ringing in the ears, tinnitus, is a very common experience. In the USA alone, about 44 million people have tinnitus, and for about 10 million it creates a problem sufficiently serious that they are seeking professional help. Typically, medical professionals are not eager to deal with the problem of tinnitus and tend to recommend that sufferers "learn to live with it." The question remains, Why is tinnitus so difficult to deal with, and why, in spite of the efforts of many people over the centuries, we have not found a cure for tinnitus?

There are many reasons for this, the first of which is that tinnitus is a phantom sound, that is, a sound perceived only by the sufferer. Even using the most advanced equipment, observers cannot hear the sound of tinnitus. This creates difficulties for work aimed at discovering the mechanisms of tinnitus and thereby a new, efficient way of reducing it. The second reason is that when we measure psychoacoustical parameters of tinnitus, for example, its loudness, pitch, and how easy it is to mask, using external sounds as a reference, there is no clear relation between this characterization of tinnitus and the extent of tinnitus-induced annoyance. In other words, even tinnitus that is perceived as a soft sound can induce an enormously high level of annoyance, while a relatively loud tinnitus might not be as annoying. Furthermore, attempts to correlate treatment outcome with these tinnitus parameters have not revealed any systematic relation. There are patients who show significant improvement and for whom tinnitus is not annoying anymore, even though the loudness remains the same, while other patients with softer tinnitus are still annoyed to a large extent.

Attempts to classify tinnitus on the basis of its origin or cause, and to find specific ways of dealing with it based on these classifications, have not been successful. Furthermore, a wide variety of drugs, from those with a specific action on the inner ear to drugs used in psychiatry, have not been systematically helpful. At the moment there is no drug that can be recommended to the average tinnitus patient that has a high chance of relieving tinnitus but does not have the likelihood of very profound side effects.

Neither have surgical approaches been systematically helpful. To make the situation worse, it has been shown that cutting the auditory nerve, which is still promoted by some as a treatment for tinnitus, actually causes tinnitus in about 50 percent of people who did not experience tinnitus before the operation.

With such a pessimistic outlook, the questions is, what can be done, and what approach might offer better help to tinnitus sufferers? In trying to answer these questions, we have promoted an approach, based on neuroscience, which was introduced by Domenneck in 1988 and formally described in 1990. This approach is based on the following reasoning.

If we are forced to accept the fact that we cannot erase the source of tinnitus and that we can have many different sources of tinnitus, even in one patient, we should turn our attention to what is happening between the events triggering tinnitus (most frequently occurring at the periphery) and the level where tinnitus (and indeed all sounds) is perceived—the cerebral cortex. In the absence of any sound we still have high levels of neuronal activity in the auditory nerve, as well as in other nerve cells in the auditory pathways, but this activity is random. The nervous system filters out this activity and therefore we do not perceive it as a sound. This random activity can be considered "a code for silence."

When we are exposed to a sound the random activity within the different fibers in the auditory nerve increases, becomes more regular and synchronized, and the patterns of electrical activity represent quite closely the complex acoustic signals that arrived at the ear drum. The processing of the information at this stage is very limited and it does not allow for selecting one piece of auditory information from another; activity within the auditory nerve reflects faithfully all the sounds that reach our ear.

However, this activity undergoes extensive processing in at least five centers within the auditory pathways before reaching the cortex, where perception of the sound occurs. The important factor to realize is that this processing of information can itself result in changes of the connections within the brain involved in transmitting signals from the ear to the cortex.

THE IMPORTANCE OF BRAIN PLASTICITY

It is well established that the brain has an enormous amount of plasticity; it is constantly undergoing change. Every time we learn something new or memorize a fact or face, small changes occur within the brain by way of modification of the neural connections. But our brain has one shortcoming. It cannot handle too much information at the same time. For example, we cannot understand two people speaking at the same time, we cannot read aloud from a book and write a different text at the same time. This can only be achieved by switching from one task to another. Although the brain is able to perform very complex tasks, it has to focus on one task at a time. Therefore the question is how, in this situation, is it possible to handle an enormous number of different signals (sounds, pictures, aromas, etc.) coming to us through our many different senses?

The solution of this problem is in the filtering capability of the nervous system. Before any information reaches the cortex, it is assessed and evaluated without our awareness. If information is classified as sufficiently important, it is allowed to reach the level of the cortex at which conscious perception of the information occurs. Alternatively, if it is judged as not sufficiently important, it is rejected. For example, when we are talking to someone in a noisy restaurant or at a party, surrounded by other people, we can focus our attention on one particular speaker and ignore, without understanding or perceiving, sounds around us, which may be even louder but that are labelled as not significant. On the other hand, even weak sounds that have special meaning, such as our given name or sounds indicating danger, are perceived even when they are weak, unexpected, and intermixed with other environmental noise. Think how many times you have turned promptly to the sound of your name mentioned in a nearby conversation, of which you have otherwise not heard or understood a single word. Our brain is able to select sounds that are important and ignore those that are not important without being in any way aware of this process.

In addition, we have conscious control over selecting the sounds that, even if not important, we have decided to "listen to." For example we do not normally hear the sound of the refrigerator in our home (except when it is brand new), but we can focus our attention on it and pick it up if we wish. Normally the decision as to whether a sound is important, and whether it is allowed to reach the level of our awareness is made without our conscious decision, in the subcortical pathways of the nervous system. Obviously our brain should work like this because if we always had to decide consciously what signal was important for us, we would have to perceive it first, which would be exactly opposite to the goal of relieving our awareness from an excess of information. Filtering of signals results in selective perception, which stops us from wasting time focusing on large amounts of information that we have already decided are unimportant.

Our brain makes these decisions based on four factors. First, if the signal is new, something that we are experiencing for the first time (like the new refrigerator), it attracts attention and triggers a reaction. Second, the brain makes decisions based on past experiences. If something was important to us because it was pleasant or unpleasant, that is, having a clear emotional message, it is given priority in reaching the level of perception. Third, it depends on what other task our brain is performing at the time. If we are very involved in some activity, stimuli not related to this activity will be ignored. However, if we are just relaxing, doing nothing much, weaker or unimportant stimuli that would normally be rejected will reach us and be drawn to our attention. Fourth, stimuli that are radically different from others being perceived at the same time, will be perceived. This last feature reflects the ability our nervous system in focusing on and enhancing contrast.

The question is, what do all these points have to do with tinnitus? The answer is that if we can utilize this enormously powerful feature of the brain to filter out signals that are not important, then we may be able to remove tinnitus from our awareness. If we can teach the brain to filter out the tinnitus sound, the person will not be aware of the presence of tinnitus even if the tinnitus related activity is still present somewhere in the periphery and would normally be able to reach the level of the cortex where it would be perceived as a sound. It is like the secretary who screens incoming telephone calls so that only a small proportion get through and are answered by the boss. A very similar task can be achieved by the nervous system. In neuroscience the disappearance of a reaction to a stimulus is called the process of habituation. Consequently, the method of handling tinnitus aimed at habituation of tinnitus perception is called a neurophysiological approach to tinnitus, since it uses neurophysiological principles applicable to the central nervous system rather than focusing on the source of tinnitus signal, which usually is in the inner ear.

The goal of the approach is to habituate tinnitus sound, for example, to create a situation in which the tinnitus sufferer is not aware of the presence of tinnitus for the majority of the time, or not at all, but still can perceive tinnitus if he or she focuses attention on the tinnitus sound. The tinnitus source or trigger is unchanged; but the signal that is normally perceived as a tinnitus sound is blocked before it reaches the cortex and our awareness.

TINNITUS HABITUATION

How can tinnitus habituation be achieved? To answer this question, we have to go back to the basic findings of neuroscience and psychology relating to how perception and learning occurs. It was mentioned already that our brain is filtering out unimportant signals. The physical strength or other parameters of the signal are only loosely related to our reaction or how easily we can ignore the sound; what is important is the meaning associated with the sound. A child learning to play the piano can offer a good example of this principle. If the child is our own and we are trying to encourage him or her to learn, the sound of the child practicing might be slightly annoying at first, but we can quickly ignore it and read the newspaper. If, on the other hand, it is the child of our neighbor with whom we do not have a particularly good relationship, even if the child is playing more quietly and better than our own, the sound can be very irritating and we will not be able to ignore it.

Phrasing it more formally, the perception of sound can be habituated only when it does not evoke any form of emotional response; the signal has to be neutral. Indeed, for nearly 80 percent of people experiencing tinnitus, it is a neutral sound. They habituate it, they perceive tinnitus only part of the time, and it is not annoying them. If, however, exactly the same perception of tinnitus is associated with something unpleasant or dangerous, then habituation cannot occur, and tinnitus results in unpleasant feelings usually described as irritation, fear, or distress.

When tinnitus is perceived for the first time, the thoughts may be "Well, perhaps I have a brain tumor. Maybe I am going crazy. I will not be able to tolerate this. I will not be able to work. I might lose my job because I will not be able to concentrate." Unfortunately, it is common that early encounters with health care professionals, far from being helpful, actually further enhance these thoughts and beliefs. For example, patients are commonly told; "It might last forever. There is nothing that can be done about tinnitus. We must do a brain scan to rule out the possibility of a tumor." At this point a vicious cycle starts with strong reinforcement of the initial negative emotional values that the individual, on their own, has attached to the tinnitus sound.

If someone is afraid that tinnitus is an indication of a medical problem, this tells the brain that the tinnitus signal is important and should be followed up and monitored, in much the same way as pain perception can be an important warning of a disease process. So the perception of tinnitus is enhanced, and the tinnitus related activity is detected all the time, instead of intermittently, allowing it to reach the cortex and be perceived all the time. Once this happens, it causes even more annoyance, prevents us from enjoying recreational pursuits, and makes concentration or sleeping more difficult. Sleeping is of particular importance because tinnitus tends to be more noticeable in the quiet. So when we are trying to sleep at night the tinnitus is in sharp contrast to the silence normally around us at that time and is, therefore, perceived more loudly and clearly. Annoyance increases the brain's focus on the tinnitus-related activity. Since the brain perceives it as a very important signal, its perception is further enhanced. If tinnitus has definite threatening properties attached to it, sleep is further prevented, as our overall safety and well-being depends on the lack of any danger or warning signal while sleeping. We cannot, and should not, go to sleep in the presence of something that might be harmful to us.

As long as tinnitus is judged to be something important, something that indicates danger, our brain cannot habituate the perception of this sound. Therefore, the first important step on the path to tinnitus habituation is to reduce the strong association of tinnitus with emotional state. It is often difficult for some people to realize that tinnitus, from the medical or physiological standpoint, is nothing of real importance beyond the unpleasant emotional effects it evokes. Although the perception of tinnitus has an enormously strong effect on people and can be absolutely devastating, it does not typically indicate anything wrong is happening within the auditory system. Actually, it usually indicates over-compensation of the auditory pathways in response to small and otherwise nonsignificant distortion in the inner ear. Tinnitus associated with a particular type of brain tumor is very uncommon; in the vast majority of cases tinnitus is not associated with pathology of this type. While the exclusion of this pathology is an essential duty of the attending otologist, this task has to be undertaken sensitively and subtly, without increasing the fears of the tinnitus sufferer about serious disease while this possibility is being ruled out. Once the investigations have been performed, the results play an important role in the process of reassurance about the harmless nature of tinnitus.

PRACTICAL ARRANGEMENTS IN THE TINNITUS CLINIC

In our centers in Baltimore and London, we are using different variations of the same procedure that we occasionally describe as Retraining Therapy. This means reversing the changes in the central nervous system involved in producing tinnitus and tinnitus distress. The differences in approach allow us to assess the relative importance of the individual parts of the therapy but do not seem to have altered the overall excellent long-term results in either center.

Measurements

First the patient undergoes an audiological evaluation, including characterization of tinnitus, that serves as a check whether anything else might be happening, as far as the auditory system is concerned, in addition to tinnitus. Furthermore, it creates a reference for future follow-up and helps in prescribing the proper treatment. The second step is the medical interview in which we try to find out if there are any problems related to tinnitus that might influence the process and outcome of our treatment. The third step is directive counseling. The fourth step is fitting of appropriate instruments or devices. The final step consists of a series of follow-up visits that combines elements of counselling, modification of the protocol to the needs of a particular case, and repeated audiological evaluation.

Our evaluation tests the basic properties of the auditory system; for example, audiogram, auditory reflexes, speech perception, as well as tests that are aimed at the characterization of tinnitus, such as tinnitus loudness, pitch, and minimal masking level. Furthermore, we evaluate the otoacoustic emission distortion product (a new clinical test) as a tool for assessing function of one of the sensory cells involved in sound transduction, the outer hair cell, in the inner ear with relevance to the discordant damage hypothesis. The test specifically measures functional integrity of the outer hair cells. While the audiogram provides us with information about the combined action of both inner and outer hair cells and all processes occurring in the inner ear, the distortion product test tells us how outer hair cells are functioning. On a number of occasions, despite normal or near normal hearing, we observe a ragged, irregular distortion product, which is very repeatable, indicating small local patches of damaged outer hair cells. This exactly fits with the discordant damage hypothesis: It is a place in the inner ear from which the tinnitus-related activity is being triggered.

Measurement of loudness discomfort (to pure tones or wideband noise) is of great importance in assessing whether hyperacusis (oversensitivity to external sounds) is present. Patients with hyperacusis form a separate category and are treated differently than other patients. By monitoring the changes in loudness discomfort level, we can determine if the process of desensitization, involving decrease of the gain in the auditory system, is progressing as planned.

In both the audiological evaluation and particularly in the medical evaluation, a number of questions are aimed at determining the extent of annoyance induced by tinnitus, the percentage of time when tinnitus is perceived, and activities prevented by tinnitus or hyperacusis. These questions create a reference for future follow-up and are needed for monitoring the progress of recovery from tinnitus and the final outcome.

Specific counseling approaches

The initial audiological and medical evaluation serves to rule out any possibility that other medical problems might contribute to tinnitus. This allows us to tell the patient with full confidence that his or her tinnitus does not indicate any serious medical problem. To get rid of the fears and concerns that all patients have, we discuss them in depth, and we explain the results of the tests. In this step, as in all subsequent steps, we have very frank discussions and are very open with the patient. It is important to realize that even faced with strong medical evidence that all is well, the tinnitus patient might still have doubts. Strongly held beliefs and concerns, like "nothing can be done for tinnitus," cannot be overcome in one session. The patient needs some time, reassurance, and, above all, to see an improvement. This stage of counselling aimed at removing the importance and potential negative association of tinnitus is crucial but usually is not sufficient on its own for inducing or facilitating habituation.

Directive counselling is an essential part of our approach and differs from traditional counselling since it is aimed at actively changing the way the patient thinks about tinnitus. In some cases there are very strong negative beliefs about the meaning of tinnitus: that it represents the onset of deafness, madness, or untreatable disease. These fears are part of the mechanism for establishing strong negative emotional associations with the tinnitus; this is the cause of tinnitus distress, and also the major reason for the inability of tinnitus habituation. To remove these fears, anxieties, and beliefs about the meaning of tinnitus, another explanation must be put in their place. For this reason we use a logical and, at the same time, simple description of the neurophysiological model that shows what we know presently about the mechanisms of tinnitus. This also shows the patient that their fears are groundless, being based on incomplete information.

In one sense tinnitus can be seen like the generation of a phobic state. For example, fear of spiders (arachnophobia) is a common experience, in which the preoccupation with a small harmless creature can totally disable the sufferer, so that no room can be entered without extensive cleaning for spiders, and every spider can be seen in sharp contrast as a large and threatening monster. It is however the irrational fear, not the attack of the spider, that produces the disability and the inability to function normally within that environment. Retraining therapy is now very effective for arachnophobic victims who need to be shown that close association with spiders is possible (even desirable) and that this can be achieved, although initially with some anxiety. Finally, the patient reaches the state in which spiders are no longer noticed, even on inspection of the environment.

As part of our approach we are using the well-established psychological rule that people are afraid of the unknown, and even if something is unpleasant but is well- understood, it is not so frightening. We are more afraid about what might be happening than what we know and understand is going to happen. Therefore as part of our counselling we teach the patient the relevant elements of both basic and advanced auditory physiology, how sound changes from sound waves in the air into electrical signals in the nervous system, and which kind of mechanism of tinnitus might be appropriate in each particular case.

RELEVANCE OF THE INNER EAR

About 80 percent of all tinnitus cases can be traced to, or associated with, some changes within the inner ear. However these changes occur naturally as a process of aging and are present even in young people. At the same time tinnitus is not necessarily associated with deafness, any more than it is with normal hearing. Thirty percent of the worst suffering from tinnitus occurs in people without any hearing difficulty, and 28 percent of those with total deafness in both ears have no tinnitus at all. Without going into too much detail, but keeping strictly to the scientific facts and their interpretation, we present each patient with a mechanism that seems to be most appropriate to their case.

Quite frequently, the trigger mechanism may be related to uneven degeneration of two types of receptor cells inside the inner ear, inner and outer hair cells. While this is, at the moment an unproven hypothesis (like all other hypotheses of tinnitus generation), nevertheless, all results of experimental work and clinical results support this idea. If we have an area on the membrane inside the inner ear where outer hair cells are damaged and inner hair cells are intact, this area is responsible for initiating a series of processes that finally yield to the perception of tinnitus. Again we repeat that these changes are NOT tinnitus, they are not the sounds that distress patients, they are only the source initiating the process that results in tinnitus perception and also that these signals are extremely weak and difficult to detect. Tinnitus itself results from the enhancement and magnification of these weak signals as they pass from the ear to the auditory cortex where they are perceived.

In this chapter we are not going to discuss this hypothesis further. It has already been presented in a number of publications and would require an extensive amount of space. Nevertheless, this hypothesis, labelled discordant damage of outer and inner hair cells, is very useful in helping the patient understand the mechanism by which tinnitus is triggered.

JUSTIFICATION FOR SOUND THERAPIES

Even if the patient fully accepts that tinnitus is not reflecting any serious medical problem and is not medically significant, it does not automatically yield to habituation. All of our senses work on the basis of contrasts and anything that is distinctively different from the background will be noticed even after repetitive exposure. We might not get annoyed by it, but we will still perceive it. In other words, if the significance of tinnitus is removed and if the sound of tinnitus no longer induces a strong emotional response, tinnitus might loose its annoyance, but it will still be heard. We will achieve habituation only in the sense of removing the negative reaction induced by tinnitus, but the tinnitus sound will still be perceived. We want to achieve the next step, habituation of tinnitus *perception.* To accomplish this we need to provide the patient with an additional auditory background. This can be achieved by instructing the patient to introduce low level, mild sounds into their auditory environment, if necessary amplified by a hearing aid, or by providing them with wearable broadband noise generators. To explain the reasoning behind these devices we would go back to the basic neuroscience and physiology underlying our approach.

There are several reasons why we need to introduce additional external sound. First, all our sensory systems work on detection and enhancement of contrasts, while at the same time adjusting amplification (gain) of incoming peripheral information. Probably the best known example of this kind of modification of sensitivity of perception is with our vision. When we are in darkness, the pupils of our eyes expand so more light reaches the retina (back of the eye), and we can perceive very weak light. On the other hand, when we are in bright light, our pupils contract, and we can still see without being blinded by the strong light. This is an example of simple mechanical increase and decrease of sensitivity in the visual system. In the auditory system we cannot see the mechanical changes as we can in the eye, but research now confirms that within the inner ear we have mechanisms that can enhance weak sounds, up to about 50 dB, and perhaps aid in the attenuation of loud sound. We cannot see it, but we can measure the process by special clinical tests, such as evaluation of the otoacoustic emission distortion products. Again, this particular aspect is explained in detail to our patients.

Let's now apply these two principles, that is, perception and enhancement of the contrast, and the regulation of the gain (amplification) in the auditory system, to tinnitus. The first principle, the perception of the contrast, is easy to apply: Simply, the weak sound will be perceived clearly when there are no other sounds. Assuming that we have a constant, tinnitus-related signal coming from the inner ear, it will be easy to detect, if there are no other sounds around, for example, when we are in a quiet environment. At the same time, if there are no other sounds around us, the central auditory system will tend to enhance any kind of signal coming from the periphery (the inner ear). If this signal happens to be tinnitus, tinnitus will be made even stronger.

This line of reasoning has been confirmed by an experiment. If we take a group of young people with normal hearing and no tinnitus and put them into an anechoic chamber (a near totally silent and echo free room) initially nothing will happen, but within a couple of minutes they will start to perceive sounds. They will start to hear their heartbeat, the movement of their clothes from breathing, and *importantly* every one of them will develop tinnitus! The reason is that when there are no other, even moderate, sound signals coming to our ears, the brain tries to get some information from the ear, whatever it may be. What is detected are fluctuations of the normal spontaneous activity within the auditory pathways that are constantly present in every one of us. Fluctuations of this activity are detected and amplified and finally perceived as tinnitus in everyone who takes part in the experiment. On leaving the anechoic chamber the tinnitus disappears immediately as it is masked by environmental noise and as the subject ceases to listen for it.

It has been found that the nerve cells (neurons) in all the auditory pathways have a high level of natural, spontaneous activity, similar to what happens in the auditory nerve. This means that even when there is no sound present, neurons still fire electrical spikes along their bodies and connecting nerve fibers leading from the inner ear. We do not perceive the firing as sound and this normal random spontaneous electrical activity can be thought of as a "code for silence." When sound is presented to us, the activity increases overall and the neuronal discharges become more regular. But even in total silence this activity is never totally random, there are always some fluctuations. Normally we do not perceive these fluctuations as sound, but when there are no external sounds coming to us and our brain is increasing the gain from the auditory pathways, we start perceiving these fluctuations as if they were sound, and we start hearing tinnitus. So potentially all of us can hear tinnitus if we are put in a quiet enough environment.

In the case of hearing loss, the auditory system is deprived of some of the information that should be coming into the central nervous system. As a result the gain in the central auditory pathways will increase in the case of permanent, or even temporary, hearing loss in exactly the same way as if you are in the sound-proof chamber. In animal experiments it has been found that neurons within the auditory pathways exhibit increased sensitivity to any type of stimulation while permanent or temporary hearing loss has been induced. On the clinical side, we have found that about 40 percent of our tinnitus patients in Baltimore and London exhibit elements of hypersensitivity to sound (hyperacusis), which can reach an extremely high level so that people are unable to tolerate normal everyday sounds. A study performed in London a few years ago also showed that some tinnitus patients become oversensitive to environmental noise, even years before tinnitus starts.

So the first reason for introducing constant, low level sound is to decrease gain within the auditory pathways. It is particularly important if the gain was already increased above normal and the patient has hyperacusis. Please note that this does not affect the hearing threshold and what we are talking about is the enhancement of signal that is already above threshold. For example, if we were to keep someone in a sound-proof chamber for a month, the person would perceive tinnitus all the time. Then when we take this person to an everyday environment and expose them to sound, the gain would decrease to the previous value and the tinnitus would disappear. Unfortunately this simplified view is only partially true. A normal increase of gain plays a significant role, but decreasing this gain is not sufficient for disappearance of tinnitus. The reason is due to another very important feature of our perception: the ability of the sensory systems to focus on and detect contrasts.

Again, the easiest example can be imagined by using the visual system. Let's imagine that we have a small birthday cake candle and we put this candle on the table in the corner of a dark room. Even though the light is weak, the candle will attract attention and be very visible. If we switch on the light we will still be able to see the candlelight, but our attention will not be attracted to it that much. Finally, when the room is illuminated by sunshine, we will probably have a problem noticing the candlelight, although we can still see it if we focus our attention on it. This example points out that the absolute strength of a physical stimulus is less important than its contrast against background. Another example is that if we look at a buff colored dog on a beige carpet, we might have a problem noticing it if we are not focusing our attention on the dog. However, if we put the same dog on a grey carpet you will see it without any problem. In this case we might have the same physical intensity, brightness of stimulus, but we have another feature, color, that makes this stimulus distinctively different. Finally, let's imagine that we have a high school picture of a class of children with different styles of hair and dress. Although we can differentiate the faces, we will see it as one general picture. But if you replace one of the children with a picture of a scarecrow, it will be noticed at once, and our attention will be attracted to it because it is out of place.

The same rules govern auditory perception. We ignore sounds that are random and natural, such as wind, rain, or the mixed sound of voices of many people. At the same time we can pick up and distinguish a melody from a clarinet quite easily from the background of these sounds, but we may not be able to do this if it is a part of a symphony orchestra with many other instruments playing at the same time and generating similar types of sound.

There is no real external sound that corresponds to tinnitus perception. It is a phantom perception of a signal coming from the auditory pathways, that is created by a process different from the normal stimulation of the ear by sound. At the same time it is important to remember that the perception of tinnitus is totally real, by definition of perception. When we are simulating tinnitus on a music synthesizer and asking someone with tinnitus to adjust the machine so it sounds like the tinnitus, we often produce strange and unusual sounds. It is practically impossible to generate sounds that are exactly the same as the perception of tinnitus. As such, tinnitus is contrastingly different to any other natural occurring sound in the environment, and because of this, the rule of contrasts applies; and it is picked up and enhanced. It is the scarecrow in the class photograph. Therefore, to reduce or remove this strange sound we have to decrease the contrast between it and general background activity of the neurons within the auditory system.

MAIN APPROACHES TO PATIENTS

We have three general ways of decreasing the contrast between the tinnitus signal and the background activity. Depending on the particular case, we usually recommend two of these three approaches: (1) enrichment of environmental sounds, (2) enrichment and enhancement of environmental sounds using hearing aids, and (3) introducing broadband noise produced by wearable noise generators.

For the majority of patients we recommend the first approach in addition to anything else we may be doing, because even if people are in a quiet environment for a short period of time, the auditory system will turn up the gain, further enhancing the tinnitus signal, that will stick out from the low background sound and will make it very difficult, if not impossible, to habituate. So we instruct people to have some sound around them all their waking hours. Many people with tinnitus have found out for themselves that this is a helpful approach. The type of sound is not important, but it is recommended that the sound covers all frequencies, for example, using a compact disc rather than a poor quality Walkman. The general idea is to have some mild sound around them all the time. We instruct people that neither excessive noise nor silence is good for their tinnitus.

The second approach, which has to be combined with the first, is using hearing aids. We use this approach when hearing loss is a significant problem. After instructing the patient to create the proper auditory environment with similar reasoning and examples as in the first approach, we additionally instruct them in the use of the hearing aids as an aid to tinnitus habituation. The hearing aids are not only used for communicating but first of all as a continuous means of sound enhancement. The hearing aid in this case is just a tool to enhance the environmental sound. It is not meant only to help in communication or listening pleasure but to amplify sounds that the ear cannot otherwise hear. Of course, by using hearing aids in this situation we are helping with communication and quality of life as well, but if the hearing aid is prescribed as a tool for tinnitus, it has a few distinctive properties compared to hearing aids that are prescribed solely for hearing loss. First, the hearing aids should be used at all times throughout all waking hours. Second, extreme care is given to prevent obstructing natural sound coming to the ear. For many people the tinnitus is enhanced and increased in loudness when they cover their ears. Therefore, we only use very open molds to attach the aid to the ear, to avoid occlusion, and to interfere as little as possible with incoming environmental noise and other external sounds.

Most frequently we use the third approach, which involves wearing wideband noise generators, generally on both ears. The noise is applied at a low level, and should not be confused with so-called tinnitus masking. This particular approach has a number of advantages that make it the most efficient and powerful tool for inducing and facilitating habituation. First, it creates a stable sound background that does not fluctuate and that patients can carry with them at all times. In this respect it shares with tinnitus similar characteristics; the patient cannot assign tinnitus to one particular point in space outside his head, but the placement of tinnitus within the head is often quite stable. Environmental sounds by definition have directional properties, and they tend to fluctuate in intensity and spectral components. Second, the applied broadband frequency noise is random. The increase of activity within the auditory pathways induced by this noise is similar, although not identical, to the random activity that normally exists as a code for silence. As such, this type of signal should be easy to habituate to; and, indeed, many of our patients are habituating to the sounds of these devices within 20 to 30 minutes, failing to perceive their sound unless focusing attention on it. Notably, we use broadband stimulation containing not one, but many different frequencies, so we are stimulating as many fibers in the auditory nerve and neurons in the auditory pathways as possible but creating only a small increase of their overall activity. This should cause first of all a decrease of gain in the auditory system, and our experimental results fully support this prediction. Furthermore, it decreases the contrast between background activity within the auditory pathways and the activity that is perceived as tinnitus. By decreasing this contrast we are starting the process of habituation and, furthermore, facilitating it once it has started.

The external signal interferes with the tinnitus signal, but must never, by definition, cover or mask it. The reason for this is based on the well-established psychological and neurophysiological principle: it is impossible to train or retrain to a stimulus that is not detected by the nervous system. If tinnitus is covered up, it is impossible to induce habituation to it. Therefore, for the process of habituation to occur it is crucial that the tinnitus sound is not masked and can still be detected. In this respect it is interesting to mention the case of a patient who had been on masking treatment for 15 years and was getting relief while tinnitus was masked, but as soon as the masker was switched off, the tinnitus came back with the same intensity and annoyance. Once the patient, with reluctant approval, was switched to habituation therapy, he developed a gradual habituation of tinnitus, and he stopped perceiving tinnitus for longer and longer periods of time. This is another crucial prediction of the neuro-physiological model that our practice has confirmed: Once habituation is achieved and stabilized, there is no longer a need for using any external noise generator. Patients are advised to avoid silence and excessive noise, but, except for this, they can carry on their normal life without thinking about tinnitus or being bothered by it.

NOT A QUICK FIX

By its nature, retraining therapy, involving the rearrangement of neural connections in the auditory system and eventual habituation of tinnitus perception cannot be achieved overnight. Although a few patients habituate rapidly once they understand what is involved, the majority require repeated instruction, with directive counselling and reinforcement of this information over a period of 12 to 18 months.

The time between the fitting of the device or hearing aid and achieving habituation is the time when the main retraining work is carried out. The initial appointment serves as a checking opportunity for other medical problems and a counselling session in which to explain to the patient in detail what is going to take place. During the 12 to 18 months of continuous treatment, the patient uses the devices for at least six hours a day, preferably longer and particularly when in a quiet environment. The sound generated by these devices induces and further promotes the process of tinnitus habituation. To help with this, we have a strict system of follow-ups, usually at four and eight weeks, three months, six months, twelve months, and eighteen months, in addition to telephone contact. During the follow-up, we check the progress of treatment: noting any new modification of tinnitus, going through the basic explanations as often as necessary, answering questions, and, if necessary, modifying the approach depending on results and progress. The recurrence of tinnitus occurs rarely after completing treatment and can be dealt with by reapplication of the original protocol for a much shorter period of time. This reflects the well-established neurophysiological principle that once training has been achieved, but its effects partially reversed, much less intensive retraining is required to restore the system to its original state.

RESULTS SO FAR

By the end of 1994, in Baltimore we have seen close to 500 patients; over 100 patients who received treatment for at least six months were surveyed to assess treatment outcome. Eighty-four percent of the patients showed significant improvement, both in decreased annoyance induced by tinnitus and in showing clear habituation of its perception. These patients perceive tinnitus a small percentage of the time, often less than 10 percent. A number of them had stopped using the devices because tinnitus ceased to be a problem. About 1200 new patients have been seen in London over the same period of time with similar results.

Nevertheless, we have cases in which despite our efforts, there is no progress, with tinnitus remaining the same or becoming worse. It seems that these difficult cases belong to a specific subcategory, and perhaps a different approach is needed to help them.

Retraining therapy is very time-consuming and creates a heavy load on all personnel involved. Our efforts both in using the animal model of tinnitus and our clinical results are working toward a speeding up of the recovery process and increasing the percentage of cases we can help.

MEDICATIONS

One of the problems we face is that tinnitus patients are frequently taking a variety of drugs. If the drugs are needed for other medical reasons, we do not interfere with their use. However, if they were prescribed because of tinnitus, we encourage the patient to slowly withdraw these medications, working in close contact with the physician who prescribed them. It is particularly difficult in cases for which the drugs have addictive properties or tinnitus as a withdrawal effect. For many years benzodiazepine tranquilizers such as valium have been widely administered to tinnitus sufferers. Among these drugs the most popular at present is Xanax, which is prescribed for anxiety, as a sleeping pill, and as a drug for tinnitus. Although Xanax was reported to attenuate tinnitus in humans, it is a drug that should not be taken for prolonged periods and never without constant appropriate medical supervision, since it has strong addictive properties and can cause personality changes. Xanax dependence is now so widespread among tinnitus patients that we have developed a special protocol for its safe withdrawal.

SUMMARY

While the approach we have presented is not "the cure" in the classical sense of the word, for the first time it provides over 80 percent of patients with relief from tinnitus by removing the perception of tinnitus from their awareness in a consistent and systematic manner. The approach is significantly different to any that have been tried before and is based on totally new principles. Moreover there are no negative side effects that have been observed or can be envisioned.

We recognize that the process requires significant resources in terms of properly trained professionals and takes an average of twelve to eighteen months to complete. However, once completed it provides patients with relief from their tinnitus without the need for continuation of treatment. Recurrence of the tinnitus problem can occur, but this is infrequent in our experience, and can be easily dealt with by applying the original protocol for a much shorter period of time.

FURTHER READING

More detailed description of the discussed issues can be found in the following papers.

Jastreboff, P.J. Phantom auditory perception (tinnitus): Mechanisms of generation and perception. *Neurosci.Res.* 8:221–254, 1990.

Jastreboff, P.J. and Hazell, J.W.P. A neurophysiological approach to tinnitus: Clinical implications. *Brit.J.Audiol.* 27:1–11, 1993.

Jastreboff, P.J., Hazell, J.W.P., and Graham, R.L. Neurophysiological model of tinnitus: Dependence of the minimal masking level on treatment outcome. *Hearing Res.* 80:216–232, 1994.

The following books can be useful for a general overview of tinnitus.

Hazell, J.W.P. (Ed.). *Tinnitus.* Edinburgh: Churchill Livingstone, 1987.

McFadden, D. *Tinnitus: Facts, theories, and treatments,* Washington, DC: National Academy Press, 1982.

Proceedings of the III International Tinnitus Seminar, Muenster, edited by Feldmann, H.Karlsruhe. Harsch Verlag, 1987.

Tinnitus 91. Proceedings of the IV International Tinnitus Seminar. Bordeaux, France, 1991, edited by J. Aran and R. Dauman. Amsterdam: Kugler Publications, 1992.

PATIENT'S QUESTIONS AND ANSWERS

1. *Question:*   I note that you say there is no drug that can be recommended with a high chance of relieving tinnitus. What about the drug Xanax suggested by Dr. Brummett in Chapter V?

   Answer: Because Xanax can be habit forming, we do not recommend its use. We have had problems withdrawing tinnitus patients from this drug, and a number of patients complained of its side effects. While Xanax is of interest for research purposes, we are not recommending it in a clinical environment.

2. *Question:*   You indicate that tinnitus is perceived at the level of the cerebral cortex. Does that mean that the brain location of the tinnitus is known?

   Answer: Tinnitus, the same as external sounds, is perceived at the cortical level. However, we believe that the tinnitus signal is present and processed in both cortical and subcortical levels. Our study on animals and humans is aimed at the precise characterization of the tinnitus related activity and delineating of all centers involved in the processing of the tinnitus signal.

3. *Question:*   Does the presence of tinnitus mean that I also have increased sensitivity to sounds or that I will develop an increased sensitivity?

   Answer: Not necessarily, although in about one-half of the tinnitus patients, we see the mechanisms are interrelated and may reflect two different manifestations of enhanced sensitivity within the auditory system.

4. *Question:* You have repeatedly cautioned tinnitus patients to avoid loud sounds. How does one know when a sound is too loud?

   Answer: Actually, silence is as bad for tinnitus patients as sounds that are too loud. In general, the rules for loud sounds are the same as for anyone with or without tinnitus. Using ear protection against normal sound levels is discouraged.

5. *Question:* The emphasis in your program is on retraining how we view our tinnitus. I have tried that; I have repeatedly told myself to ignore my tinnitus but most of the time I cannot.

   Answer: I am sorry to say that you have totally misunderstood our approach. It has nothing to do with how a person views his or her tinnitus. This is a complex issue that is described in the chapter and other literature. It concerns changes in relationships between auditory limbic and autonomic nervous systems in a way that reduces first the reaction to tinnitus and finally the perception of tinnitus. The expected outcome is that a patient, even when perceiving tinnitus, is no longer annoyed by it, and, furthermore, the percentage of time of awareness of tinnitus is gradually reduced.

23

Microvascular Decompression Surgery for Tinnitus

PETER J. JANNETTA, M.D.
Department of Neurologic Surgery
University of Pittsburgh Medical Center
Pittsburgh, Pennsylvania

The symptom of tinnitus means that something has gone wrong somewhere, or anywhere, within the auditory system. Tinnitus is comparable to pain in other sensory departments; it is the signal of damage or impairment to the hearing mechanism. The American Tinnitus Association estimates that 12 million Americans suffer from severe tinnitus and that is about 20 percent of the people who experience tinnitus in milder forms. It is important for patient and clinic alike to realize that many people have tinnitus in a minor form that does not bother them nor does it mean that their tinnitus will become a severe case. Also, the presence of tinnitus does not mean that the patient will become deaf.

The incidence of tinnitus is presently increasing as the population continues to increase and as longevity also continues to increase. For the patients seen in our Department of Neurologic Surgery, tinnitus is usually not their primary problem. Nevertheless, it has occurred often enough to bring our attention and concern to it. Tinnitus can result from many different types of insults; overdose of medication, direct injury to the inner ear or hearing centers of the brain, acoustic overloads to the ear, and for many the cause is probably unknown. It is only in recent years that a remediable reversible cause for some forms of tinnitus has been known.

Most patients with tinnitus, at lease those whom we see in our practice at the University of Pittsburgh, have unilateral tinnitus, which is in sharp contrast to the patient population seen at the Tinnitus Clinic at the Oregon Hearing Research Center in Portland, Oregon. There, in a study of 1932 tinnitus patients, 1062 (55%) presented with bilateral tinnitus, 21 percent with unilateral tinnitus and the rest with tinnitus perceived as being located in the head. Tinnitus may spread to the opposite ear as the condition continues or as it becomes more intense. In our experience in Pittsburgh, rarely is tinnitus bilateral and symmetrical at its onset. We, of course, see only patients with the chief complaint of tinnitus; those who are having major problems with the tinnitus symptom. These people have difficulties with their daily activities, with their work, with their socializing, their sleeping, with concentration, and in short, with living in general. They describe their tinnitus in a variety of ways, indeed, so much so as to suggest that there may not be two cases of identical tinnitus. For the majority, tinnitus is a high-pitched tone and for others it is a low-pitched sound. For the majority it is loud, and for some it is soft. If our ability to precisely duplicate the quality of tinnitus was more accurate, it is likely that each patient would be distinctive, much like finger prints. In general, tinnitus is irritatingly loud and high pitched, and it is that high pitch that makes the tinnitus sound not only unacceptable but very difficult to ignore.

There is a common subgroup of tinnitus sufferers who present primarily with balance problems and associated tinnitus. In these patients the tinnitus is treated incidentally by the operation used for the balance problem. It was the results of this approach, as well as initial observations on other adjacent cranial nerves, that led to the development of a specific and definitive surgery for the disabling problem of tinnitus. The present day surgical technique evolved gradually as technical advances became available. First, there was the binocular surgical microscope that offered needed and sufficient magnification. Then came the ability to visually communicate surgical findings and surgical procedures using 35mm color slides, followed by 16mm movies and finally color videotapes with sound. These technical advances have enabled one to train others as well as to present one's own data in an objective manner.

As early as 1932 work by Dr. Dandy demonstrated it was possible that the severe facial pain of trigeminal neuralgia (tic douloureux) was apparently caused by blood vessels impinging on the trigeminal nerve in the cerebral portion angle. Similarly, in 1962 Gardner and Sava showed that in some cases of hemifacial spasm, a symptom of twitching on one side of the face was caused by a blood vessel compressing the facial nerve. Unfortunately because of inadequate technology (lack of magnification), the findings were inadequate and partial. The current approach to these nerves is through a small incision and bony opening about the size of one's thumb print made behind the mastoid area, that is, a retro mastoid craniectomy. The technique utilized to identify and remove the offending blood vessel(s) away from the nerve was termed Microvascular Decompression (MVD).

Inasmuch as compression upon the fifth cranial nerve by blood vessels was demonstrated to produce pain, it seemed reasonable to assume that a similar compression upon the hearing nerve (VIII nerve) could produce tinnitus. This theory of vascular compression suggests that blood vessels come to exert a force upon the nerve and the real question then becomes, What are these forces? There are probably two forces that can contribute to the compression problem. The first is the sagging of the brain as a simple and straightforward aging process. As we age, our brains sag just as does our chin, stomach, and other tissues. This changes venous-neural relationships. The second force is exerted by the elongation of our arteries that may be the result of arteriosclerosis. Arteries at the base of the brain are small and numerous so as to surround the base of the brain and the cranial nerves that exit the brain in that region. As the brain sags in a posterior direction and the accompanying arteries increase in length, they begin to loop, which in turn allows them to impinge upon one or more cranial nerves. When the brain sags and/or the arterial impingement presses upon the cochlear portion of the VIII cranial nerve, tinnitus is the result. The VIII nerve is arranged so that the fibers carrying the high frequency (pitch) signals are on the outer layer of the fiber, thus the initial tinnitus produced by this mechanical compression will usually be a high pitched tone or a high pitched hiss.

The sagging of the brain and the involvement of the accompanying arteries are the main factors that produce vascular compression tinnitus and other compression disorders. However, there is another factor as well, and it is a congenital factor. The problems produced by vascular compression tend to run in families because we inherit our parents' blood vessels, their configuration and location.

Very early on, when I had begun to perform microvascular decompression of the VIII cranial nerve for the relief of vertigo and disequilibrium, it was observed that some of these patients also had tinnitus that was relieved by the vascular decompression operation. It turned out that 80 percent of the patients who had tinnitus got relief of their tinnitus by the MVD of the cranial nerve. As might be expected, we then began to perform microvascular decompression operations for tinnitus alone. Initially, we were disappointed in the results of the decompression operation for tinnitus because the results were nowhere as good as those for facial pain, spasm, vertigo, or other symptoms. We found that less than 40 percent of the patients with severe tinnitus were relieved by our surgical intervention. That result was far short of our expectations and thus we initiated an investigation in an effort to determine the reason for the shortfall. Review of operative photographs and notes revealed that these patients did not lack vascular compression of the VIII nerve. There were blood vessels in abundance compressing the cochlear portion of the VIII nerve for these patients. The mobilization of the compression blood vessels was adequate and not faulty. As far as could be determined, there was no nerve injury that could account for the lack of success. Careful survey of our patient data files, however, revealed that the critical element was the duration of the tinnitus symptom. Those patients who had an average tinnitus duration of 7.9 years did poorly with the microvascular decompression technique while those who had an average duration of 2.7 years obtained complete or near complete tinnitus relief. Our patient review involved 72 patients, all of whom had undergone operative treatments for tinnitus. Four of these patients had severe postoperative hearing impairment. The remaining 68 demonstrated no hearing loss after the operation, and many improved slowly from their preoperative status. Indeed, it may be that our surgical procedure corrected or delayed the aging process to such an extent as to delay or even prevent presbyacusias. Of the 72 patients, one demonstrated a facial weakness, which gradually improved. Two patients demonstrated worsening of their tinnitus, a result for which we are unable to account but probably just a continuation of their problem. Women did much better in our patient population than did the men. We think this was because they had vascular pathology that was easier to treat.

We caution each patient who opts for the microvascular decompression operation that it is a physiological operation that may require considerable time to become effective. Some patients have obtained tinnitus relief almost immediately, postoperatively. Other patients experience a gradually improving tinnitus over a period as long as two years.

One final word. As yet we have not been able to devise a definitive test that would indicate when vascular compression of the VIII nerve is the cause of tinnitus. There are many causes for tinnitus, but if one of these causes can be identified in a given case, it may then be profitable to entertain the possibility of vascular decompression.

PATIENT'S QUESTIONS AND ANSWERS

1. *Question:*   The implication is that vascular compression is an effect of aging. Is it possible that vascular compression can occur in young patients?
   Answer: Trauma to the head region can produce vascular compression at any age. The patient's medical history would be the critical aspect of inquiry. Microvascular compression might be suspected in any tinnitus where there is no known cause but reason to suspect vascular accidents.

2. *Question:*   Does vascular compression show up on X–ray or any of the brain scanning techniques?
   Answer: At this stage of technical capability, the scanning devices are not sufficiently refined to detect very small vessels but that day is coming, and when it does, much of our guess work will be eliminated.

3. *Question:*   If you surgically correct microvascular compression, what assurance is there that the same thing will not occur at some other nerve location with other blood vessels?
   Answer: What you propose is not likely, at least we have not seen such an occurrence. I suppose it is always possible, but I would say it is highly unlikely.

4. *Question:*   If a wedge is placed under the offending blood vessel would not that increase the pressure rather then decrease it?
   Answer: The wedge distributes the pressure so that it is not discretely applied to a restricted area of the nerve.

5. *Question:* Is there any characteristic of the tinnitus that results from microvascular compression that is distinctive?

   Answer: It is well known that the nerve fibers that carry the high frequencies are located on the periphery of the VIII nerve. Therefore, it may be the case that the initial tinnitus produced by microvascular compression would be a very high pitched tinnitus.

6. *Question:* If microvascular compression has produced tinnitus, will microvascular decompression immediately relieve or cure the tinnitus?

   Answer: No, a recovery time is necessary and the duration of that recovery period depends upon such things as the degree of compression and the extent of the trauma to the nerve.

24

Treatment For Hyperacusis

JACK VERNON, Ph.D., and LINDA PRESS
Oregon Hearing Research Center
Oregon Health Sciences University
Portland, Oregon

It is off the subject of treatments for tinnitus to introduce the topic of hyperacusis, however, we find that some tinnitus patients also suffer with hyperacusis; and in such cases it is the hyperacusis that is often considered the more severe of the two problems. In a survey conducted by the American Tinnitus Association, 1 of 112 patients with both tinnitus and hyperacusis, 53 percent listed hyperacusis as worse than their tinnitus while 25 percent listed both problems as equally disturbing, leaving 16 percent who placed tinnitus as the worst and 6 percent who were unsure. Thus, when both conditions are present, we usually attempt to treat the hyperacusis first, and fortunately there is a potential treatment to offer the hyperacusis patient.

Most patients and many health–care professionals describe hyperacusis as "exceptionally sensitive hearing ability," and we feel that is an *incorrect definition.* In Dorland's Medical Dictionary (26th Edition) hyperacusis is defined as "an exceptionally acute sense of hearing, the hearing threshold being unusually low." Dorland's definition is not only totally incorrect but most likely the source of much present day confusion. *Hyperacusis is best defined as the collapse of loudness tolerance* so that almost all sounds produce loudness discomfort even though the actual sound intensity is well below that judged to be uncomfortable by others. Not only is hyperacusis not increased hearing sensitivity but many hyperacusis patients actually display hearing impairment. In the survey mentioned above, by Gloria Reich, Ph.D. and Susan Griest, M.A., which was mentioned at the Fourth International Tinnitus Seminar, Bor-

223

deaux, France 1991, 70 percent of the hyperacusis patients reported some form of hearing loss. Some patients with hearing loss display recruitment and not infrequently recruitment is mistaken for hyperacusis.

Hyperacusis means that *the tolerance for the loudness of sounds has collapsed* so that almost all sounds are uncomfortably loud. The hyperacusis patient experiences a great deal of discomfort and for that reason they seek quiet and protected places. In the normal hearing ear when the intensity of a sound is progressively increased there will be a level at which the sound is uncomfortably loud and that point is termed The Uncomfortable Loudness Level (UCL). Usually the UCL for normal hearing people is around 100 dB to 110 dB sound pressure level. In contrast to the normal loudness function, when very low intensity sounds produce an exaggerated loudness, discomfort, it is most likely an example of hyperacusis. In the hyperacusis patient the threshold of loudness discomfort is inversely related to the pitch of the test sounds. The higher the pitch of the sound the less the loudness tolerance. Typically the threshold of discomfort for hyperacusis patients is on the order of 20 to 25 dB above threshold for low pitched sounds (200 Hz or so) and progressively declines until it is only about 3 to 5 dB, or less, above threshold for sounds at 10,000 Hz and above.

TREATMENT OF HYPERACUSIS: DESENSITIZATION

There are two parts to the treatment for hyperacusis, one of which most patients object to. First the objection. We insist that *over protection of the ears* will cause a worsening of the hyperacusis. Most hyperacusis patients continuously wear ear plugs in an attempt to make their every day situations more tolerable. In the above survey patients were asked if they constantly wear ear plugs and 93 percent answered *yes*. This type of protection is false security and one way to almost surely make hyperacusis worse. On the other hand, hyperacusis patients, like tinnitus patients, must avoid truly loud sounds and this distinction often presents a problem for hyperacusis patients. We estimate that hearing protection is required for those sounds that are sufficiently loud as to cause one to raise the level of one's voice in order to be heard. Absence of ear plugs when exposed to normal environmental sounds may produce some discomfort for the hyperacusic patient, but that kind of loudness discomfort will probably gradually habituate.

Many hyperacusis patients dread going out of doors for fear of encountering loud sounds such as car horns, sirens, signals, truck noise, backfires, and so on. To this end Jim Nunley, Jonathan Lay and Grayson Silaski (our electronics staff) are currently developing a special hearing aid (*2000) with extensive compression so that sounds of any sort cannot rise above approximately 65 dB SPL and very low intensity sounds are amplified up to a comfortable level that is adjustable. With such a device the hyperacusis patient should be able to travel out and about without fear of an accidental loud exposure. The prototype of *2000 is currently being tested on a hyperacusis patient and so far reports have been favorable.

The second phase of the desensitizing procedure is to listen, under earphones, to pink noise (200 Hz through 6000 Hz) for about two hours each day. The listening level is determined by the patient in the following manner. Under ear phones the patient increases the loudness of the pink noise until it just begins to reach the loudness discomfort level and then the loudness is *immediately* reduced to the highest, loudest level that is *comfortable*. Once that level is established the patient listens to it for two hours each day. If desired, the patient may break the listening period into shorter intervals, as long as a new listening level is established each time a new listening period is introduced.

Desensitizing the hyperacusis patient is a very slow process that probably depends upon how long the patient has had hyperacusis and how severe it is. The most rapid retraining we have experienced required three months; the longest desensitization period to date was two years; and the average is probably much closer to two years than to three months.

We have provided pink noise cassette tapes to a score of hyperacusis patients. Recently we mailed a questionnaire to 30 of these patients from whom we have had 20 (67%) responses. Of these 20 there were 13 (65%) who had used the tape repeatedly and of that 13 there were 7 (54%) who estimated that their hyperacusis was improved. Several patients indicated they were afraid to use the tape for fear it would exacerbate their hyperacusis and/or tinnitus and, therefore, did not try it. A few patients simply indicated that they had not yet gotten around to using the tape. Two patients indicated that by not overprotecting the ears, they had improved enough so that they felt no need to use the pink noise tape.

From these findings we conclude that we have something on the order of a 54 to 69 percent success rate. Obviously we would like to develop a more effective treatment procedure, but for the present, this is the best we can offer. When treatment is successful for hyperacusis, caution is still required, for if the patient is exposed to very loud sounds, they are apt to have a return of their hyperacusis.

SOME SURVEY DATA ABOUT HYPERACUSIS PATIENTS

The hyperacusis survey conducted by the American Tinnitus Association involved 35,000 patients from which 112 (0.3%) hyperacusis patients were revealed. The average age of these hyperacusis patients was 43.6 years of which 65 percent were male and 35 percent were female. We have not seen any children with hyperacusis, but it is our guess that hyperacusis is present among children, especially those with Williams syndrome, and perhaps some tend to grow out of it.

The possibility of TMJ dysfunction was indicated by one or more of the following symptoms in 65 patients: (1) jaw problems in 58 percent, (2) jaw pain in 43 percent, (3) bad bite in 51 percent, (4) bruxism in 52 percent and (5) jaw clicking in 58 percent. A feeling of fullness in the ears was experienced by 83 (74%) of those with hyperacusis.

Of those presenting with these possible TMJ problems, 33 (51%) had been treated for TMJ dysfunction. Of that number, 4 (12%) obtained relief of their hyperacusis, 17 (51%) obtained no hyperacusis relief, and 12 (36%) were unsure about the outcome. It is our estimate that TMJ dysfunction can be a potential cause of hyperacusis.

Although 31 patients could not recall anything as being associated with the onset of their hyperacusis, 29 attributed it to a brief intense noise exposure, 11 attributed it to long-term noise exposure, 4 attributed it to ear infections, 6 to illness, 6 to head trauma, 4 to medications, and 20 to various other causes. Clearly there is no established primary cause for hyperacusis.

On the topic of noise exposure, 50 percent of the patients in the survey reported that they were exposed to occupational noise at an objectionably loud level, 72 percent were exposed to recreational noise, and 17 percent were exposed to military noise. These data seem at odds with those that patients report as being associated with the onset of their hyperacusis, which may mean that noise exposure could possibly exert its influence relative to hyperacusis at a considerable latency after exposure.

For 49 percent the onset of hyperacusis was sudden, for 45 percent it was gradual, and 6 percent were unsure. In 86 percent both ears were affected and in 14 percent only one ear was affected, and when only one ear was affected, it was in the right ear for 5 percent and in the left ear for 9 percent. Hyperacusis was not constant, being shown to fluctuate in 71 percent of the cases. Hyperacusis altered social relationships for 91 percent and caused an occupational change for 56 percent. Leisure activities were altered or terminated for 97 percent. Medical help was sought, usually in vain, by 93 percent of these patients. One patient claimed his hyperacusis was completely removed by the drug Paxil. To our certain knowledge, Paxil has not been the subject of a properly controlled study for the possible relief of hyperacusis.

SUMMARY

Hyperacusis is a collapse of one's loudness tolerance. In some cases it can be defeated by desensitization, which is a simple listening exercise utilizing pink noise. The patient must be persistent and diligent in conducting the desensitization exercises. In addition the hyperacusis patient must not overprotect his ears.

We recommend that hyperacusis patients join Dan Malcore's Hyperacusis Network, 444 Edgewood Drive, Green Bay, Wisconsin 54302 (414/468–4663).

PATIENT'S QUESTIONS AND ANSWERS

1. *Question:*   Does hyperacusis come on very suddenly so that it is absent one day and suddenly present the next?

Answer: Both things can happen. That is, the hyperacusis can come on either suddenly or gradually, and as indicated in this chapter, 49 percent had a sudden onset while 45 percent had a gradual onset. The more pertinent question is the cause of each type of onset, and here we have no answers.

2. *Question:*   Does the onset function of hyperacusis determine the degree of the response to treatment? Is it suddenly in and suddenly out?

   Answer: Unfortunately we have no information on that matter. We suspect, however, that the nature of the onset is not as important as the duration of the condition. For those who start treatment early, the recovery seems to be more rapid than for those who had endured the condition for a long time. Unfortunately, those who have a gradual onset usually wait for some time before seeking help.

3. *Question:*   How can one's loudness tolerance be severely depressed and yet one's hearing ability be unaffected?

   Answer: To correctly answer this question would require much more knowledge than is available for either of these functions. However, an overly simplified explanation is that two different aspects of the auditory system are involved. Hearing ability is related to the functioning capability of the hair cells of the inner ear and in the normal ear the loudness function is also related to the action and number of hair cells available. But in the hyperacusis ear something has gone wrong with the loudness regulator. Since loudness tolerance can be retrained, we assume that hyperacusis is not necessarily a permanent chronic intractable condition.

4. *Question:*   Why does the lack of loudness tolerance increase?

   Answer: We think the hyperacusis can increase because patients understandably tend to overprotect their ears so that less and less sound is needed to produce discomfort. We have very few cases to support the position that lack of overprotection speeds the recovery process but that most certainly seems to be the case. Like most of the things stated here this is yet another item that requires properly controlled study.

5. *Question:*   Is there any medication available for the relief of hyperacusis?

   Answer: There is no medication that has been properly tested and found to be effective. There are, however, several patient reports about drugs that have been helpful to them. One report mentions the drug Risperidone, and another report mentions the drug Valporic Acid. Let me repeat, these are patient anecdotal reports and not the results of properly controlled studies. If, however, you and your primary physician agree, I see no reason why these medications should not be given a trial under the supervision of the physician.

Index